Lecture Notes in Computer Science 9581

Commenced Publication in 1973
Founding and Former Series Editors:
Gerhard Goos, Juris Hartmanis, and Jan van Leeuwen

More information about this series at http://www.springer.com/series/7409

Nikolaj Bjørner · Sanjiva Prasad
Laxmi Parida (Eds.)

Distributed Computing and Internet Technology

12th International Conference, ICDCIT 2016
Bhubaneswar, India, January 15–18, 2016
Proceedings

 Springer

Editors
Nikolaj Bjørner
Microsoft Research
Redmond, WA
USA

Laxmi Parida
IBM Thomas J. Watson Research Center
Yorktown Heights, NY
USA

Sanjiva Prasad
Indian Institute of Technology Delhi
New Delhi
India

ISSN 0302-9743   ISSN 1611-3349   (electronic)
Lecture Notes in Computer Science
ISBN 978-3-319-28033-2   ISBN 978-3-319-28034-9   (eBook)
DOI 10.1007/978-3-319-28034-9

Library of Congress Control Number: 2015957781

LNCS Sublibrary: SL3 – Information Systems and Applications, incl. Internet/Web, and HCI

This Springer imprint is published by SpringerNature
The registered company is Springer International Publishing AG Switzerland

Preface

The 12th International Conference on Distributed Computing and Internet Technology, ICDCIT-2016, took place in Bhubaneswar, India, during January 15–18, 2016. It was hosted and sponsored by the Kalinga Institute of Information Technology (KIIT) University.

The ICDCIT conference series focusses on three broad areas of computer science, namely, distributed computing, Internet technologies, and societal applications. It provides a platform for academicians, researchers, practitioners, and developers to present and publish their research findings and also deliberate on contemporary topics in the area of distributed computing and Internet technology. From the very inception of the ICDCIT series the conference proceedings have been published by Springer as *Lecture Notes in Computer Science*; vol. 3347 (year 2004), 3816 (2005), 4317 (2006), 4882 (2007), 5375 (2008), 5966 (2010), 6536 (2011), 7154 (2012), 7753 (2013), 8337 (2014), 8956 (2015), and 9581 (2016).

In response to the call for submissions, ICDCIT 2016 received 165 abstracts. Subsequently, 129 submissions with full versions were reviewed by an international Program Committee (PC) consisting of 35 members from 12 countries. Each submission was peer reviewed by up to three PC members with the help of external reviewers. After receiving the reviews of the papers, the PC meeting was conducted electronically over a period of ten days in the latter part of September 2015 to discuss and finalize the acceptance of submissions under different categories. We included a poster paper category in order to encourage participation and presentation of ongoing research activities. Based on their relevance to the conference theme, and the quality of the technical contents and presentation style, a total of 24 papers (19%) were accepted for presentation and publication in the LNCS proceedings, out of which six papers (5%) are under the category of regular papers each with a maximum length of 12 pages, seven short papers, and 11 poster papers. We wish to thank all the PC members and external reviewers for their hard work, dedication, and timely submission of the reviews without which it would have been difficult to maintain the publication schedule.

The program also included invited lectures by six distinguished speakers: Benny Chor (Tel Aviv University, Israel), Eric Jonasch (University of Texas, USA), Shriram Krishnamurthi (Brown University, USA), John Rushby (SRI International, USA), Assaf Schuster (Technion, Israel), and Andrei Voronkov (University of Manchester, UK). We express our sincere thanks to all the invited speakers for accepting our invitation to share their expertise and also submit insightful and thought-provoking papers for inclusion in the proceedings. We are very sad to report that one of our original invited speakers, Alberto Apostolico, passed away while he was attending a conference in Lipari, Italy. He is missed dearly by all his friends, colleagues, and co-authors, and he was in our thoughts during this meeting.

Our sincere thanks to Achyuta Samanta (Founder of KIIT University) for his patronage and constant support with hosting the ICDCIT conference series. We are grateful to the Vice-Chancellor and administration of the KIIT University for providing us with the infrastructure and logistics to organize this international event. We are indebted to the Advisory Committee members for their constant guidance and support. We would like to place on record our appreciation of the invaluable service and tireless efforts of the organizing chair, finance chair, publicity chair, registration chair, session management chair, the publications chair, and all members of various committees. We would also like to thank the chairs of the satellite events, the student symposium, and the industry symposium. We would like to thank Arup Acharya in particular, for his help on communicating all matters related to registration and submissions. Our special thanks to Hrushikesha Mohanty, N. Raja, and D.N. Dwivedy for their valuable advice and wholehearted involvement in all activities.

We wish to acknowledge and thank all the authors for their scholarly contributions to the conference, which stimulated interesting discussions during the technical sessions. Our thanks are also due to the technical session chairs for managing the sessions effectively. We acknowledge the service rendered by EasyChair for efficient and smooth handling of all activities starting from paper submissions to preparation of the proceedings. We sincerely thank Alfred Hofmann and Anna Kramer from Springer for their cooperation and constant support throughout the publication process of this LNCS volume.

Last but not the least, we thank all the participants and people who directly or indirectly contributed to making ICDCIT 2016 a memorable event.

January 2016

Nikolaj Bjørner
Sanjiva Prasad
Laxmi Parida

Organization

Program Committee

Karthikeyan Bhargavan	Inria, France
Chiranjib Bhattacharyyaa	Indian Institute of Science, India
Nikolaj Bjørner	Microsoft Research, USA
Hung Dang Van	UET, Vietnam National University, Hanoi
Günter Fahrnberger	University of Hagen, North Rhine-Westphalia, Germany
Marc Frincu	University of Southern California, USA
Vijay Ganesh	University of Waterloo, Canada
Deepak Garg	Max Planck Institute for Software Systems, Germany
Arie Gurfinkel	Software Engineering Institute, Carnegie Mellon University, USA
Karthick Jayaraman	Microsoft, USA
Ranjit Jhala	University of California San Diego, USA
Kishore Kothapalli	IIIT, Hyderabad, India
Laura Kovacs	Chalmers University of Technology, Sweden
Paddy Krishnan	Oracle, Australia
Ratul Mahajan	Microsoft Research, USA
Hrushikesha Mohanty	University of Hyderabad, India
Krishnendu Mukhopadhyaya	Indian Statistical Institute, India
Madanlal Musuvathi	Microsoft Research, USA
Laxmi Parida	IBM, USA
Manas Ranjan Patra	Berhampur University, India
Dana Petcu	West University of Timisoara, Romania
Tatjana Petrov	IST Austria
Ruzica Piskac	Yale University, USA
Sanjiva Prasad	IIT Delhi, India
P. Radha Krishna	SET Labs, Infosys Technologies Limited, Hyderabad, India
N. Raja	TIFR, India
S. Ramaswamy	ABB Inc., India
Krishna S.	IIT Bombay, India
Smruti Sarangi	IIT Delhi, India
Nishant Sinha	IBM Research Labs, India
Jun Sun	Singapore University of Technology and Design
Hideyuki Takahashi	Tohoku University, Japan
Mahesh Tripunitara	University of Waterloo, Canada
Yakir Vizel	Princeton University, USA

Additional Reviewers

Akshay, S.
Babiceanu, Radu
Bai, Guangdong
Berezish, Murphy
Bégay, Pierre-Léo
Dang Duc, Hanh
De, Swades
Gauthier, Francois
Gorain, Barun
Hollitt, Christopher
Kalra, Prem
Li, Li
Liang, Jimmy
Malakar, Preeti

Mandal, Partha Sarathi
Mukhopadhyaya, Srabani
Narasimhan, Lakshmi
Negi, Atul
Nejati, Saeed
Paul, Kolin
Rathinasamy,
   Bhavanandan
Santolucito, Mark
Sau, Buddhadeb
Sen, Sagnik
Subramanian,
   Vimalathithan
Subramanyan, Pramod

Sudarsan, Sithu
Sur-Kolay, Susmita
Tran, Thi Minh Chau
Truong, Hoang
Utro, Filippo
Veerubhotla, Ravi Sankar
Zhai, Ennan
Zhang, Shuyuan
Zhu, Charlie Shucheng
Zulkoski, Ed

Invited Talks

Teaching Computer Science in the Community

Benny Chor[1(✉)] and Assaf Zaritsky[1,2(✉)]

[1] School of Computer Science Tel Aviv University Tel Aviv 69978, Israel
benny@cs.tau.ac.il, assafzar@gmail.com
[2] Present Address: Department of Cell Biology,
UT Southwestern Medical Center,
Dallas, TX 75390, USA

Abstract. The School of Computer Science at Tel Aviv University, Israel, has initiated and carried out a project titled "Teaching Computer Science in the Community". The project aims to introduce scientific thinking and basic computer science concepts in an informal setting to school children from low socio-economic background. The project is implemented as a single semester undergraduate elective course, in which third year computer science students teach in schools and community centers. Here, we describe the spirit, content, and structure of the course and discuss insight we have gained over the last four years of teaching it.

Attacks in the Resource-as-a-Service (RaaS) Cloud Context

Danielle Movsowitz, Orna Agmon Ben-Yehuda, and Assaf Schuster[✉]

Technion—Haifa Institute of Technology,
Haifa, Israel
dani.movso@campus.technion.ac.il,
{ladypine, assaf}@cs.technion.ac.il,
http://www.cs.technion.ac.il

Abstract. The Infrastructure-as-a-Service (IaaS) cloud is evolving towards the Resource-as-a-Service (RaaS) cloud: a cloud which requires economic decisions to be taken in real time by automatic agents. Does the economic angle introduce new vulnerabilities? Can old vulnerabilities be exploited on RaaS clouds from different angles? How should RaaS clouds be designed to protect them from attacks? In this survey we analyze relevant literature in view of RaaS cloud mechanisms and propose directions for the design of RaaS clouds.

Static and Dynamic Reasoning for SDNs

Tim Nelson and Shriram Krishnamurthi

Brown University

In a traditional network, switches collectively decide on forwarding behavior. In contrast, a Software-Defined Network [5] (SDN) obeys a logically centralized controller program. Centralization and programmability grant unparalleled visibility and control, but also pose challenges to reasoning about network behavior. This talk presents some recent work [10, 11, 12, 13, 14] in both static and dynamic reasoning for SDNs and lays out a landscape for thinking about these issues.

Correct-by-Construction Switch Updates SDNs have prompted a surge in network programming-languages research [1, 9, 11, 15] aimed at helping operators more easily write safe, trustworthy controllers. For performance reasons, controller programs often install *persistent* behavior on switches. In effect, this means that these programs *must themselves generate programs*. Manually managing this process opens the programmer to numerous subtle bugs: controllers can be flooded with unnecessary traffic or fall behind on important updates, leading to still more incorrect behavior. Fortunately, this issue can be mitigated by language runtimes that manage switch updates automatically.

Static Reasoning: Verification Even if switch behavior is correct with respect to the program, the program itself may have bugs—many of which can be detected with static program reasoning (e.g., [2, 4, 7, 8]). Reasoning about network programs may be either in context of the network they control or in isolation. For instance, we might check that the program preserves reachability in a particular network, but we might also want to confirm that the program properly implements round-robin load-balancing—a property that depends only on the behavior of switches, independent from network topology.

Static Reasoning: Differential Analysis Humans are notoriously poor at stating formal properties, especially without training. Moreover, many correctness properties shift in subtle ways as a program evolves over time. In the absence of properties, it is useful to recall that property verification is only one means to an end: building confidence in the program being checked. Often, an operator may have an initial program that "works", and wishes to *transfer their confidence* in the old version onto the new version. They may have only an intuitive notion of what the change should (and should not) accomplish; we discuss techniques that leverage this intuition by presenting examples of differential behavior.

Dynamic Reasoning Dynamic, rather than static, reasoning (e.g., [3, 6, 14, 16]) is also powerful in certain cases, such as testing the use of third-party libraries or validating hardware behavior. *Interactive* dynamic tools let operators iteratively refine their understanding and locate faults step by step. The downside of interactivity is that it can become repetitive, and thus we believe that dynamic tools should also be *scriptable*.

References

1. Anderson, C.J., Foster, N., Guha, A., Jeannin, J.-B., Kozen, D., Schlesinger, C., Walker, D.: NetKAT: semantic foundations for networks. In: Principles of Programming Languages (POPL) (2014)
2. Ball, T., Bjørner, N., Gember, A., Itzhaky, S., Karbyshev, A., Sagiv, M., Schapira, M., Valadarsky, A.: VeriCon: towards verifying controller programs in software-defined networks. In: Programming Language Design and Implementation (PLDI) (2014)
3. Beckett, R., Zou, X.K., Zhang, S., Malik, S., Rexford, J., Walker, D.: An assertion language for debugging SDN applications. In: Workshop on Hot Topics in Software Defined Networking (2014)
4. Canini, M., Venzano, D., Perešíni, P., Kostić, D., Rexford, J.: A NICE way to test OpenFlow applications. In: Networked Systems Design and Implementation (2012)
5. Feamster, N., Rexford, J., Zegura, E.: The road to SDN: an intellectual history of programmable networks. ACM Comput. Commun. Rev. **44**(2) (2014)
6. Handigol, N., Heller, B., Jeyakumar, V., Mazières, D., McKeown, N.: I know what your packet did last hop: using packet histories to troubleshoot networks. In: Networked Systems Design and Implementation (2014)
7. Kazemian, P., Varghese, G., McKeown, N.: Header space analysis: static checking for networks. In: Networked Systems Design and Implementation (2012)
8. Khurshid, A., Zou, X., Zhou, W., Caesar, M., Godfrey, P.B.: VeriFlow: verifying network-wide invariants in real time. In: Networked Systems Design and Implementation (2013)
9. Monsanto, C., Reich, J., Foster, N., Rexford, J., Walker, D.: Composing software-defined networks. In: Networked Systems Design and Implementation (2013)
10. Nelson, T., Ferguson, A.D., Krishnamurthi, S.: Static differential program analysis for software-defined networks. In: International Symposium on Formal Methods (FM) (2015)
11. Nelson, T., Ferguson, A.D., Scheer, M.J.G., Krishnamurthi, S.: Tierless programming and reasoning for software-defined networks. In: Networked Systems Design and Implementation (2014)
12. Nelson, T., Ferguson, A.D., Yu, D., Fonseca, R., Krishnamurthi, S.: Exodus: toward automatic migration of enterprise network configurations to sdns. In: Symposium on SDN Research (SOSR) (2015)
13. Nelson, T., Guha, A., Dougherty, D.J., Fisler, K., Krishnamurthi, S.: A balance of power: expressive, analyzable controller programming. In: Workshop on Hot Topics in Software Defined Networking (2013)
14. Nelson, T., Yu, D., Li, Y., Fonseca, R., Krishnamurthi, S.: Simon: scriptable interactive monitoring for sdns. In: Symposium on SDN Research (SOSR) (2015)
15. Voellmy, A., Wang, J., Yang, Y.R., Ford, B., Hudak, P.: Maple: simplifying SDN programming using algorithmic policies. In: Conference on Communications Architectures, Protocols and Applications (SIGCOMM) (2013)
16. Wundsam, A., Levin, D., Seetharaman, S., Feldmann, A.: OFRewind: enabling record and replay troubleshooting for networks. In: USENIX Annual Technical Conference (2011)

Trustworthy Self-Integrating Systems

John Rushby[(✉)]

Computer Science Laboratory
SRI International
333 Ravenswood Avenue
Menlo Park, CA 94025 USA
rushby@csl.sri.com

Abstract. Patients in intensive care often have a dozen or more medical devices and sensors attached to them. Each is a self-contained system that operates in ignorance of the others, and their integrated operation as a system of systems that delivers coherent therapy is performed by doctors and nurses. But we can easily imagine a scenario where the devices recognize each other and self-integrate (perhaps under the guidance of a master "therapy app") into a unified system. Similar scenarios can be (and are) envisaged for vehicles and roads, and for the devices and services in a home. These self-integrating systems have the potential for significant harm as well as benefit, so as they integrate they should adapt and configure themselves appropriately and should construct an "assurance case" for the utility and safety of the resulting system. Thus, trustworthy self-integration requires autonomous adaptation, synthesis, and verification at integration time, and this means that embedded automated deduction (i.e., theorem provers) will be the engine of integration.

The Design of EasyChair (Abstract)

Andrei Voronkov

University of Manchester, Chalmers University of Technology, EasyChair

EasyChair started in 2002 as a small collection of scripts helping the author to organise submission and reviewing for the conferences LPAR and CADE. Since then it has served over 41,000 conferences and 1,500,000 users. The system has over 297,000 lines of source code (mainly in Perl) and automates paper submission, reviewing, proceedings generation, publishing, conference registration and conference programme generation. Several new modules are under development.

The design and architecture of every very large Web service is unique, and EasyChair is not an exception. This talk overviews design features of EasyChair, which may be interesting for the software engineering community.

Highly agile development methodology. EasyChair development is highly user-oriented. There are essentially no major releases. Even very large modules, such as program generation, are initially released in a minimal form, and then extended, updated and bug-fixed depending on its acceptance by users, user feedback and discovered bugs. For example, the initial version of program generation contained about 8,000 lines of source code, now contains about 32,000 lines and will probably reach over 50,000 lines in the next year. There are frequent updates, normally performed without stopping the server. In the last calendar year there were nearly 1,400 updates, that is, about 4 updates per day.

Design centred around a small number of concepts. EasyChair is uniformly designed. All pages, apart from home pages, have the same logic and structure and contain the same components. There are several programming techniques that are consistently used and supported by libraries.

Semantic page generation. EasyChair design is not based on writing pages as text, as PHP suggests. The page content is an object consisting of components, which are also objects. A typical statement in the program is "add this paragraph to the page summary" or "add this link to the page context menu".

The visual design of pages follows the logic of the design. We are preparing a new design for mobile devises and expect no changes in the code for concrete pages, since visual design is totally separated from page generation.

Automatic generation of efficient and secure code. Nearly all libraries in EasyChair (which constitute about 40% of all code) are generated automatically from SQL table descriptions. This code automates access to tables, object-relational mapping and caching of objects. This eliminates any possibility of SQL injection and guarantees that a large part of the code is correct and efficient.

The fact that the page content (and HTML in general) is an object essentially eliminates a possibility of JavaScript injection.

An object caching technique eliminating mismatch between objects and relational data. Data handled by EasyChair is very complex, thanks to the logic of the application and a variety of conference management models it suports. When a user accesses a page, it may easily result in access to 20 to 60 different relational tables.

Database access in EasyChair uses no joins and is still efficient, thanks to the use of object-relational mapping and object caching technique. Before this technique was implemented, EasyChair had frequent deadlocks (with a much smaller number of users). Maintaining code on database schema changes was a time-consuming and error-prone work. With the new technique we estimate that a ten-fold increase of the number of users will make no effect on the EasyChair performance.

Server-side generation of client-side code. Although EasyChair uses JavaScript extensively, programming dynamic pages or AJAX calls in EasyChair normally requires no knowledge of JavaScript - the JavaScript code is generated by server-side libraries.

Automation of code management. More than 10% of EasyChair code is metacode, dedicated to supporting EasyChair programming, maintaining and analyzing code and making updates. EasyChair has its own code maintenance and versioning implementation used in addition to Git.

Light-weight code analysis. EasyChair contains several modules for code analysis, trying to find common problems (simple examples are the use of uninterpolated variables in strings, or database access outside of library modules) and also generating information for programmers (e.g., sophisticated cross-link analysis).

We also plan an implementation of light-weight dataflow analysis intended to find potential information leaks.

Automatic generation of documentation. In addition to user-provided Doxygen documentation, EasyChair generates Doxygen documentation automatically from the SQL code. It also generates documentation about how pages are accesses from other pages, including access parameters and the type of their values.

Integrity constraint management. In EasyChair one can specify nearly arbitrary integrity constraints on objects, including their relations to other objects (for example, "a submission should have at least one corresponding author" or "a submission on a PC member watch list cannot be on her or his conflict list"). The code for enforcing these constraints is generated automatically. Any updates violating integrity constraints will be rejected. This powerful technique uncovered a number of subtle problems in the EasyChair code. Now adding any new class to EasyChair is necessarily followed by specification of integrity constraints.

Runtime analysis. EasyChair code execution is analysed at runtime, including statistics on database queries, script use and timing to ensure efficiency, understanding of how it is used, and security.

Nearly 50% of EasyChair code is now generated automatically. The high level of code management automation of EasyChair has allowed the author to increase the code size by around 50,000 lines in the last 16 months and also make the code less error-prone and easier to maintain and understand.

Contents

Invited Talks

Teaching Computer Science in the Community

Benny Chor[1]([⊠]) and Assaf Zaritsky[1,2]([⊠])

[1] School of Computer Science, Tel Aviv University, 69978 Tel Aviv, Israel
benny@cs.tau.ac.il, assafzar@gmail.com
[2] Department of Cell Biology, UT Southwestern Medical Center,
Dallas, TX 75390, USA

Abstract. The School of Computer Science at Tel Aviv University, Israel, has initiated and carried out a project titled "Teaching Computer Science in the Community". The project aims to introduce scientific thinking and basic computer science concepts in an informal setting to school children from low socio-economic background. The project is implemented as a single semester undergraduate elective course, in which third year computer science students teach in schools and community centers. Here, we describe the spirit, content, and structure of the course and discuss insight we have gained over the last four years of teaching it.

1 Background

Teaching Computer Science in the Community is an elective course offered in 2008–2014 by the school of Computer Science (CS) at Tel Aviv University (TAU) as part of the regular undergraduate CS curriculum. The course combines academic content and social involvement, with the basic underlying theme of introducing scientific thinking and CS concepts in an informal setting to school children. The course engages three layers of participants:

1. School children (250 in 2014).
2. Undergraduate CS students (33 in 2014), acting as instructors to these school children.
3. Course staff (3 in 2014), responsible for the course academic contents, pedagogical aspects, and administration.

Most school children participating in the project are 10 to 14 years old, and come from low socio-economic neighborhoods in the Tel Aviv metropolitan area. The ultimate goals of the project are to attract the children to sciences and technology, CS in particular, to increase their accessibility to higher education. Most parents of the participating children did not have the opportunity to obtain higher education. Thus, an implicit goal is to present this option, by having the undergraduate students become role models for the children. A secondary goal is to empower the students-instructors, who must deal with challenging and often unexpected educational situations, and to broaden their social awareness.

In this paper, we describe the content and administration of the course based on our experience in the last four years, starting from 2011, when we became in charge of the course.

© Springer International Publishing Switzerland 2016
N. Bjørner et al. (Eds.): ICDCIT 2016, LNCS 9581, pp. 3–9, 2016.
DOI: 10.1007/978-3-319-28034-9_1

2   Activities Content

Initially, during 2011 and 2012, the activities carried out in schools and community centers were mostly taken from Computer Science Unplugged (see below), and consequently were "computer free". During these two years, we witnessed a strong demand by the school children to include some hands-on activities, where they can "touch the keyboards". Consequently, we incorporated introductory programming classes in the curriculum. In addition, as of 2014, every group of school children visited the offices of a high-tech company and was introduced to its activities. In the following sections, we elaborate on these three components.

2.1   Computer Science Unplugged

Much of the teaching material is taken from the program Computer Science Unplugged (CSU), developed by Tim Bell, Ian Witten and Michael Fellows [1] (http://csunplugged.org/activities/). CSU teaches concepts of scientific thinking and problem solving, especially in computer science, through games and activities that do not require computers. Activities include topics such as the binary number system and how it is used to represent text and images, error correction codes, digital images representation and processing, information theory, cryptography, graphs and graph algorithms. Many activities were translated to Hebrew by Benny Chor and Shimon Schocken (http://www.csunplugged.org.il/), and some original activities were added as well. The informal nature and flexibility of this program, as well as the ability to adjust the expositions and activities to varying ages, makes it suitable for our purposes.

One of the popular activities, the Card Flip Magic, is briefly described here (see http://csunplugged.org/error-detection/#Card_Flip_Magic). The activity starts with a discussion about transmission of digital messages (text, audio, or video) between computers, cell phones, and other electronic devices. In particular, how messages are received intact, despite noise and errors that may be introduced when the message moves through the communication path. This discussion is followed by a concrete game, employing 25 large cards, each with a black side and a white side. The game proceeds as follows:

1. A volunteer is selected and asked to place the cards in a 5-by-5 square pattern on a board, choosing arbitrarily if the white or black side of each card will face the audience.
2. The student-instructor leaves the classroom for a short while, saying that during this time a second volunteer will flip one of the cards, and that upon returning to class, the student-instructor will guess which card was flipped. The instructor explains that the 5-by-5 pattern is large enough so that a guess cannot be carried out successfully by memorizing the initial arrangement.
3. Before leaving the classroom, the student-instructor announces that he/she will make this task even harder by adding a row and a column of cards to the 5-by-5 pattern, making it a 6-by-6 pattern, noting that this surely makes the guessing task even harder. The student-instructor adds that the second volunteer is allowed to flip any of the 36 cards in the resulting 6-by-6 pattern.

4. The student-instructor leaves the classroom, the door is shut, and the second volunteer flips one card.
5. The student-instructor returns to the classroom and "miraculously" succeeds in guessing the flipped card.

The key to this successful educated guess are the cards in the additional row and column: they define parity bits for error detection and correction, whereas the original 25 cards constitute the message, or information bits. The additional cards are placed so that the number of black-sided cards in each row and column is even (parity bits), allowing detection and correction of a single bit error, and detection (without correction) in the case of two or three bit errors. There are configurations of four bit errors that cannot be detected, and these are later demonstrated to the class.

A couple of additional rounds of this game are performed, and the children discuss how the student-instructor correctly guessed the flipped card. Next, the student-instructor explains the "trick", and this is followed by hands-on activity by the children using smaller size versions of the cards. Finally, the class discusses error detection and correction in a more general setting, including examples from day-to-day life, such as barcodes, ID and credit card numbers.

2.2 Preparing New Activities

In addition to using existing activity outlines, students-instructors design and prepare new activities. This constitutes their major academic task in the course. Examples of such activities include search engines, artificial intelligence, the Turing test, representing audio using numbers (and bits), online privacy, and computer game design. These new activities are added to an activity pool that is accessible to other students and is available online (http://www.csunplugged.org.il, in Hebrew) under the Creative Commons Attribution-ShareAlike 3.0 United States license (CC BY-SA 3.0 US).

2.3 Introductory Programming

Feedback from school children and their instructors suggested that children are interested in learning programming and that it was difficult for them to concentrate on theoretical aspects for the entire course. Responding to this feedback, we added hands-on activities using Scratch , a widely used first programming language for children (https://scratch.mit.edu), to complement the theoretical CSU activities. Scratch's interface fully supports a variety of languages, including Hebrew, which is very helpful for children. Various resources were used by the students-instructors to teach Scratch. The main resources were detailed presentations, prepared by former students of the course, a textbook written at the Weizmann Institute of Science [2], and numerous projects that are featured on the Scratch web site (https://scratch.mit.edu).

2.4   Visits to High-Tech Companies

Israel has a thriving information technology (IT) and start-up industry. Introducing the children to computer science in the real world has two benefits: raising interest and enthusiasm about CS, and inspiring long term career goals. We held a successful pilot during the 3rd year of our project (2013), which served as a model, and became a regular part of the program in the 4th year (2014). Every group of children visited an IT company. These visits were guided by company employees, most of whom were alumni of the Computer Science in the Community course. Typically, one of the class activities before the visit was devoted to an explanation of concepts related to high-tech industry in general, and start-up companies in particular. Remarkably, this addition to the project was initiated and arranged (completely voluntarily) by a former student in the course, highlighting the long-term commitment of students to the project (see http://kidstartupday.wix.com/kidstartupday).

3   Graduation Ceremony

Soon after the end of the semester, we hold a graduation event at the university. The school children are invited, together with their families and representatives from the schools and community centers. University officials (head of CS school, head of the unit for social intervention, dean of the faculty of Exact Sciences, and the deputy rector) are also invited. The event begins with a guided tour of the campus. Each group of school children is led by the same team of students that instructed them during the semester. The ceremony that follows includes greetings by TAU and CS School officials, and a popular science guest lecture. The children are then awarded graduation certificates signed by representatives of the School of Computer Science and the Unit of Community Involvement at TAU. These certificates are greatly valued by the children and their families. Approximately 250 guests attended the event that concluded the 2014 activity.

Following the graduation event, we hold an informal concluding session for the course stuff and the students-instructors. In this session, we encourage criticism and suggestions regarding the course activities and operations. This feedback is valuable for maintaining the course standards and further improving this project. The relationships between the course staff and students are informal and open throughout the semester, and a sentiment of true partnership is formed.

This has led to sincere, constructive feedback that substantially helped improving the project over the years. For example, in the first year we ran this project, we required an extensive review process of each new activity by other students. Following students' criticism that this process was slow, tedious, and not very effective, we modified the review process. The students complained that this process was slow and caused too much overhead. Consequently, we modified the review process. The students also commented that some of the texts we used as examples were written in an old fashion linguistic style, not accessible to most children. These texts were consequently simplified substantially.

4   Course Administration

Many administrative decisions and details should be taken care of while planning and executing this course. Below, we briefly list a number of important ones.

- Collaborations and Funding
  - Recruiting a course staff member from TAU unit for social intervention, and administrative support from the School of CS.
  - Securing funding to the project via university and external resources.
  - Collaborations with several non-profit organizations that provide direct link to schools and community centers.
- Interaction with the schools and community centers
  - Selection and coordination of schools and community centers. The major criteria are genuine interest in the project and the availability of appropriate facilities (e.g., having functioning computers).
  - Reaching an understanding on mutual commitments with schools/community centers. For example, notifying the students-instructors in advance if a planned meeting is cancelled due to school activity, or help with discipline problems by having a teacher present in class during activities.
  - Setting up a network of contacts people (typically teachers or deputy school principals) in each school/community center.
  - Contacting schools/community centers in cases of persistent problems such as continued misbehavior of the children.
- Interaction between course staff and students
  - Recruiting students: This includes advertising the course by sending introductory emails, inviting 2nd and 3rd year CS students who are interested to participate in the project for group meetings with the academic staff. These meetings provide a framework to disseminate detailed information to the students, and an opportunity to assess the abilities and potential of every candidate.
  - Assigning students to teams – in most cases two students per team, and very few singleton teams.
  - Assigning students' teams to schools and community centers, based on students' scheduling constraints, teaching experience and potential.
  - Intensive, brief teaching training for students (4 meetings, 3 h each, during the first 2 weeks of the semester). We note that this is the only formal teaching training CS students get as part of their university studies.
  - Setting a mechanism to track progress of every team of students in each center by filling online reports on a weekly basis.
  - Supplying timely pedagogical advice and assistance to students in cases of difficulties in the classrooms, as well as advice regarding the teaching materials.
  - A mid-semester meeting with the students for sharing experiences, discussing difficulties, resolving problems, and raising awareness to the fact that despite frequent friction points and occasional frustration, the program is highly appreciated by the school children and the school teachers.

- Fostering sincere and open communication between the course staff and the students-instructors.
- Recording new and improved activities in the course website for use by future students and other interested parties.
- Collecting students' feedback and acting to improve the following round of the course accordingly.
- Defining a grading policy, based on a combination of students' activities during the training, feedback from schools and community centers, and the quality, originality, and readability of the academic task.

These administrative aspects are crucial to the successful operation of such projects, and are as important to its success as the academic contents. We decided not to elaborate more on these aspects in this manuscript, as many of them will vary in different contexts and locations. Detailed descriptions of these aspects are available (in Hebrew) [3]. The activities developed by the students-instructors are available only in Hebrew. However, the central educational components on which our program is based, Computer Science Unplugged and Scratch, are readily accessible. Interested educators are encouraged to contact the authors of this paper, BC and AZ, for further details.

5   Concluding Remarks

We did not have the resources and means to conduct a rigorous evaluation of the project using accepted statistical and educational tools. Yet, we did formulate and distribute feedback forms annually, and collected them from participating children and students-instructors. Many students reflected that participation in the course was an important challenge and an enriching experience. Some described it as the most meaningful course throughout their undergraduate Computer Science studies. A number of school children commented that this project exposed them to science and technology and encouraged them to register to elective computer and science courses (in their schools). Some children expressed interest in future academic studies.

Projects of a similar spirit were adopted in Israel by the Ashkelon Academic College and by the University of Haifa. In both cases, our course staff provided guidance, advice and teaching material.

The main long term goal of this project is making science, particularly computer science, accessible to children from low socio-economical backgrounds. Despite the lack of rigorous statistical evidence, we hope and believe that this project will achieve its goals and serve as a model bridging students, academia, science, technology and education.

Funding. This project was supported by the School of Computer Science, Tel-Aviv University, by Google project CS@HS, and by the Council of Higher Education in Israel.

Acknowledgements. We are proud to thank many friends, colleagues, and students, for help and support during the development and operation of this project.

Benny Chor wishes to thank Tim Bell and Mike Fellows, initiators of the Computer Science Unplugged project, for their friendship, support, and many hours of discussions and debates. Many thanks to Shimon Schocken from the Inter Disciplenary Center in Hertzeliya for co-translating CSU material to Hebrew, and running together a similar, initial project during the years 2009 and 2010.

We would like to thank Rachel Warshavsky, Idit Helman, and Nadia Belkind from the Unit of Community Involvement at the Dean of Students Office, Tel-Aviv University, for the fruitful partnership, which substantially improved the quality of our project. Special thanks to Yasmin Denenberg from the Unit of Community Involvement, who was an essential part of the course staff during the three years 2012 to 2014, and provided indispensable knowledge and experience on the pedagogical aspects of this operation. Thanks to Pnina Neria-Barzilay from the School of Computer Science at Tel Aviv University, who helped solving numerous administrative and logistical problems that occurred during our activities, and to the School of Computer Science at Tel Aviv University, whose support made this project possible.

Thanks to Matan Hadadi, our former student, for his KidStartUpDay initiative. Thanks to the many former course students who participated in our intensive training for newer students, shared their experience, and hosted school children groups in visits to high tech companies, where they are employed. Yoav Ram, Noy Rotbart, Amir Rubinstein, Arieh Zaritsky, and Hilla Zaritsky provided helpful comments on earlier drafts of this manuscript. Thanks to Noga Levy-Oron and David Amar, who were the teaching assistants in 2013–2014. Last but not least, we thank the 110+ TAU CS students who took on this challenge (during the years 2011 to 2014) and carried it out remarkably.

References

1. Bell, T.C., Witten, I.H., Fellows, M.: Computer Science Unplugged ... Off-line activities and games for all ages (1998). http://csunplugged.org/wp-content/uploads/2015/01/unplugged-book-v1.pdf
2. Meerbaum-Salant, O., Armoni, M., Ben-Ari, M.: Learning computer science concepts with Scratch. Comput. Sci. Educ. **23**, 239–264 (2013)
3. Zaritsky, A., Chor, B.: Teaching Computer Science in the Community at Tel Aviv University, Hebetim in Computer Science (in Hebrew), pp. 5–13 (2014)

Attacks in the Resource-as-a-Service (RaaS) Cloud Context

Danielle Movsowitz, Orna Agmon Ben-Yehuda, and Assaf Schuster[✉]

Technion—Israel Institute of Technology, Haifa, Israel
dani.movso@campus.technion.ac.il, {ladypine,assaf}@cs.technion.ac.il
http://www.cs.technion.ac.il

Abstract. The Infrastructure-as-a-Service (IaaS) cloud is evolving towards the Resource-as-a-Service (RaaS) cloud: a cloud which requires economic decisions to be taken in real time by automatic agents. Does the economic angle introduce new vulnerabilities? Can old vulnerabilities be exploited on RaaS clouds from different angles? How should RaaS clouds be designed to protect them from attacks? In this survey we analyze relevant literature in view of RaaS cloud mechanisms and propose directions for the design of RaaS clouds.

Keywords: Cloud computing · Privacy · Security · RaaS

1 Introduction

The Resource-as-a-Service (RaaS) cloud [1] is an economic model of cloud computing that allows providers to sell individual resources (such as CPU, memory, and I/O resources) for a few seconds at a time. In the RaaS cloud, clients are able to purchase exactly the resources they need when they need them. In light of global trends and economic incentives driving the providers to a price war [3], we anticipate that the RaaS cloud will gradually replace the IaaS cloud. In the RaaS cloud, e-commerce is quick and frequent. It is impossible for a human to make the economic decisions required to optimize the resource purchases. Hence, in the RaaS cloud, clients will deploy automatic agents to conduct the e-commerce for them. This e-commerce may be centralized (an auction, for example) or decentralized (as in a marketplace or negotiations).

Commercial cloud users are selfish economic entities, with secrets and potentially conflicting preferences. Since some clients may be malicious, most clients expect a certain level of privacy and security within the system. The more private and secure the cloud is, the more motivated the users are to trust the cloud with important tasks. In the past few years, numerous studies have been published on different attack methods (side channel, escape to hypervisor, etc.), levels of isolation in cloud computing systems, and how to detect and limit attacks.

The introduction of economic aspects into the hypervisor, the basic layer of the cloud's operating system, may introduce new vulnerabilities. In addition, known attacks may be launched in different ways against an economically driven

© Springer International Publishing Switzerland 2016
N. Bjørner et al. (Eds.): ICDCIT 2016, LNCS 9581, pp. 10–18, 2016.
DOI: 10.1007/978-3-319-28034-9_2

machine, or may be combined in different ways with economic attacks. In this paper we survey non-economic attacks in the context of the RaaS cloud, in order to learn how a successful, undetected attack may be launched, and what can be done to defend against it.

We begin this paper with a description of Ginseng, an example of an economic resource allocation mechanism in the hypervisor, in Sect. 2. In Sect. 3 we survey cloud attacks which may prove relevant in the context of the RaaS cloud. We conclude in Sect. 4.

2   Allocating RAM Using an Auction

The division of resources according to economic mechanisms is discussed in several academic works [4,15,16,18,26] and implemented in several commercial clouds. Amazon's spot instances are sold using an auction, in which entire IaaS machines are rented. In CloudSigma's burst price method, clients pay a fast-changing price.[1] Both pricing mechanisms are declared to be affected by supply and demand, but their exact algorithm is kept secret [2]. In this work we use the terminology and mechanism used by Ginseng [4], the first economy-driven cloud system that allocates memory efficiently to selfish cloud clients. It does so by using the Memory Progressive Second Price (MPSP) auction, which is based on the Progressive Second Price (PSP) auction [16].

In a RaaS cloud, each guest has a different, changing, private (secret) *valuation* for memory: how much benefit it expects to gain from different quantities of memory. This is what guides the agent's actions in any economic transaction it performs (i.e., negotiations or auction bidding). We define the aggregate benefit of a memory allocation to all guests—their satisfaction from auction results—using the game-theoretic measure of *social welfare*. The social welfare of an allocation is defined as the sum of all the guests' valuations of the memory they receive in this allocation. An efficient memory auction allocates the memory to the guests such that the social welfare is maximized.

VCG [6,13,25] auctions optimize social welfare by incentivizing even selfish participants with conflicting economic interests to inform the auctioneer of their true valuation of the auctioned items. They do so by the *exclusion compensation* principle, which means that each participant is charged for the damage it inflicts on other participants' social welfare, rather than directly for the items it wins. VCG auctions are used in various settings, including Facebook's repeated auctions [14,17].

The Memory Progressive Second Price (MPSP) auction, which Ginseng uses, resembles a VCG auction. It is a repeated auction in which each auction round takes 12 s. In each auction round the participants bid in order to rent memory for the following 12 s. The MPSP protocol is illustrated in Fig. 1. To work at this rate, the participants are not human clients who own the guest virtual machines, but rather software agents which work on their behalf, according to the valuation

---

[1] CloudSigma's Pricing https://www.cloudsigma.com/pricing/, accessed October 2015.

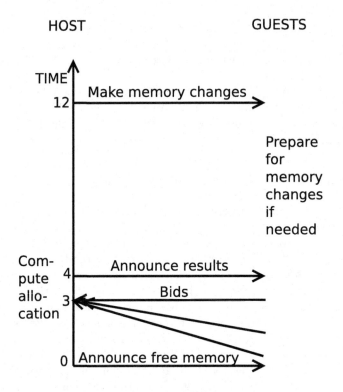

Fig. 1. Ginseng's MPSP protocol.

functions and business-logic algorithms embedded in them by their respective owners. Accordingly, the auction is orchestrated by the host's auctioneer, which is a software agent working on behalf of the cloud provider. Ginseng's structure in illustrated in Fig. 2.

An MPSP auction round begins with the host's auctioneer announcing the quantity of memory which is up for rent in this round. Then, during the following 3 s, each participant may bid by stating a maximal unit price it is willing to pay for the memory (in terms of dollars per MB per second), and desired ranges of quantities it is willing to accept. The limitation of ranges allows the guest to refuse to get and pay for quantities from which it cannot benefit: for example, if the guest requires 1 GB to avoid thrashing, and can enjoy up to 1.5 GB, it can refuse to get any memory quantity in the range 0–1 GB, but be willing to rent any quantity from 1–1.5 GB.

During the fourth second, the host's auctioneer determines the allocation and the bills each guest will have to pay. The host's auctioneer chooses the allocation which optimizes the social welfare according to the bids. The bills are computed according to the exclusion compensation principle: each guest pays according to the damage it causes other guests, as per their own reported valuation. For each guest i, the host's auctioneer computes the social welfare of all guests except

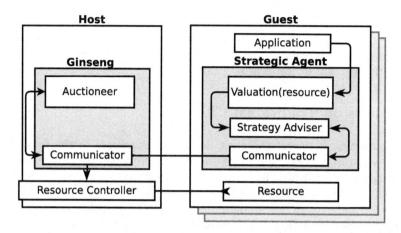

Fig. 2. Ginseng's structure. The auctioneer is a smart agent working for the host. It interacts with the strategic agent within the guest. Once the auction's results are determined, the host actually changes the resource allocation for the guest. The guest uses the resource to operate its applications (presumably one or more main applications, whose performance matters).

guest i. Then it computes what the optimal allocation would be, had guest i not participated in the auction at all, and what the social welfare of all the other guests would be in that case. Guest i's bill is determined as the difference between these two computations. This method of computing payments and choosing an optimal allocation makes truthful bidding the best strategy for the guests: to state the real value they attach to getting a certain quantity of RAM.

Then the host announces the result of the auction to the guests, and gives them 8 s to prepare for a change in the memory allocation (e.g., release memory from the main application), before the change actually takes place. Finally, at the end of the 12 s, the host actually changes the memory allocation (if necessary).

When the host announces the results, each guest hears in private how much memory it won, and for what price. In addition, the host informs all guests of the lowest bid price among those whose bidders won any memory (denoted by P_{min_in}), and the highest bid price among those whose bidders did not win any memory (denoted by P_{max_out}). This information is broadcast for three reasons. First, the guest agents use this information to plan their next bids: they use it to approximate the borderline unit price bid, below which they are not likely to win any memory in the next round. Second, guest agents can acquire this information over time through the rejection or acceptance of their bids, so it is futile to try to hide it. Third, helping the guest agents learn the borderline unit price bid quickly can help the system stabilize, and thus reach the maximal social welfare quickly.

Although we refer in this work to MPSP terminology used in Ginseng, many of the observations we make here are also relevant to other mechanisms which mimic market pressure. In Ginseng, resource pressure is felt by participants in the bill they pay, which reflects the damage they caused to the social welfare. In mechanisms which rely on computing a clearing price (the highest price for which the demand is equal to the supply or exceeds it), resource pressure is felt through the increase in the clearing price.

3   Attacks on Traditional Clouds

Cloud computing is one of the most dominant paradigms in the information technology industry nowadays. More and more companies are moving to cloud computing solutions, which in turn requires attackers to find new and inventive ways to attack cloud computing systems. In this section we will classify attack types and explain how to map the internal system infrastructure, how to determine levels of isolation, and how to detect and limit attacks.

3.1   Classifying Attack Types

Many types of attacks can be launched against cloud computing systems. These include attacks aimed at obtaining information from innocent users or resource-freeing attacks (RFAs) to improve personal cloud performance. Younis et al. [27] survey the different types of cache based side channel attacks and point out weaknesses in currently researched solutions. Varadarajan et al. [23] show how to improve a VM's performance by forcing a competing VM to saturate some bottleneck (a resource used by the VM). This can slow down or shift the competing applications' use of a desired resource.

Our goal is to determine which of the above attacks are most likely to be launched against Ginseng, which are irrelevant, and which are most likely to succeed. Is it possible, for example, that an attack analogous to the RFA attack can be launched against Ginseng in order to obtain a maximum amount of memory at the expense of other system guests? This might be done, for instance, by slowly raising P_{max_out} and forcing the rest of the guests to exhaust their resources up to the point where they need to bid for a smaller amount of memory, thus freeing memory that the attacker can obtain for a lower bid. This type of attack can be carried out either by an attacker who is the highest bidder not allocated memory, or as a part of a grand-scheme collusion with other agents.

3.2   Mapping the Internal System Infrastructure and Determining Levels of Isolation

A successful attack within a cloud computing system usually requires a profound understanding of the internal system infrastructure and the capability to map the system's users and their level of isolation. Ristenpart et al. [20] showed that one can inexpensively probe and explore the system to determine the location of an instance in the cloud infrastructure, determine whether two instances are co-resident on the same physical machine, launch instances that will be co-resident with other users instances, and exploit cross-VM information leakage once co-resident.

Today it would be very hard—though not impossible—to do what Ristenpart et al. did in 2009. One reason is that the spot instances of only one zone can contain tens of thousands of machines. Moreover, machines today are live migrated and their IP may no longer indicate the IP or identity of guest machines co-located with them on the same physical machine. Finally, machine types are mixed on physical machines. All of this makes it harder to get a machine co-resident with a predesignated victim machine. However, on a RaaS cloud machine an attacker can directly gain from attacking guests sharing the same physical machine. We can learn from Ristenpart et al. that **if** the population is small and there are no migrations (as in the case of Ginseg today), **then** it is easier to learn about neighbors.

Zhang et al. [28] introduced a system called HomeAlone that allows guests to use cache-based side channel probing in order to determine their level of isolation. The HomeAlone system allows users to silence their activity in a selected cache region for a period of time, in which they can monitor cache usage and detect unexpected activity. This system can be used to find information on other virtual machines that share the same hardware but do not belong to the same owner.

Caron et al. [5] proposed a placement heuristic that allows guests to determine the level of security they require by stating co-residency requirements (alone, friends, enemies) or by stating the level of privacy/security they need. Ginseng does not currently take into consideration guest preferences regarding security/privacy levels or their co-residency requirements. This opens the door to numerous types of attacks that do not exploit the Ginseng protocol itself. In the future, it might be interesting to explore the option of determining the level of security/privacy and isolation between guests by allowing them to state bidding borders (for example a price/memory range that will define co-residency).

3.3 Detecting and Limiting Attacks

Security measures to detect and limit attacks can range from simple alarm systems (such as alarms triggered when trying to access an unauthorized area) to complex systems that monitor and learn user actions and performance over time.

1. Dolgikh et al. [7] showed that malicious users (attackers) can be detected in two phases: the training phase and the detection phase. In the training phase the system learns and classifies the "normal" behavior of system users. In the detection phase, user activities are monitored and observed; any deviation from the "normal" behavior is detected. This work is relevant to Ginseng in two manners:

   (a) Detection of malicious behavior. The attacker may also use the two phase approach. During the training phase, the attacker gathers information about the system's behavior, the neighboring guests, and their bid needs. Furthermore, the attacker can collect information regarding user schedules that can influence changes in supply and demand. It may even figure out the best time to attack. This information can be used to plan the attack, and in particular, the best cues for timing costly attacks. During the detection phase, the attacker will hunt for those cues, and launch the attack at the perfect time.

During the training phase, the attacker may be monitored and certain actions may be considered as "out of the ordinary behavior" and thus stopped. However, this approach has its risks, as benign agents who online-learn their best strategy may be misidentified as attackers.

(b) Automatic prevention of malicious behavior. Several mechanisms were proposed to prevent rapid memory allocation changes. These include an affine-maximizer based method, which taxes the difference between allocations [19], and a reclaim factor method [19], which controls the fraction of the memory that is reclaimed by the system to be sold by the next auction. This method resembles Waldspurger's tax on unused memory [26]. This means that an attack on Ginseng might fail due to the system's sluggishness.

We note that the sluggishness fails actions according to the action and not the intention behind it. Hence, it might also fail benign guest actions, if they are considered harmful to the system.

2. Shi et al. [22] presented Chameleon, a non-intrusive, low-overhead dynamic page coloring mechanism that provides strict cache isolation only during security-critical operations. If an attack on Ginseng is cache based, implementing the Chameleon mechanism may obstruct attempts to attack the system.

3. Varadarajan et al. [24] introduced the concept of soft isolation—reducing the risks of sharing through better scheduling. They show that a minimum run time guarantee for VM virtual CPUs that limits the frequency of preemptions can effectively prevent existing prime+probe cache-based side-channel attacks. This particular work is relevant to RaaS machines that use economic measures to allocate CPU resources, such as CloudSigma, which uses CPU burst prices. It is not directly relevant to the memory allocation method used by Ginseng.

Note that Varadarajan et al.'s method protects the system at the cost of introducing an inefficiency in resource allocation. In that, it resembles the sluggish mechanisms, which protect the system against quick changes, at the expense of reducing its responsiveness.

4   Conclusion

We have reviewed several kinds of attacks on traditional clouds and on the new RaaS cloud. In addition to its vulnerability to regular attacks, an economically driven hypervisor is also vulnerable to attacks designed specifically for economic systems, using the special features of the system against it. Therefore, economic cloud systems have to be designed while considering both types of attacks, and include built-in defenses. This design might consist of patches to the original

designs, protecting against specific vulnerabilities. It may even require a whole
new mechanism, which prioritizes privacy and security over other considerations.
There is a large volume of work addressing privacy in distributed systems where
no trusted entity exists [9,11,12,21]. However, it might be enough to assume
that the resource provider, the host and its auctioneer are trusted entities. Data
mining which preserves client privacy [8,10] may be used to reduce the amount
of information that leaks by announcing global data about the auction's result,
such as P_{min_in} or P_{max_out}.

Acknowledgment. This work was partially funded by the Prof. A. Pazi Joint Research
Foundation. We thank Dr. Eran Tromer, Prof. Katrina Ligett, Dr. Arik Friedman and
Shunit Agmon for fruitful discussions.

References

1. Agmon Ben-Yehuda, O., Ben-Yehuda, M., Schuster, A., Tsafrir, D.: The resource-
   as-a-service (RaaS) cloud. In: USENIX Conference on Hot Topics in Cloud Computing (HotCloud) (2012)
2. Agmon Ben-Yehuda, O., Ben-Yehuda, M., Schuster, A., Tsafrir, D.: Deconstructing
   Amazon EC2 spot instance pricing. ACM Trans. Econ. Comput. **1**(3), 16:1–16:20
   (2013)
3. Agmon Ben-Yehuda, O., Ben-Yehuda, M., Schuster, A., Tsafrir, D.: The rise of
   RaaS: the resource-as-a-service cloud. Commun. ACM **57**(7), 76–84 (2014)
4. Agmon Ben-Yehuda, O., Posener, E., Ben-Yehuda, M., Schuster, A., Mu'alem, A.:
   Ginseng: market-driven memory allocation. ACM SIGPLAN Not. **49**(7), 41–52
   (2014)
5. Caron, E., Cornabas, J.R.: Improving users' isolation in IaaS: virtual machine
   placement with security constraints. In: IEEE International Conference on Cloud
   Computing (CLOUD), pp. 64–71 (2014)
6. Clarke, E.H.: Multipart pricing of public goods. Public Choice **11**(1), 17–33 (1971)
7. Dolgikh, A., Birnbaum, Z., Chen, Y., Skormin, V.: Behavioral modeling for suspi-
   cious process detection in cloud computing environments. In: IEEE International
   Conference on Mobile Data Management (MDM), vol. 2, pp. 177–181 (2013)
8. Friedman, A., Schuster, A.: Data mining with differential privacy. In: ACM International Conference on Knowledge Discovery and Data Mining (SIGKDD), pp.
   493–502 (2010)
9. Friedman, A., Sharfman, I., Keren, D., Schuster, A.: Privacy-preserving distributed
   stream monitoring. In: Annual Network and Distributed System Security Symposium (NDSS) (2014)
10. Friedman, A., Wolff, R., Schuster, A.: Providing k-anonymity in data mining.
    VLDB J. **17**(4), 789–804 (2008)
11. Gilburd, B., Schuster, A., Wolff, R.: k-ttp: a new privacy model for large-scale dis-
    tributed environments. In: ACM International Conference on Knowledge Discovery
    and Data Mining (SIGKDD), pp. 563–568 (2004)
12. Gilburd, B., Schuster, A., Wolff, R.: Privacy-preserving data mining on data grids
    in the presence of malicious participants. In: International Symposium on High-
    Performance Distributed Computing (HPDC), pp. 225–234 (2004)
13. Groves, T.: Incentives in teams. Econometrica **41**(4), 617–631 (1973)

14. Hegeman, J.: Facebook's ad auction. Talk at Ad Auctions Workshop, May 2010
15. Kelly, F.: Charging and rate control for elastic traffic. Eur. Trans. Telecommun. **8**, 33–37 (1997)
16. Lazar, A., Semret, N.: Design and analysis of the progressive second price auction for network bandwidth sharing. Technical report, Columbia University (1998). http://econwpa.repec.org/eps/game/papers/9809/9809001.pdf
17. Lucier, B., Paes Leme, R., Tardos, E.: On revenue in the generalized second price auction. In: International Conference on World Wide Web (WWW) (2012)
18. Maillé, P., Tuffin, B.: Multi-bid auctions for bandwidth allocation in communication networks. In: IEEE INFOCOM (2004)
19. Posener, E.: Dynamic memory allocation in cloud computers using progressive second price auction. Master's thesis, Technion (2013)
20. Ristenpart, T., Tromer, E., Shacham, H., Savage, S.: Hey, you, get off of my cloud: exploring information leakage in third-party compute clouds. In: ACM Conference on Computer and Communications Security (SIGSAC), pp. 199–212 (2009)
21. Schuster, A., Wolff, R., Gilburd, B.: Privacy-preserving association rule mining in large-scale distributed systems. In: Cluster, Cloud and Grid Computing (CCGrid), pp. 411–418 (2004)
22. Shi, J., Song, X., Chen, H., Zang, B.: Limiting cache-based side-channel in multi-tenant cloud using dynamic page coloring. In: IEEE/IFIP International Conference on Dependable Systems and Networks Workshops (DSN-W), pp. 194–199 (2011)
23. Varadarajan, V., Kooburat, T., Farley, B., Ristenpart, T., Swift, M.M.: Resource-freeing attacks: improve your cloud performance (at your neighbor's expense). In: ACM Conference on Computer and Communications Security (SIGSAC), pp. 281–292 (2012)
24. Varadarajan, V., Ristenpart, T., Swift, M.: Scheduler-based defenses against cross-vm side-channels. In: Usenix Security (2014)
25. Vickrey, W.: Counterspeculation, auctions, and competitive sealed tenders. J. Finance **16**(1), 8–37 (1961)
26. Waldspurger, C.A.: Memory resource management in Vmware ESX server. USENIX Symp. Operating Syst. Des. Implementation (OSDI) **36**, 181–194 (2002)
27. Younis, Y., Kifayat, K., Merabti, M.: Cache side-channel attacks in cloud computing. In: International Conference on Cloud Security Management (ICCSM), p. 138. Academic Conferences Limited, (2014)
28. Zhang, Y., Juels, A., Oprea, A., Reiter, M.K.: Homealone: co-residency detection in the cloud via side-channel analysis. In: IEEE Symposium on Security and Privacy (SP), pp. 313–328. IEEE (2011)

Trustworthy Self-Integrating Systems

John Rushby$^{(\boxtimes)}$

Computer Science Laboratory, SRI International,
333 Ravenswood Avenue, Menlo Park, CA 94025, USA
rushby@csl.sri.com

Abstract. Patients in intensive care often have a dozen or more medical devices and sensors attached to them. Each is a self-contained system that operates in ignorance of the others, and their integrated operation as a system of systems that delivers coherent therapy is performed by doctors and nurses. But we can easily imagine a scenario where the devices recognize each other and self-integrate (perhaps under the guidance of a master "therapy app") into a unified system. Similar scenarios can be (and are) envisaged for vehicles and roads, and for the devices and services in a home. These self-integrating systems have the potential for significant harm as well as benefit, so as they integrate they should adapt and configure themselves appropriately and should construct an "assurance case" for the utility and safety of the resulting system. Thus, trustworthy self-integration requires autonomous adaptation, synthesis, and verification at integration time, and this means that embedded automated deduction (i.e., theorem provers) will be the engine of integration.

1 Introduction

An invited paper provides an opportunity for more speculative inquiry than usual, and I will use this chance to sketch some of the challenges and opportunities in a class of systems that I think is just around the corner, but that does not seem to be widely recognized.

We are familiar with systems built from components, and are becoming so with systems of systems. Components are intended as parts of a larger whole and their interfaces and functionality are designed with that in mind. *Systems*, on the other hand, are intended to be self-sufficient and to serve a specific purpose, so they often cooperate awkwardly when combined as systems of systems. *Open* systems are intended to cooperate with others and they restore some of the characteristics of components while still operating as self-sufficient individually purposeful systems. Open *Adaptive* Systems (OAS), a popular topic of current interest, are open systems that are capable of adjusting their behavior to function better in systems of systems.

The systems that I am interested in here take this one step further: they do not merely adapt to cooperate better with their neighbors, but *self-integrate* to deliver some new capability or service, possibly under the direction of an application designed for that purpose. The integrating application or its surrogates

© Springer International Publishing Switzerland 2016
N. Bjørner et al. (Eds.): ICDCIT 2016, LNCS 9581, pp. 19–29, 2016.
DOI: 10.1007/978-3-319-28034-9_3

will seek useful capabilities among its peers, cause them to adapt or configure appropriately, and synthesize suitable wrappers, shims, or glue. This behavior has something in common with Service Oriented Architecture (SOA) as well as OAS, but what I want to posit is that the capabilities and services so constructed will be used for somewhat critical purposes where assurance of function and safety should be provided. Skeptics may concur that self-integrating systems are likely, but not their application as critical systems that require assurance. Accordingly, in the next section I sketch some scenarios proposed by others and then, in Sect. 3 outline some current and recent work. In Sect. 4, I explain why I believe that automated verification and synthesis are required at integration-time and I describe how modern developments in automated deduction can provide these. Section 5 summarizes and concludes that embedded automated deduction is the enabling engine for trustworthy self-integration.

2   Scenarios

We can build quite complex software-intensive systems that are individually safe: civil aircraft are a good example, as there have been no serious aircraft incidents due to faulty software.[1] There is a price to this record of safety, however, for current methods of safety assurance are based on strongly predictable, often deterministic, behavior. This prohibits even simple kinds of adaptive or intelligent behavior, such as control laws that optimize for the circumstances of each flight (e.g., weight and weight distribution, stiffness of actuators, etc.).

Furthermore, assurance applies to each system in isolation: there are no guarantees that the interaction of individually safe systems will be safe. Thus, although individual aircraft are safe, their interaction is managed by another, separate system for air traffic management. The move to NextGen, where individual aircraft take more responsibility for the safety of their interactions, as cars do on the road, is proving to be a challenging endeavor.

The future will be about interacting systems. Interaction will come about because, as systems become more ubiquitous and embedded in our lives, so they necessarily interact with each other through the "plant." For example, cars and traffic lights interact to create, or to avoid, traffic jams. Currently, there is (at least in the USA) essentially no management of this interaction, so cars waste gasoline accelerating and decelerating from one uncoordinated red light to another, or lights show green while traffic cannot move because it is backed up from the uncoordinated red light ahead. As systems become better able to communicate, so we expect them to become more open and to integrate in a productive manner, so that traffic lights and cars should communicate and respond to changing traffic and the behavior of neighboring lights. Later, conventional traffic lights can be replaced or supplemented by virtual traffic lights that interact directly with car systems and can be deployed whenever and wherever needed.

---

[1] Due to faulty requirements, there have been incidents in systems implemented in software, but there have been no incidents due to software development.

Integration of large scale systems such as air and ground transportation presents formidable challenges, so it is not likely they will self-integrate any time soon, but it seems quite plausible for smaller systems. We already see this in the nascent "Internet of Things" (IoT). For example, I recently added a Chromecast to the large TV display in my living room, turned on the DLNA server built in to the Windows machine that stores my digital photos, and installed an app on my Android phone; I can now view my photos on the large display (transmitted over WiFi from the PC in another room) while using my phone to control everything from my couch. It is remarkable that this works at all, still more remarkable how easy it is to set up, but sadly it does not work very well. The photos are transmitted at full resolution despite the limited (1920 × 1080) resolution of the display. My WiFi is slow and the PC is in a room distant from the router; as a result one photo may still be in the process of transmission when the timer in the Android app calls for the next one; then everything hangs; sometimes a restart is sufficient, and sometimes a full reboot is needed. Viewing my photos is hardly a critical endeavor, but it is not uncommon for things that work "well enough" to undergo "mission creep" and become part of some critical enterprise (e.g., we could imagine my setup for home photos being used to display images needed during medical procedures), which is fine—until things fail.

Goldman and colleagues describe several intriguing applications for a more trustworthy IoT in a hypothesized "Operating Room of the Future" and "Intensive Care Unit of the Future" [1]. I sketch a few of these.

Some seriously ill patients are maintained on a heart-lung machine while undergoing surgery. And sometimes an X-ray is required during the procedure. Surgeons may temporarily turn off the heart-lung machine so the patient's chest is still while the X-ray is taken. They must then remember to turn it back on. We can posit a scenario where the heart-lung machine and the X-ray camera recognize each other and negotiate their safe interaction. In the simplest case, the camera could request a still period from the heart-lung machine; in a more attractive approach, the heart-lung machine could notify the camera of the null points during its inflation and deflation of the chest.

A patient under general anesthesia is generally provided an enriched oxygen supply. Some throat surgeries use a laser and this can cause burning (or even fire) in the presence of abundant oxygen, so the human anesthetist does not enrich the oxygen supply in this case. There is an obvious risk of human error in this scenario. Accordingly, it would surely be good if the laser and the anesthesia machine could recognize each other so that the laser could request reduced oxygen. Of course, we do not want other (possibly faulty) devices to cause the oxygen supply to be reduced. It is also possible that a faulty anesthesia machine may not reduce the oxygen, so we would like a safety interlock that does not allow the laser to light unless the oxygen has actually been reduced. Conversely, there may be emergency scenarios where the patient's health or survival urgently needs enriched oxygen (this may be detected by a "pulse oximeter," the third component of a larger integrated system) and we would like the combined system to support this, either by an override that autonomously shuts off the laser and enriches the air supply, or by alerting the human operators.

Accurate blood pressure sensors can be inserted into an intravenous (IV) fluid supply. The reading needs to be corrected for the difference in height between the sensor (which can be standardized by the height of the IV pole) and the patient. Some hospital beds have a height sensor, but this is a fairly crude device to assist nurses in their activities. We can imagine an ICU where blood pressure data from IV sensors and height measurements from the beds are available on the local network and integrated by monitoring and alerting services. These services need to be sure the bed height and blood pressure sensor readings are from the same patient, and there needs to be an ontology that distinguishes height-corrected and uncorrected sensor readings. The noise- and fault-characteristics of the bed height sensor mean that alerts should be probably driven from changes in the uncorrected reading; alternatively, since bed height will seldom change, it is possible that a noise and fault-masking wrapper could be synthesized for this value.

A machine for Patient Controlled Analgesia (PCA) administers a pain-killing drug to patients on demand (when the patient presses a button). To prevent overdoses, PCA devices will not deliver the drug when thresholds in a built-in model (whose parameters can be programmed by a nurse) are exceeded. The thresholds are conservative, so patients may sometimes experience unrelieved pain unnecessarily. A pulse oximeter (PO) attached to the patient provides a specific indication of overdose, so the combination of a PCA and PO could provide safer and greater relief. We can imagine the combination of a standard PCA, a PO, and an application that manipulates the thresholds of the PCA based on data from the PO to allow this improved capability. As with the blood pressure example, we need to be sure that the two devices are attached to the same patient, and that all parties interpret the measurements consistently (i.e., there is a shared ontology). Furthermore, the integrating app and its assurance case must deal suitably with new hazards due to integration and possible faults therein. For example, if the app works by blocking button presses when an approaching overdose is indicated, then loss of communication could remove the safety function. If, on the other hand, it must approve each button press, then loss of communication may affect pain relief but not safety. In both cases, it is necessary to be sure that faults in the blocking or approval mechanism cannot generate spurious button presses.

Most will agree, I think, that the integrated systems sketched above could be readily constructed as bespoke systems by suitably skilled teams. But what I have in mind is that these systems "self assemble" from their separate component systems given little more than a sketch of the desired integrated function. The sketch might be a formal specification, or an idealized reference implementation that assumes fault-free and safe operation of the individual systems.

Beyond automation of this self assembly, the challenge is to provide assurance for safety of the integrated system. The state of the art in safety assurance is the assurance "case," which is an argument, based on evidence about the system and its design and construction, that certain claims (usually about safety but possibly about other important properties such as security or performance) are true [2]. When systems interact, we would like the assurance case for their composition to be assembled in a modular or compositional way from the cases for the individual systems. This is difficult because, as we noted previously, safety generally does not compose: that is to say the composition of safe systems it not necessarily safe, primarily because their interaction may introduce new hazards. For example, the laser and anesthesia machine may be individually safe, but their integration has a new hazard (burning in an oxygen-enriched air supply). The construction of the joint assurance case is therefore a fairly difficult process, typically requiring human insight, which presupposes that system integration is a deliberate and planned procedure.

For the near term, I expect that system self-integration will be initiated by an application that embodies the purpose of the integration (e.g., a "safe analgesia app" that integrates a PCA and PO) but we can imagine that future systems will integrate spontaneously as they discover each other, similar to the way that human teams assemble to solve difficult problems (although even here there must be some agreed purpose for the teaming). And as with human teams, the integration may involve exchange of assumptions and claims, negotiation, and some relinquishing of autonomy and acceptance of constraints. Clearly this is an ambitious vision, but there is recent and current work that addresses many of the precursor challenges.

3   Recent Work

DEOS (Dependable Operating Systems for Embedded Systems Aiming at Practical Applications) was a large project in Japan that ran from 2008 to 2013. The overall ambition of DEOS was to ensure the dependability of open systems subject to change [3]; thus, it focuses on the evolution of systems rather than their self-integration. In DEOS, a system assurance case is maintained as part of the system and is used to guide its adaptation to failure and to changed requirements. For local adaptation (e.g., responding to failure), an online representation of the assurance case (called a D-Case) is used to guide adjustments to the system, potentially automatically, under the guidance of a scripting language call D-Script and associated tools [4]. Human intervention is required for larger adaptations, but this is assisted by, and maintains, the assurance case.

The Semantic Interoperability Logical Framework (SILF) was developed by NATO to facilitate dependable machine-to-machine information exchanges among Command and Control systems [5]. SILF employs an extensive ontology to describe the content of messages exchanged, and a mediation mechanism to translate messages as needed. The mediation can be performed by a centralized hub, or by wrappers at either the sender or receiver. ONISTT [6] is an SRI project that developed and prototyped many of the ideas in SILF; it was primarily employed to enable the integration of live and virtual simulation systems for military training. Using ontological descriptions, ONISTT is able automatically to synthesize adapters that allow incompatible message streams to be connected (e.g., different time representations, or different accuracies or units of measurement). It can also decide when incompatibilities are too great to meet the purpose of integration.

The Frauenhofer Institute for Experimental Software Engineering in Kaiserslautern, Germany, has done much work on the safety assurance of OAS, mostly in the context of farm tractors and the very sophisticated implements that attach to them. Trapp and Schneider provide a comprehensive survey of safety assurance for OAS [7]. They frame their survey in the context provided by Models@Runtime (M@RT), which is an emerging framework for organizing OAS. The idea is that if open systems are to adapt to each other, they need to know something about each other, and one way to do this is to exchange models for their individual behavior and assumptions. It is a matter for negotiation what constitutes a "model" in this context. In DEOS, for example, it is the D-CASE representation of an assurance case, in SILF and ONISTT it is ontologies in some standardized description logic (none of DEOS, SILF and ONISTT describe themselves in M@RT terms, but they fit the paradigm).

Trapp and Schneider extend the M@RT idea to *Safety* Models@Runtime (SM@RT) for self-integrating systems. They distinguish four levels of sophistication and difficulty according to how ambitious is the integration, and note that only the first two are feasible at present. The simplest class "Safety Certificates at Runtime" applies when it is sufficient for system safety that each component system maintains its own local safety objective. Then come "Safety Cases at Runtime" where component system safety cases guide adaptation and are integrated dynamically to deliver a safe and assured assembly (e.g., one system may need to demonstrate that it delivers properties assumed by another). Next is "V&V at Runtime," where it may be that one system cannot deliver the assumptions required by another, so more extensive adjustment are needed (e.g., wrapping or runtime monitoring to exclude some class of faults). Finally, "Hazard Analysis and Risk Assessment at Runtime" applies when essentially the full procedure of safety assurance (e.g., identification and elimination or mitigation of hazards, and assurance that this has been done, accurately and completely) is performed on integration. Personally, I am not convinced the "at Runtime" appellation is suitable for all these notions; certainly runtime monitoring is one way to ensure certain properties, but the generic process employed here is analysis, adaptation, and assurance at *integration-time*.

4   Prospects

The recent work outlined above provides some impressive accomplishments and attractive frameworks in which to view the issues of self-integration. What I wish to propose is that automated deduction provides the capabilities needed to realize the more challenging classes of trustworthy self-integration, and that such capabilities (essentially, theorem provers) will be the engines of integration.

From the scenarios in Sect. 2, we see that ontology matching is an important capability: all parties need to be talking about the same things (patient identity, blood pressure, oxygen levels, drug dosage) in the same way and using the same units. As mentioned in Sect. 3, SILF proposes that mediation mechanisms are employed to ensure this and ONISTT constructs such mechanisms automatically using ontological specifications for the data streams. The purpose of the integration is similarly represented in a task ontology. These ontological specifications are given in a description logic (the Web Ontology Language, OWL) and construction of the mediators is accomplished by a dedicated program written in Prolog.

Going beyond this, we can imagine that systems document not only the ontologies for their data streams, but specifications of their properties (e.g., those they assume and those they guarantee). Mediators may then have to provide more complex services than ontology matching: for example, they may need to enforce a certain invariant. A "runtime monitor" provides a simple way to do this: it is separate function that observes state variables of the system and evaluates a predicate representing the desired invariant. Should the predicate ever evaluate to false, then the monitor signals an alarm (to be handled by another part of the system, or by a human operator) or halts the system. If the invariant predicate is available in a suitably formal form (perhaps in the local assurance case) then software for the monitor can be synthesized automatically. Runtime monitors are the core of *Runtime Verification* and associated methods of assurance [8,9], whose guarantees can be very strong [10].

The ideas of runtime mediation and monitoring can be extended from ontology matching and invariant checking to more complex functions such as masking some kinds of faults or providing supervisory control. The software to accomplish these functions is more complex than simply implementing a given predicate, but modern methods of synthesis can often automate its construction. These methods are based on automated deduction (i.e., theorem proving).

Checking the satisfiability of propositional (i.e., Boolean) formulas is the simplest problem in automated deduction, and is also the quintessential NP-Complete problem, meaning its worst computational complexity is probably exponential. Yet modern satisfiability (SAT) solvers are remarkably efficient on realistic problems, often solving examples with thousands of variables in fractions of a second. Their efficiency, and the generality of the SAT problem, are such that the best way to solve many search problems is first to transform them to a SAT instance, then solve that, and finally transform back to the original problem. Satisfiability Modulo Theories (SMT) extends SAT by adding support for useful theories such as real and integer arithmetic, uninterpreted functions, arrays, and several other datatypes used in software. SMT solvers are at the core of many modern tools for automated program analysis and verification, including static analyzers, model checkers, and test generators.

Efficient automated verification methods open the door to effective automated synthesis: crudely, this is done by enumerating candidate solutions, applying automated verification to each in turn, and selecting the first that succeeds. Of course, this crude approach must be refined to yield a practical synthesis procedure. The first required refinement is a way for a human user to suggest the space of likely solutions. An attractive way to do this is for the user to specify a sketch or template and leave the synthesis search procedure to fill in the details.

The "glue" elements needed in self-integration are generally straightline programs and single loops, and the formulas that correspond to these (e.g., invariants). A trivial example of the template for an invariant is $Ax + By < C$ for some parameters A, B, and C. Formally, this can be expressed as

$$\exists A, B, C : \forall x, y : Ax + By < C \qquad (1)$$

where x and y are program variables, and the parameters A, B, C must be instantiated by the synthesis procedure. Variants on this formulation can be used to express assumption synthesis (find the weakest environment in which a given component meets its requirements), supervisory controller synthesis (design an algorithm to selectively disable component actions so that it satisfies some goal in the face of uncontrollable actions by the environment), and full synthesis (design an algorithm to achieve some goal).

The second refinement to the crude synthesis procedure sketched above is an efficient way to search for suitable values for the parameters A, B, and C. Observe the Exists-Forall (EF) two-level quantification in the formulation (1) above. Standard SMT solvers solve single-level Exists and Forall problems, but recent developments extend this to EF solving using refinements of the search procedure sketched above [11]. An EF-SMT solver uses an ordinary SMT solver as a component and works by iteratively performing two steps.

1. Guessing (cleverly) instantiations for the Exists variables and querying the SMT solver with the resulting Forall formula. If this succeeds, we are done.
2. If it fails, use the result (i.e., counterexample) of the Forall query to help in finding the next instantiation of the Exists variables.

The key in making this iteration efficient is to use (i.e., learn from) the result of failed verification (Forall) steps to prune the search space for subsequent synthesis (Exists) steps. There is a tradeoff between generality and performance in formal synthesis. EF-SMT handles richer logics than the description logics of ONISTT, but the specialized synthesis procedure of the latter outperforms EF-SMT within its domain. Nonetheless, we can expect continued progress in EF and standard SMT solving and this will eventually lead to superior synthesis performance.[2]

Both SMT and EF-SMT solvers use learning from failed candidate solutions to optimize their search. Self-integrating systems can also use explicit learning methods to cope with noisy sensors, erratic components, or external attack [12]. The idea is to learn a "safety envelope" for the system under controlled, quiescent, conditions and then monitor this in operation. The safety envelope is an invariant (which may consist of sub-invariants for each learned "mode" of the system) and its violation can indicate an attack, noise, or erratic (faulty) behavior. Depending on context, response to violation of a safety envelope could be to

---

[2] We should note that the ONISTT technology also evolves, and the current system uses the FLora-2 reasoning system for F-logic.

raise an alarm or to replace "bad" values by recent "good" ones, or by defaults. The idea of a learned safety envelope (i.e., a conservative model) is quite different than the predictive models (e.g., Kalman filters) popular in control theory and serves a different and novel purpose.

Given the ingredients described above, we can propose that as self-integrating systems come together they exchange ontologies, models, specifications of their assumptions and guarantees, and assurance arguments. All of these are potentially formal descriptions; although an assurance case is generally expected to be a persuasive rather than deductively valid argument, a case can be made that its uncertainties should be restricted to the interpretation of evidence, not the application of argument to its claims [13].

We can then further propose that the mechanisms of automated formal verification, synthesis, and learning should go to work with the aim of establishing and maintaining local and global safety properties and their attendant assurance arguments.

This raises the question what is the purpose of the integrated system and what is the safety claim of the integrated system. As a first step (corresponding to Trapp and Schneider's "Safety Certificates at Runtime" and "Safety Cases at Runtime") we might suppose that the goal is for each component system to maintain its local safety claim despite the stresses of interaction. For example, a farm tractor must continue to brake safely when an implement is attached, and to do this it needs to know the weight and center of gravity of the implement, and its braking performance.

Construction of an assurance case for the integrated system will employ automated deduction and synthesis: deduction to detect potential violations of individual safety claims in the integrated system (e.g., due to a property mismatch in an assume-guarantee argument), and synthesis to construct monitoring and recovery procedures to overcome these.

For more advanced integration, I propose that the purpose and safety claim of the integrated system will be associated with an "integration app" that guides the assembly. This might approach Trapp and Schneider's "V&V at Runtime," where the component systems not only maintain safety in each other's presence, but also deliver some new, integrated (i.e., positively emergent) behavior. For example, a standard pulse oximeter and PCA will not do anything interesting when integrated unless a suitable "safe analgesia app" takes the initiative to close the loop. We can imagine that the design and purpose of the "safe analgesia app" are indicated as formal templates or sketches, whose details are filled in using EF-SMT synthesis that uses the capabilities and properties announced by the attached PO and PCA.

5   Conclusion

I have described a view of self-integrating systems that draws on many current ideas in the Internet of Things, Service Oriented Architecture, Open Adaptive Systems, and Models@Runtime. I then argued that in many applications, these self-integrating systems need to be trustworthy and I outlined some examples in medical devices.

I hope then to have made the case that trustworthy self-integration requires automated verification and automated synthesis of monitors, adapters, and mediators at integration-time. I sketched how modern technology for automated deduction, specifically SMT and EF-SMT solvers, can perform these tasks.

Pulling these various threads together, I propose that a modest but useful class of trustworthy self-integrating systems is within reach, and that embedded automated deduction is the enabling engine for this development.

Looking further into the future, we can speculate on self-integration of systems that are individually highly adaptive or intelligent. I believe this will be a challenging endeavor: almost all crashes of modern aircraft are due to flawed interaction between automated aircraft systems and the intelligent human crew. Although usually ascribed to human error, a more nuanced assessment sees flaws in the manner of interaction, with each party having insufficient insight into the other's state and intentions. Thus, it may be that the information that must be exchanged between such advanced systems is of a more strategic character than the tactical information discussed here. For the most advanced kinds of systems, it may be that what is needed is agreement on a shared system of ethics.

Acknowledgments. This work was partially funded by SRI International. Many of the ideas assembled here originated in discussions with Dave Hanz of SRI, who also provided helpful comments on the paper.

References

1. Whitehead, S.F., Goldman, J.M.: Getting connected for patient safety: how medical device "plug-and-play" interoperability can make a difference. Patient Safety and Quality Healthcare (2008). http://www.psqh.com/janfeb08/connected.html
2. Rushby, J.: The interpretation and evaluation of assurance cases. Technical report SRI-CSL-15-01, Computer Science Laboratory, SRI International, Menlo Park, CA (2015)
3. Tokoro, M.: Open systems dependability-dependability engineering for ever-changing systems. CRC Press, Boca Raton (2013)
4. Kuramtisu, K.: D-script: dependable scripting with DEOS process. In: 3rd International Workshop on Open Systems Dependability (WOSD), Workshop held in association with ISSRE 2013, Pasadena, CA, pp. 326–330 (2013)
5. NATO Science and Technology Organization, Neuilly-Sur-Seine, France: Framework for Semantic Interoperability. STO Technical report TR-IST-094 (2014)
6. Ford, R., Hanz, D., Elenius, D., Johnson, M.: Purpose-aware interoperability: the ONISTT ontologies and analyzer. In: Simulation Interoperability Workshop. Number 07F-SIW-088, Simulation Interoperability Standards Organization (2007)
7. Trapp, M., Schneider, D.: Safety assurance of open adaptive systems – a survey. In: Bencomo, N., France, R., Cheng, B.H.C., Assmann, U. (eds.) Models@run.time. LNCS, vol. 8378, pp. 279–318. Springer, Heidelberg (2014)
8. Rushby, J.: Kernels for safety? In: Anderson, T. (ed.) Safe and Secure Computing Systems, pp. 210–220. Blackwell Scientific Publications (1989). (Proceedings of a Symposium held in Glasgow, October 1986)

9. Rushby, J.: Runtime certification. In: Leucker, M. (ed.) RV 2008. LNCS, vol. 5289, pp. 21–35. Springer, Heidelberg (2008)
10. Littlewood, B., Rushby, J.: Reasoning about the reliability of diverse two-channel systems in which one channel is "possibly perfect". IEEE Trans. Softw. Eng. **38**, 1178–1194 (2012)
11. Dutertre, B.: Solving Exists/Forall problems with Yices. In: SMT Workshop 2015 (held in association with CAV), San Francisco, CA (2015)
12. Tiwari, A., Dutertre, B., Jovanović, D., de Candia, T., Lincoln, P.D., Rushby, J., Sadigh, D., Seshia, S.: Safety envelope for security. In: Proceedings of the 3rd International Conference on High Confidence Networked Systems (HiCoNS), pp. 85–94. ACM, Berlin (2014)
13. Rushby, J.: On the interpretation of assurance case arguments. In: 2nd International Workshop on Argument for Agreement and Assurance (AAA 2015), Kanagawa, Japan (2015)

Contributed Papers

HiRE - A Heuristic Approach for User Generated Record Extraction

S. Chandrakanth and P. Santhi Thilagam[(✉)]

National Institute of Technology Karnataka, Surathkal, Karnataka, India
{chandrakanthselvakumar,santhisocrates}@gmail.com

Abstract. User Generated Content extraction is the extraction of user posts, viz., reviews and comments. Extraction of such content requires the identification of their record structure, so that after the content is extracted, proper filtering mechanisms can be applied to eliminate the noises. Hence, record structure identification is an important prerequisite step for text analytics. Most of the existing record structure identification techniques search for repeating patterns to find the records. In this paper, a heuristic based approach is proposed. This method uses the implicit logical organization present in the records and outputs the record structure.

Keywords: Web content mining · User posts · Record boundary · Record extraction · Heuristics

1 Introduction

Record boundary identification is a problem associated with mining records from web sites. This paper aims to concentrate extensively on the record boundary identification and extraction of user generated (UG) records. The user generated records are entries like blogs, reviews, posts on discussion forums, etc. The user generated records are a good source for business intelligence inference. Web search engines could use them to provide value added services such as result collation or summarization.

Record structure identification is the process of isolating the records from the source html documents and thereby the information contained in them. It can also be viewed as a problem of noise filtering where the noises are the other information such as ads, scripts etc., that might be found on a web page. Structural information of the record is helpful in analyzing the meta-data and user generated post. Hence there is a need to conserve the structure and the formatting data of the page. A new heuristic based algorithm is proposed to identify and extract user generated records that conserves the structural organization of the record. The structural organization of the pages containing such UG records is exploited to find individual records.

© Springer International Publishing Switzerland 2016
N. Bjørner et al. (Eds.): ICDCIT 2016, LNCS 9581, pp. 33–37, 2016.
DOI: 10.1007/978-3-319-28034-9_4

2   Related Works

OMINI [1], one of the earliest heuristic based methods, uses a lot of heuristics developed based on assumed characters of a record. RoadRunner [2] compares multiple pages from the same site to find record structure. IEPAD [3] identify repeating structures using Patricia trees which are constructed based on the tag structure of the page. MDR [4] identifies the repeating tag structures that are likely to be present in regions containing multiple records. DEPTA [5] and NET [6] were improvements on MDR. TPC [7] uses visual cues and the intuition that data region to be extracted. MiBAT [8] uses several similarity metrics to identify anchor points, which are regions that are similar across the records. Then MiBAT grows from those points on either direction till the boundary of each record is determined.

Most of the works in web content extraction have concentrated on extracting product data records. These records have similar structure with least deviation in structure between one another. These methods may not be suitable for user generated records due to the highly irregular structure which is the challenge that is addressed in this paper.

3   Proposed Method a Heuristic Algorithm for Record Extraction (HiRE)

In this paper a heuristic based method (HiRE) is proposed for record boundary identification. The proposed heuristic is based on the logical organization of the web page, and is a modified version of the heuristic proposed in Text to Tag Ratio (TTR) [9]. The TTR heuristic points to the sections that contain the most text. This property/heuristic namely "the more the TTR value, the higher will be the text content" has been modified and used in this paper. The modification is the calculation of TTR at node level instead of at line level, which is known as Node-Level Text to Tag Ratio (NTTR).

Instead of searching for the records, we find the root of the records. The NTTR is used to narrow down to the region that contains the records. The root of the records is identified by examining the html address patterns obtained from the region pointed by the NTTR metric and by extracting similar address patterns. Then, all the records are obtained by exploiting the parent-child relationship among them. There may be nodes that are child to the root of the records node that are not actually records. To filter these nodes, a text based similarity metric called Jaro-Winkler distance [10] is used. XML parsers are used on html tags of the source document and html tags are considered as Xpath tags to access and process the document. The steps that are incorporated in HiRE are as follows:

Step 1: Clean the input document. The input document is checked for formatting and unwanted tags are removed. Attributes are added to uniquely identify the tags.

Step 2: Apply NTTR on document and get Xpath address of node. Once the NTTR values of all the nodes in the document are calculated, the node with the maximum NTTR value is found and the Xpath of this node is obtained.

Step 3: Extract Xpaths of nodes with similar address structure. The Xpaths of the nodes in the document are compared with the Xpath of the node with the maximum NTTR and similar addresses are extracted.

Step 4: Identify the root records. On the list of similar Xpath addresses, the root of records is the node with the longest and highest occurrence count. The level one child nodes of the root node are the record nodes.

Step 5: Remove non-record nodes. The Xpath address of the child nodes are analyzed using the Jaro-Winkler distance. The nodes with most deviation are ignored.

Table 1. Sample Results of HiRE

Website	Records present	Records found	Precision (%)	Recall (%)	Running time (seconds)
http://broadbandforum.in/airtel-broadband/30121-airtel-broadband-please-help-me/	9	9	100	100	1.037
http://www.wargamer.com/forums/posts.asp?t=581598	6	6	100	100	.650
http://www.sitepoint.com/forums/showthread.php?773093-Please-Review-My-Webmaster-Blog	4	4	100	100	.863
http://bikeshops.mtbr.com/cat/united-states/alabama/bikeshop/cahaba-cycles/prd_368898_6213crx.aspx	5	0	0	0	.853
http://www.notebookforums.com/t/238619/hp-ultrabook-folio-13-9hrs-battery-performance	1	0	0	0	.872
http://www.physicsforums.com/showthread.php?t=296748	16	16	100	100	1.464
http://www.battlefront.com/community/showthread.php?t=95968	8	8	100	100	1.145
http://windows7forums.com/windows-7-games/23292-running-32bit-games-64bit.html	4	4	100	100	1.130
http://www.tomshardware.com/forum/7734-63-installing-programs-windows	10	10	97.78	100	1.175

4   Discussion on Results

The tests were done on system running Windows 7 OS with 8 GB RAM. HiRE is coded in Java. The sites for testing are chosen randomly with varying number of posts and with different types of page templates. The overall percentage of pages on which HiRE gave 100 percent precision and recall was around 85 percent of the total number of websites tested [11]. Table 1 lists a subset of the test results.

The method works when the following conditions are met: (i) the page has only user generated records (ii) the page contains more than one record and (iii) the region within the record has the highest NTTR. These requirements are satisfied in case of forum and discussion pages. The system fails when the page contains only one user generated record or if any section other than the one containing the record has the highest NTTR. However, our testing results show that the possibility of the latter occurring is very low.

5   Conclusion

The HiRE proposed in this paper is an extension of TTR heuristic to extract record boundaries for records from web pages. The contributions in HiRE are as follows:

- Proposition of NTTR metric to identify nodes with highest text content
- Finding the root of the records using the Xpath address and NTTR
- The usage of Jaro-Winkler distance on Xpath for noise removal

The proposed method HiRE is experimentally tested and found to perform well in terms of precision, recall, and running time. The HiRE algorithm can also be extended to work on review pages.

References

1. Buttler, D., Liu, L., Pu, C.: A fully automated object extraction system for the world wide web. In: 21st International Conference on Distributed Computing Systems, pp. 361–370. IEEE (2001)
2. Crescenzi, V., Mecca, G., Merialdo, P., et al.: Roadrunner: towards automatic data extraction from large web sites. VLDB 1, 109–118 (2001)
3. Chang, C.H., Lui, S.C.: Iepad: information extraction based on pattern discovery. In: Proceedings of the 10th International Conference on World Wide Web, pp. 681–688. ACM (2001)
4. Liu, B., Grossman, R., Zhai, Y.: Mining data records in web pages. In: Proceedings of the ninth ACM SIGKDD International Conference on Knowledge Discovery and Data Mining, pp. 601–606. ACM (2003)
5. Zhai, Y., Liu, B.: Web data extraction based on partial tree alignment. In: Proceedings of the 14th International Conference on World Wide Web, pp. 76–85. ACM (2005)
6. Liu, B., Zhai, Y.: NET – a system for extracting web data from flat and nested data records. In: Ngu, A.H.H., Kitsuregawa, M., Neuhold, E.J., Chung, J.-Y., Sheng, Q.Z. (eds.) WISE 2005. LNCS, vol. 3806, pp. 487–495. Springer, Heidelberg (2005)
7. Miao, G., Tatemura, J., Hsiung, W.P., Sawires, A., Moser, L.E.: Extracting data records from the web using tag path clustering. In: Proceedings of the 18th International Conference on World Wide Web, pp. 981–990. ACM (2009)

8. Song, X., Liu, J., Cao, Y., Lin, C.Y., Hon, H.W.: Automatic extraction of web data records containing user-generated content. In: Proceedings of the 19th ACM International Conference on Information and knowledge Management, pp. 39–48. ACM (2010)
9. Weninger, T., Hsu, W.H.: Text extraction from the web via text-to-tag ratio. In: 19th International Workshop on Database and Expert Systems Application. DEXA 2008, pp. 23–28. IEEE (2008)
10. Winkler, W.E.: String comparator metrics and enhanced decision rules in the fellegi-sunter model of record linkage (1990)
11. Chandrakanth, S., Thilagam, P.S.: User generated content extraction from web. Master's thesis, National Institute of Technology Karnataka, Surathkal, India (2012)

Optimization of Service Rate in a Discrete-Time Impatient Customer Queue Using Particle Swarm Optimization

Pikkala Vijaya Laxmi$^{(\boxtimes)}$ and Kanithi Jyothsna

Department of Applied Mathematics, Andhra University,
Visakhapatnam 530003, India
{vijaya_iit2003,mail2jyothsnak}@yahoo.co.in

Abstract. This paper investigates a discrete-time balking, reneging queue with Bernoulli-schedule vacation interruption. Particle swarm optimization which is a biologically inspired optimization technique mimicking the behavior of birds flocking or fish schooling is implemented to determine the optimum service rate that minimizes the total expected cost function per unit time. A potential application of the considered queueing problem in an inbound email contact center is also presented.

Keywords: Discrete-time · Balking · Reneging · Bernoulli-schedule vacation interruption · Particle swarm optimization

1 Introduction

In impatient customer queues, customers either decide not to join the queue (i.e., balk) or depart after joining the queue without getting service (i.e., renege). In queueing systems with working vacations (WV), the server is allowed to take WV whenever the system becomes empty. During WV the server renders service at a different rate. At the end of a WV, if the queue is non-empty a regular service period begins; otherwise, another WV commences. A discrete-time WV queue with balking and reneging has been studied by Goswami [1]. Under the Bernoulli-schedule vacation interruption $(BS - VI)$, the server may continue the WV with probability q or interrupt the WV and resume regular service period with probability $1 - q$. An impatient customer queue with $BS - VI$ has been analyzed by Vijaya Laxmi and Jyothsna [5].

The main objectives of this article are: (i) to derive the steady-state probabilities of a discrete-time queue with balking, reneging and $BS - VI$, (ii) to construct a total expected cost function per unit time and use particle swarm optimization (PSO) to search for the optimum service rate during regular service period. PSO is an evolutionary computation technique developed by Kennedy and Eberhart [2] based on the social behavior of animals such as bird flocking, fish schooling, etc. The main advantages of the algorithm are its simple structure, ease of implementation, robustness and speed in acquiring solutions. The complexity of PSO is $O(nm)$, where m being the number of particles and n the number of iterations. For a detailed algorithm, refer Rao [3].

© Springer International Publishing Switzerland 2016
N. Bjørner et al. (Eds.): ICDCIT 2016, LNCS 9581, pp. 38–42, 2016.
DOI: 10.1007/978-3-319-28034-9_5

2   Model Description and Analysis

We consider a finite buffer discrete-time queue with balking, reneging and $BS-VI$ under an early arrival system. We assume that the capacity of the system is N. On arrival, a customer either decides to join the queue with probability b_i or balks with probability $\bar{b}_i = 1 - b_i$. Further, we assume that $0 < b_{i+1} \le b_i \le 1, 1 \le i \le N - 1, b_0 = 1$ and $b_N = 0$. The waiting time of a customer before reneging is geometrically distributed with parameter α and the average reneging rate is given by $(i - 1)\alpha, 1 \le i \le N$. The server interrupts the vacation under the Bernoulli rule. The inter-arrival times, regular service times, service times during WV and vacation times are geometrically distributed with parameters λ, μ, η and ϕ, respectively. The customers are served according to FCFS discipline.

The present queueing model has potential application in an inbound email contact center where the potential customers transmit emails across the network through an office automation system such as LAN. An email contact center is a communication network wherein email sending, preprocessing and processing of requests are done in discrete slots. The emails received are processed immediately when the server is idle; otherwise, they are placed in a queue. When the server is busy, there is a probability that requests may be terminated by users before arriving at the email server and if an email is not processed within a certain duration it is lost. To keep the functioning of the email server well and efficient, maintenance activities (MAs) such as virus scans, disk cleaning, etc., can be done when the server is idle. During the MAs, the server can still process emails at a lower speed. After processing an email during the MAs, if there are emails waiting to be processed, the server may interrupt or continue the MAs with some probability. On the other hand, when the MAs are completed and emails are waiting in the queue, they are processed with regular speed. In this scenario, the requests terminated by users, lost emails, the email server and the MAs correspond to balking, reneging, server and WV with $BS-VI$, respectively.

At steady-state, let $\pi_{i,0}(0 \le i \le N)$ represent the probability of i customers in the system and the server in WV and $\pi_{i,1}(1 \le i \le N)$ be the probability of i customers in the system and the server in regular busy period. Based on the one-step transition analysis, we obtain the following steady-state equations:

$$\pi_{0,0} = \left(\bar{\lambda} + \lambda\eta \right) \pi_{0,0} + \mathbf{s}_1(\eta)\pi_{1,0} + \mathbf{t}_2(\eta)\pi_{2,0} + \mathbf{s}_1(\mu)\pi_{1,1} + \mathbf{t}_2(\mu)\pi_{2,1}, \tag{1}$$

$$\pi_{i,0} = \bar{\phi}\mathbf{u}_i(\eta)\pi_{i,0} + \bar{\phi}\mathbf{m}_{i-1}(\eta)\pi_{i-1,0} + \bar{\phi}\mathbf{w}_{i+1}(\eta)\pi_{i+1,0} + \bar{\phi}\mathbf{f}_{i+2}(\eta)\pi_{i+2,0},$$
$$1 \le i \le N - 2, \tag{2}$$

$$\pi_{N-1,0} = \bar{\phi}\mathbf{u}_{N-1}(\eta)\pi_{N-1,0} + \bar{\phi}\mathbf{m}_{N-2}(\eta)\pi_{N-2,0} + \bar{\phi}\mathbf{w}_N(\eta)\pi_{N,0}, \tag{3}$$

$$\pi_{N,0} = \bar{\phi}\mathbf{u}_N(\eta)\pi_{N,0} + \bar{\phi}\mathbf{m}_{N-1}(\eta)\pi_{N-1,0}, \tag{4}$$

$$\pi_{i,1} = \mathbf{r}_i(\mu)\pi_{i,1} + \mathbf{s}_{i+1}(\mu)\pi_{i+1,1} + \mathbf{m}_{i-1}(\mu)\pi_{i-1,1} + \mathbf{t}_{i+2}(\mu)\pi_{i+2,1} + \phi\mathbf{r}_i(\eta)\pi_{i,0}$$
$$+\phi\mathbf{m}_{i-1}(\eta)\pi_{i-1,0} + \phi\mathbf{s}_{i+1}(\eta)\pi_{i+1,0} + \phi\mathbf{t}_{i+2}(\eta)\pi_{i+2,0} + \bar{\phi}\mathbf{v}_i(\eta)\pi_{i,0}$$
$$+\bar{\phi}\mathbf{z}_{i+1}(\eta)\pi_{i+1,0} + \bar{\phi}\mathbf{g}_{i+2}(\eta)\pi_{i+2,0}, 1 \le i \le N - 2, \tag{5}$$

$$\pi_{N-1,1} = \mathbf{r}_{N-1}(\mu)\pi_{N-1,1} + \mathbf{s}_N(\mu)\pi_{N,1} + \mathbf{m}_{N-2}(\mu)\pi_{N-2,1} + \phi\mathbf{r}_{N-1}(\eta)\pi_{N-1,0}$$
$$+\phi\mathbf{m}_{N-2}(\eta)\pi_{N-2,0} + \phi\mathbf{s}_N(\eta)\pi_{N,0} + \bar\phi\mathbf{v}_{N-1}(\eta)\pi_{N-1,0}$$
$$+\bar\phi\mathbf{z}_N(\eta)\pi_{N,0}, \tag{6}$$
$$\pi_{N,1} = \mathbf{r}_N(\mu)\pi_{N,1} + \mathbf{m}_{N-1}(\mu)\pi_{N-1,1} + \phi\mathbf{r}_N(\eta)\pi_{N,0} + \phi\mathbf{m}_{N-1}(\eta)\pi_{N-1,0}, \tag{7}$$

where for any $x \in [0,1], \bar x = 1 - x$,

$$\mathbf{u}_i(x) = \bar\lambda\bar{x}\overline{(i-1)\alpha} + \lambda\bar{b}_i\bar{x}\overline{(i-1)\alpha} + \lambda b_i q\overline{x(i-1)\alpha} + \lambda b_i\bar{x}(i-1)\alpha,$$
$$i = 1,\ldots,N;$$
$$\mathbf{v}_i(x) = \lambda b_i\bar{q}\overline{x(i-1)\alpha}, \ i = 1,\ldots,N; \ \mathbf{r}_i(x) = \mathbf{u}_i(x) + \mathbf{v}_i(x);$$
$$\mathbf{w}_i(x) = \bar\lambda q\overline{x(i-1)\alpha} + \lambda\bar{b}_i q\overline{x(i-1)\alpha} + \bar\lambda\bar{x}(i-1)\alpha + \lambda\bar{b}_i\bar{x}(i-1)\alpha$$
$$+\lambda b_i q x(i-1)\alpha,$$
$$i = 1,\ldots,N-1;$$
$$\mathbf{z}_i(x) = \bar\lambda\bar{q}\overline{x(i-1)\alpha} + \lambda\bar{b}_i\bar{q}\overline{x(i-1)\alpha} + \lambda b_i\bar{q}x(i-1)\alpha, i = 1,\ldots,N-1;$$
$$\mathbf{s}_i(x) = \mathbf{w}_i(x) + \mathbf{z}_i(x);$$
$$\mathbf{f}_i(x) = \lambda\bar{b}_i q x(i-1)\alpha + \bar\lambda q x(i-1)\alpha, i = 3,\ldots,N;$$
$$\mathbf{g}_i(x) = \lambda\bar{b}_i\bar{q}x(i-1)\alpha + \bar\lambda\bar{q}x(i-1)\alpha, i = 3,\ldots,N; \ \mathbf{t}_i(x) = \mathbf{f}_i(x) + \mathbf{g}_i(x);$$
$$\mathbf{m}_0(\eta) = \lambda\bar\eta; \mathbf{m}_0(\mu) = 0; \mathbf{m}_i(x) = \lambda b_i\bar{x}\overline{(i-1)\alpha}, i = 1,\ldots,N-1.$$

Solving (2) to (7) recursively, the steady-state probabilities are obtained as $\pi_{i,0} = \xi_i\pi_{N,0}$; $\pi_{i,1} = (k\zeta_i + \gamma_i)\pi_{N,0}$ where $\pi_{N,0} = 1/(\sum_{n=0}^N \xi_n + \sum_{n=1}^N(k\zeta_n + \gamma_n))$;

$$\xi_N = 1; \ \xi_{N-1} = \left(1 - \bar\phi\mathbf{u}_N(\eta)\right)/\bar\phi\mathbf{m}_{N-1}(\eta); \ \zeta_N = 1; \ \gamma_N = 0;$$
$$\xi_{N-2} = \left(\left(1 - \bar\phi\mathbf{u}_{N-1}(\eta)\right)\xi_{N-1}/\bar\phi - \mathbf{w}_N(\eta)\xi_N\right)/\mathbf{m}_{N-2}(\eta);$$
$$\xi_i = \left(\left(1 - \bar\phi\mathbf{u}_{i+1}(\eta)\right)\xi_{i+1}/\bar\phi - \mathbf{f}_{i+3}(\eta)\xi_{i+3}\right.$$
$$\left. -\mathbf{w}_{i+2}(\eta)\xi_{i+2}\right)/\mathbf{m}_i(\eta), i = N-3,\ldots,0;$$
$$\zeta_{N-1} = \left(1 - \mathbf{r}_N(\mu)\right)/\mathbf{m}_{N-1}(\mu);$$
$$\zeta_{N-2} = \left(\left(1 - \mathbf{r}_{N-1}(\mu)\right)\zeta_{N-1} - \mathbf{s}_N(\mu)\right)/\mathbf{m}_{N-2}(\mu);$$
$$\gamma_{N-1} = -\phi\left(\mathbf{m}_{N-1}(\eta)\xi_{N-1} + \mathbf{r}_N(\eta)\right)/\mathbf{m}_{N-1}(\mu);$$
$$\gamma_{N-2} = \left(\left(1 - \mathbf{r}_{N-1}(\mu)\right)\gamma_{N-1} - \phi\mathbf{m}_{N-2}(\eta)\xi_{N-2} - \left(\phi\mathbf{s}_N(\eta) + \bar\phi\mathbf{z}_N(\eta)\right)\right.$$
$$\left. - \left(\phi\mathbf{r}_{N-1}(\eta) + \bar\phi\mathbf{v}_{N-1}(\eta)\right)\xi_{N-1}\right)/\mathbf{m}_{N-2}(\mu);$$
$$\zeta_i = \left(\left(1 - \mathbf{r}_{i+1}(\mu)\right)\zeta_{i+1} - \mathbf{s}_{i+2}(\mu)\zeta_{i+2} - \mathbf{t}_{i+3}(\mu)\zeta_{i+3}\right)/\mathbf{m}_i(\mu), i = N-3,\ldots,1;$$
$$\gamma_i = \left(\left(1 - \mathbf{r}_{i+1}(\mu)\right)\gamma_{i+1} - \mathbf{s}_{i+2}(\mu)\gamma_{i+2} - \mathbf{t}_{i+3}(\mu)\gamma_{i+3} - \phi\mathbf{m}_i(\eta)\xi_i\right.$$
$$- \left(\phi\mathbf{r}_{i+1}(\eta) + \bar\phi\mathbf{v}_{i+1}(\eta)\right)\xi_{i+1} - \left(\phi\mathbf{s}_{i+2}(\eta) + \bar\phi\mathbf{z}_{i+2}(\eta)\right)\xi_{i+2}$$
$$\left. - \left(\phi\mathbf{t}_{i+3}(\eta) + \bar\phi\mathbf{g}_{i+3}(\eta)\right)\xi_{i+3}\right)/\mathbf{m}_i(\mu), i = N-3,\ldots,1;$$
$$k = \left(\mathbf{s}_2(\mu)\gamma_2 + \mathbf{t}_3(\mu)\gamma_3 + \left(\phi\mathbf{r}_1(\eta) + \bar\phi\mathbf{v}_1(\eta)\right)\xi_1 + \phi\lambda\bar\eta\xi_0 + \left(\phi\mathbf{s}_2(\eta)\right.\right.$$
$$\left.+\bar\phi\mathbf{z}_2(\eta)\right)\xi_2 + \left(\phi\mathbf{t}_3(\eta) + \bar\phi\mathbf{g}_3(\eta)\right)\xi_3 - \left(1 - \mathbf{r}_1(\mu)\right)\gamma_1)/\left(\left(1 - \mathbf{r}_1(\mu)\right)\zeta_1\right.$$
$$\left. -\mathbf{s}_2(\mu)\zeta_2 + \mathbf{t}_3(\mu)\zeta_3\right).$$

The outside observer's observation probabilities $\pi_{i,j}^o$ that the outside observer finds i customers in the system and server in state j are given by

$$\pi_{0,0}^o = \bar{\lambda}\pi_{0,0}; \ \pi_{i,0}^o = (1 - \lambda b_i)\pi_{i,0} + \lambda b_{i-1}\pi_{i-1,0}, \ 1 \le i \le N;$$
$$\pi_{1,1}^o = (1 - \lambda b_1)\pi_{1,1}; \ \pi_{i,1}^o = (1 - \lambda b_i)\pi_{i,1} + \lambda b_{i-1}\pi_{i-1,1}, \ 2 \le i \le N.$$

Taking $\alpha = 0, q = 1$, our results match with those of Vijaya Laxmi et al. [4].

3   Performance Measures and Cost Model

The average system length at an arbitrary epoch (L_s), at an outside observer's observation epoch (L_s^o), the probability that the server is in WV (P_{wv}), in regular busy period (P_b), the average reneging rate ($R.R.$), the average balking rate ($B.R.$), the average rate of customer loss ($L.R.$) are given by $L_s = \sum_{i=1}^{N} i(\pi_{i,0} + \pi_{i,1}); L_s^o = \sum_{i=1}^{N} i(\pi_{i,0}^o + \pi_{i,1}^o); P_{wv} = \sum_{i=0}^{N} \pi_{i,0}; P_b = \sum_{i=1}^{N} \pi_{i,1}; R.R. = \sum_{i=1}^{N} (i-1)\alpha(\pi_{i,0} + \pi_{i,1}); B.R. = \sum_{i=1}^{N} \lambda \bar{b}_i(\pi_{i,0} + \pi_{i,1}); L.R. = B.R. + R.R.$

We develop a total expected cost function with an objective to determine the optimum regular service rate (μ^*). Let the total expected cost function per unit time be $F(\mu) = C_\mu \mu + C_\eta \eta + C_{ls} L_s^o + C_{lr} L.R$, where C_μ, C_η, C_{ls} and C_{lr} are the costs per unit time during regular busy period, during WV, when a customer joins the queue and when a customer balks or reneges, respectively. We employ PSO coded in Mathematica to solve the optimization problem. Table 1 presents the optimum values of μ, the minimum expected cost $F(\mu^*)$, along with the corresponding performance measures $L_s^*, L_s^{o*}, P_{wv}^*, P_b^*$ and $L.R.^*$ for various values of η and α. For obtaining the numerical results, we have arbitrarily chosen the following parameters: $N = 10, b_0 = 1, b_i = 1 - (i/N^2), 1 \le i \le N-1, b_N = 0, \lambda = 0.4, \mu = 0.6, \phi = 0.2, q = 0.4, C_{ls} = 45, C_\mu = 40, C_\eta = 25$ and $C_{lr} = 15$. From the table, we observe that except P_b^* and $L.R.^*$ all other optimum values decrease with the increase of α for fixed η. Further, for fixed α, μ^* and P_{wv}^* increase with the increase of η whereas other optimum values decrease with η.

Table 1. Optimum values for various values of η and α using PSO

	$\eta = 0.1$			$\eta = 0.3$		
$\alpha \rightarrow$	0.05	0.07	0.1	0.05	0.07	0.1
μ^*	0.77157	0.74010	0.69875	0.77816	0.75500	0.72274
$F(\mu^*)$	115.069	112.442	109.106	97.8809	96.6992	95.1007
L_s^*	1.40803	1.37378	1.33126	0.91357	0.90582	0.89606
L_s^{o*}	1.80238	1.76828	1.72593	1.30991	1.30220	1.29248
P_{wv}^*	0.58795	0.58511	0.58154	0.67398	0.67135	0.66761
P_b^*	0.41205	0.41489	0.41846	0.32603	0.32865	0.33239
$L.R.^*$	0.03994	0.05101	0.06594	0.02057	0.02667	0.03532

References

1. Goswami, V.: A discrete-time queue with balking, reneging and working vacations. Int. J. Stoch. Anal. **2014**, 8 p. (2014). Article ID 358529, http://dx.doi.org/10. 1155/2014/358529
2. Kennedy, J., Eberhart, R.: Particle swarm optimization. In: IEEE International Conference on Neural Networks, Canberra, Australia, vol. 4, pp. 1942–1948 (1995)
3. Rao, S.S.: Engineering Optimization: Theory and Practice. Wiley, New Jersey (2009)
4. Vijaya Laxmi, P., Goswami, V., Jyothsna, K.: Analysis of discrete-time single server queue with balking and multiple working vacations. Qual. Tech. Quan. Manage. Int. J. **10**(4), 443–456 (2013)
5. Vijaya Laxmi, P., Jyothsna, K.: Impatient customer queue with Bernoulli schedule vacation interruption. Comput. Oper. Res. **56**, 1–7 (2015)

A Wait-Free Stack

Seep Goel, Pooja Aggarwal, and Smruti R. Sarangi$^{(\boxtimes)}$

Indian Institute of Technology, New Delhi, India
seep.goyal@gmail.com, {pooja.aggarwal,srsarangi}@cse.iitd.ac.in

Abstract. In this paper, we describe a novel algorithm to create a concurrent wait-free stack. To the best of our knowledge, this is the first wait-free algorithm for a general purpose stack. In the past, researchers have proposed restricted wait-free implementations of stacks, lock-free implementations, and efficient universal constructions that can support wait-free stacks. The crux of our wait-free implementation is a fast *pop* operation that does not modify the stack top; instead, it walks down the stack till it finds a node that is unmarked. It marks it but does not delete it. Subsequently, it is lazily deleted by a *cleanup* operation. This operation keeps the size of the stack in check by not allowing the size of the stack to increase beyond a factor of W as compared to the actual size. All our operations are wait-free and linearizable.

1 Introduction

In this paper, we describe an algorithm to create a wait-free stack. A concurrent data structure is said to be wait-free if each operation is guaranteed to complete within a finite number of steps. In comparison, the data structure is said to be lock-free if at any point of time, at least one operation is guaranteed to complete in a finite number of steps. Wait-free stacks have not received a lot of attention in the past, and we are not aware of algorithms that are particularly tailored to creating a generalized wait-free stack. However, approaches have been proposed to create wait-free stacks with certain restrictions [1,3,7,8], and with universal constructions [4,10]. The main reason that it has been difficult to create a wait-free stack is because there is a lot of contention at the stack top between concurrent *push* and *pop* operations. It has thus been hitherto difficult to realize the gains of additional parallelism, and also guarantee completion in a finite amount of time.

The crux of our algorithm is as follows. We implement a stack as a linked list, where the *top* pointer points to the stack top. Each *push* operation adds an element to the linked list, and updates the *top* pointer. Both of these steps are done atomically, and the overall operation is linearizable (appears to execute instantaneously). However, the *pop* operation does not update the *top* pointer. This design decision has been made to enable more parallelism, and reduce the time per operation. It instead scans the list starting from the *top* pointer till it reaches an unmarked node. Once, it reaches an unmarked node, it marks it and returns the node as the result of the *pop* operation. Over time, more and more

© Springer International Publishing Switzerland 2016
N. Bjørner et al. (Eds.): ICDCIT 2016, LNCS 9581, pp. 43–55, 2016.
DOI: 10.1007/978-3-319-28034-9_6

nodes get marked in the stack. To garbage collect such nodes we implement a *cleanup* operation that can be invoked by both the *push* and *pop* operations. The cleanup operation removes a sequence of W consecutively marked nodes from the list. In our algorithm, we guarantee that at no point of time the size of the list is more than W times the size of the stack (number of pushes - pops). This property ensures that *pop* operations complete within a finite amount of time. Here, W is a user defined parameter and it needs to be set to an optimal value to ensure the best possible performance.

The novel feature of our algorithm is the *cleanup* operation that always keeps the size of the stack within limits. The other novel feature is that concurrent *pop* and *push* operations do not cross each others' paths. Moreover, all the *pop* operations can take place concurrently. This allows us to have a linearizable operation. In this paper, we present our basic algorithm along with proofs of important results. Readers can find the rest of the pseudo code, asymptotic time complexities, and proofs in the full paper posted on Arxiv [5].

2   Related Work

In 1986, Treiber [14] proposed the first lock-free linked list based implementation of a concurrent stack. In his implementation, both the *push* and *pop* operations modified the *top* pointer using CAS instructions. Subsequently, Shavit et al. [13] and Hendler et al. [6] designed a linearizable concurrent stack using the concept of software combining. Here, they group concurrent operations, and operate on the entire group. In 2004, Hendler et al. [9] proposed a highly scalable lock-free stack using an array of lock-free exchangers known as an elimination array. If a *pop* operation is paired with a *push* operation, then the baseline data structure need not be accessed. This greatly enhances the amount of available parallelism. This technique can be incorporated in our design as well. Subsequently, Bar-Nissan et al. [2] have augmented this proposal with software combining based approaches.

The restricted wait-free algorithms for the stack data structure proposed so far by the researchers are summarized in Table 1. The *wait-free* stack proposed in [1] employs a semi-infinite array as its underlying data structure. A *push* operation obtains a unique index in the array (using getAndIncrement()) and writes its value to that index. A *pop* operation starts from the top of the stack, and traverses the stack towards the bottom. It marks and returns the first unmarked node that we find. Our *pop* operation is inspired by this algorithm. Due to its unrestricted stack size, this algorithm is not practical.

David et al. [3] proposed another class of restricted stack implementations. Their implementation can support a maximum of two concurrent *push* operations. Kutten et al. [7,8] suggest an approach where a wait-free shared counter can be adapted to create wait-free stacks. However, their algorithm requires the DCAS (double CAS) primitive, which is not supported in contemporary hardware.

Wait-free universal constructions are generic algorithms that can be used to create linearizable implementations of any object that has valid sequential

Table 1. Summary of existing restricted wait-free stack algorithms

Author	Primitives	Remarks
Herlihy 1991 [10]	CAS	1. Copies every global update to the private copy of every thread 2. Replicates the stack data structure N times ($N \rightarrow$ # threads)
Afek et al. [1] 2006]	F&A, TAS	1. Requires a semi-infinite array (impractical) 2. Unbounded stack size
Hendler et al. [7] 2006]	DCAS	1. DCAS not supported in modern hardware 2. Variation of an implementation of a shared counter
Fatourou et al. [4] 2011]	LL/SC, F&A	1. Copies every global update to the private copy of every thread 2. Relies on wait-free implementation of F&A in hardware
David et al. 2011 [3]	BH object	1. Supports at the most two concurrent pop operations

CAS $\rightarrow$ compare-and-set, TAS $\rightarrow$ test-and-set, LL/SC $\rightarrow$ load linked-store conditional
DCAS $\rightarrow$ double location CAS, F&A $\rightarrow$ fetch-and-add, BH Object (custom object [3])

semantics. The inherent drawback of these approaches is that they typically have high time and space overheads (create local copies of the entire (or partial) data structure). For example, a recent proposal by Fatourou et al. [4] can be used to implement stacks and queues. The approach derives its performance improvement over the widely accepted universal construction of Herlihy [10] by optimizing on the number of shared memory accesses.

3   The Algorithm

3.1   Basic Data Structures

Algorithm 1 shows the *Node* class, which represents a node in a stack. It has a *value*, and pointers to the next (*nextDone*) and previous nodes (*prev*) respectively. Note that our stack is not a doubly linked list, the next pointer *nextDone* is only used for reaching consensus on which node will be added next in the stack.

To support *pop* operations, every node has a *mark* field. The *pushTid* field contains the id of the thread that created the request. The *index* field and *counter* are atomic integers and are used to clean up the stack. Initially, the list contains only the *sentinel* node, which is a dummy node.

Algorithm 1. The Node Class
---
1 **class Node**
2   *int value*
3   *AtomicMarkableReference* $< Node >$ *nextDone*
4   *AtomicReference* $< Node >$ *prev*
5   *AtomicBoolean mark*
6   *int pushTid*
7   *AtomicInteger index*
8   *AtomicInteger counter* /* initially set to 0 */

3.2 High Level Overview

The *push* operation starts by choosing a phase number (in a monotonically increasing manner), which is greater than the phase numbers of all the existing push operations in the system. This phase number along with a reference to the node to be pushed and a flag indicating the status of the *push* operation are saved in the *announce* array in an atomic step. After this, the thread t_i scans the *announce* array and finds out the thread t_j, which has a *push* request with the least phase number. Note that, the thread t_j found out by t_i in the last step might be t_i itself. Next, t_i helps t_j in completing t_j's operation. At this point of time, some threads other than t_i might also be trying to help t_j, and therefore, we must ensure that t_j's operation is applied exactly once. This is ensured by mandating that for the completion of any *push* request, the following steps must be performed in the exact specified order:

1. Modify the state of the stack in such a manner that all the other *push* requests in the system must come to know that a *push* request p_i is in progress and additionally they should be able to figure out the details required by them to help p_i.
2. Update the *pushed* flag to **true** in p_i's entry in the *announce* array.
3. Update the *top* pointer to point to the newly pushed node.

The *pop* operation has been designed in such a manner that it does not update the *top* pointer. This decision has the dual benefit of eliminating the contention between concurrent *push* and *pop* operations, as well as enabling the parallel execution of multiple *pop* operations. The *pop* operation starts by scanning the linked list starting from the stack's top till it reaches an unmarked node. Once, it gets an unmarked node, it marks it and returns the node as a result of the *pop* operation. Note that there is no helping in the case of a *pop* operation and therefore, we do not need to worry about a *pop* operation being executed twice. Over time, more and more nodes get marked in the stack. To garbage collect such nodes we implement a *clean* operation that can be invoked by both the *push* and *pop* operations.

3.3   The Push Operation

The first step in pushing a node is to create an instance of the *PushOp* class. It contains the reference to a Node (*node*), a Boolean variable *pushed* that indicates the status of the request, and a phase number (*phase*) to indicate the age of the request. Let us now consider the *push* method (Line 14). We first get the phase number by atomically incrementing a global counter. Once the *PushOp* is created and its phase is initialized, it is saved in the *announce* array. Subsequently, we call the function *help* to actually execute the *push* request.

The *help* function (Line 19) finds the request with the least phase number that has not been pushed yet. If there is no such request, then it returns. Otherwise it helps that request (*minReq*) to complete by calling the *attachNode* method. After helping *minReq*, we check if the request that was helped is the same as the request that was passed as an argument to the *help* function (*request*) in Line 19. If they are different requests, then we call *attachNode* for the request *request* in Line 26. This is a standard construction to make a lock-free method wait-free (refer to [11]).

In the *attachNode* function, we first read the value of the *top* pointer, and its *next* field. If these fields have not changed between Lines 31 and 32, then we try to find the status of the request in Line 34. Note that we check that *next* is equal to null, and *mark* is equal to false in the previous line (Line 33). The *mark* field is made true after the *top* pointer has been updated. Hence, in Line 33, if we find it to be true then we need to abort the current iteration and read the *top* pointer again.

After, we read the status of the request, and find that it has not completed, we proceed to update the *next* field of the stack top in Line 36 using a compare-And-Set (CAS) instruction. The aim is to change the pointer in the *next* field from *null* to the node the push request needs to add. If we are successful, then we update the *top* pointer by calling the function, *updateTop*. After the *top* pointer has been updated, we do not really need the *next* field for subsequent *push* requests. However, concurrent requests need to see that *last.nextDone* has been updated. The additional compulsion to delete the contents of the pointer in the *next* field is that it is possible to have references to deleted nodes via the *next* field. The garbage collector in this case will not be able to remove the deleted nodes. Thus, after updating the top pointer, we set the *next* field's pointer to *null*, and set the *mark* to true. If a concurrent request reads the mark to be true, then it can be sure, that the *top* pointer has been updated, and it needs to read it again.

If the CAS instruction fails, then it means that another concurrent request has successfully performed a CAS operation. However, it might not have updated the *top* pointer. It is thus necessary to call the *updateTop* function to help the request complete.

The *updateTop* method is shown in Algorithm 3. We read the *top* pointer, and the *next* pointer. If *next* is non-null, then the request has not fully completed. After having checked the value of the *top* pointer, and the value of the *next* field, we proceed to connect the newly attached node to the stack by updating

Algorithm 2. The Push Method

```
 9  class PushOp
10      long phase
11      boolean pushed
12      Node node
13  AtomicReferenceArray < PushOp > announce
14  push(tid, value)
15  phase ← globalPhase.getAndIncrement()
16  request ← new PushOp(phase, false, new Node(value, tid))
17  announce[tid] ← request
18  help(request)
19  help(request)
20  (minTid, minReq) ← min_{req.phase} { (i, req) | 0 ≤ i < N, req = announce[i], !req.pushed }
21  if  (minReq == null) || (minReq.phase > request.phase) then
22  |   return
23  end
24  attachNode(minReq)
25  if minReq ≠ request then
26  |   attachNode(request)
27  end
28  attachNode(request)
29  while !request.pushed do
30  |   last ← top.get()
31  |   (next, done) ← last.nextDone.get()
32  |   if last == top.get() then
33  |   |   if next == null && done = false then
34  |   |   |   if !request.pushed then
35  |   |   |   |   myNode ← request.node
36  |   |   |   |   res ← last.nextDone.compareAndSet( (null, false), (myNode, false))
37  |   |   |   |   if res then
38  |   |   |   |   |   updateTop()
39  |   |   |   |   |   last.nextDone.compareAndSet ( (myNode, false), (null, true))
40  |   |   |   |   |   return
41  |   |   |   |   end
42  |   |   |   end
43  |   |   end
44  |   |   updateTop()
45  |   end
46  end
```

its *prev* pointer. We set the value of its *prev* pointer in Line 54. Every node in the stack has an index that is assigned in a monotonically increasing order. Hence, in Line 55, we set the index of *next* to 1 plus the index of *last*. Next, we set the *pushed* field of the *request* equal to true. The point of linearizability is Line 57, where we update the *top* pointer to point to *next* instead of *last*.

We have a cleanup mechanism that is invoked once the index of a node becomes a multiple of a constant, *W*. We invoke the *tryCleanUp* method in Line 60. It is necessary that the *tryCleanUp*() method be called by only one thread. Hence, the thread that successfully performed a CAS on the top pointer calls the *tryCleanUp* method if the index is a multiple of *W*.

Algorithm 3. The *updateTop* method

```
47  updateTop()
48  last ← top.get()
49  (next, mark) ← last.nextDone.get()
50  if next ≠ null then
51      request ← announce.get(next.pushTid)
52      if last == top.get() && request.node == next then
53          /* Add the request to the stack and update the top pointer */
54          next.prev.compareAndSet(null, last)
55          next.index ← last.index +1
56          request.pushed ← true
57          stat ← top.compareAndSet(last, next)
58          /* Check if any cleaning up has to be done */
59          if next.index % W == 0 && stat == true then
60              tryCleanUp(next)
61          end
62      end
63  end
```

3.4 The Pop Operation

Algorithm 4 shows the code for the *pop* method. We read the value of the *top* pointer and save it in the local variable, *myTop*. This is the only instance in this function, where we read the value of the *top* pointer. Then, we walk back towards the sentinel node by following the *prev* pointers (Lines 67 – 73). We stop when we are successfully able to set the mark of a node that is unmarked. This node is logically "popped" at this instant of time. If we are not able to find any such node, and we reach the sentinel node, then we throw an *EmptyStackException*.

Algorithm 4. The Pop Method

```
64  pop()
65  mytop ← top.get()
66  curr ← mytop
67  while curr ≠ sentinel do
68      mark ← curr.mark.getAndSet(true)
69      if !mark then
70          break
71      end
72      curr ← curr.prev
73  end
74  if curr == sentinel then
75      /* Reached the end of the stack */
76      throw new EmptyStackException()
77  end
78  /* Try to clean up parts of the stack */
79  tryCleanUp(curr)
80  return curr
```

After logically marking a node as popped, it is time to physically delete it. We thus call the *tryCleanUp* method in Line 79. The *pop* method returns the node that it had successfully marked.

3.5 The CleanUp Operation

The aim of the *clean* method is to clean a set of W contiguous entries in the list (indexed by the *prev* pointers). Let us start by defining some terminology. Let us define a range of W contiguous entries, which has four distinguished nodes as shown in Fig. 1.

A range starts with a node termed the *base*, whose index is a multiple of W. Let us now define *target* as *base.prev*. The node at the end of a range is *leftNode*. Its index is equal to $base.index + W - 1$. Let us now define a node *rightNode* such that $rightNode.prev = leftNode$. Note that for a given range, the *base* and *leftNode* nodes are fixed, whereas the *target* and *rightNode* nodes keep changing. *rightNode* is the base of another range, and its index is a multiple of W.

The *push* and *pop* methods call the function *tryCleanUp*. The *push* method calls it when it pushes a node whose index is a multiple of W. This is a valid *rightNode*. It walks back and increments the counter of the *base* node of the previous range. We ensure that only one thread (out of all the helpers) does this in Line 59. Similarly, in the *pop* function, whenever we mark a node, we call the *tryCleanUp* function. Since the *pop* function does not have any helpers, only one thread per node calls the *tryCleanUp* function. Now, inside the *tryCleanUp* function, we increment the counter of the *base* node. Once, a thread increments it to $W + 1$, it invokes the *clean* function. Since only one thread will increment the counter to $W + 1$, only one thread will invoke the *clean* function for a range.

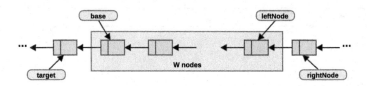

Fig. 1. A range of W entries

The functionality of the *clean* function is very similar to the *push* function. Here, we first create a *DeleteRequest* that has four fields: *phase* (similar to phase in *PushOp*), *threadId*, *pending* (whether the delete has been finished or not), and the value of the *base* node. Akin to the *push* function, we add the newly created *DeleteRequest* to a global array of *DeleteRequests*. Subsequently, we find the pending request with the minimum phase in the array *allDeleteRequests*.

Note that at this stage it is possible for multiple threads to read the same value of the request with the minimum phase number. It is also possible for different sets of threads to have found different requests to have the minimum

---

Algorithm 5. The *tryCleanUp* method

---

81 **tryCleanUp(myNode)**
82 $temp \leftarrow myNode.prev$
83 **while** $temp \neq sentinel$ **do**
84   **if** $temp.index() \% W == 0$ **then**
85   **if** $temp.counter.incrementAndGet == W + 1$ **then**
86 | $clean(getTid(), temp)$
87   **end**
88          $break$
89   **end**
90      $temp \leftarrow temp.prev()$
91 **end**

---

phase. For example, if a request with phase 2 (R_2) got added to the array before the request with phase 1 (R_1), then a set of threads might be trying to complete R_2, and another set might be trying to complete R_1. To ensure that our stack remains in a consistent state, we want that only one set goes to the next stage.

To achieve this, we adopt a strategy similar to the one adopted in the function *attachNode*. Interested readers can refer to the full paper at [5] for a detailed explanation of how this is done. Beyond this point, all the threads will be working on the same *DeleteRequest* which we term as *uniqueRequest*. They will then move on to call the *helpFinishDelete* function that will actually finish the delete request.

Let us describe the *helpFinishDelete* function in Algorithm 6. We first read the current request from the atomic variable, *uniqueRequest* in Line 93. If the request is not pending, then some other helper has completed the request, and we can return from the function. However, if this is not the case, then we need to complete the delete operation. Our aim now is to find the *target*, *leftNode*, and *rightNode*. We search for these nodes starting from the stack top.

The index of the *leftNode* is equal to the index of the node in the current request (*currRequest*) + $W - 1$. *endIdx* is set to this value in Line 97. Subsequently, in Lines 101–106, we start from the top of the stack, and keep traversing the *prev* pointers till the index of *leftNode* is equal to *endIdx*. Once, the equality condition is satisfied, Lines 101 and 102 give us the pointers to the *rightNode* and *leftNode* respectively. If we are not able to find the *leftNode*, then it means that another helper has successfully deleted the nodes. We can thus return.

The next task is to find the *target*. The *target* is W hops away from the *leftNode*. Lines 108–111 run a loop W times to find the target. Note that we shall never have any issues with null pointers because *sentinel.prev* is set to *sentinel* itself. Once, we have found the target, we need to perform a CAS operation on the *prev* pointer of the *rightNode*. We accomplish this in Line 112. If the *prev* pointer of *rightNode* is equal to *leftNode*, then we set it to *target*. This operation removes W entries (from *leftNode* to *base*) from the list. The last step is to set the status of the *pending* field in the current request (*currRequest*) to false (see Line 113).

Algorithm 6. The *helpFinishDelete* method

92 **helpFinishDelete()**
93 $currRequest \leftarrow uniqueRequest.get()$
94 **if** $!currRequest.pending$ **then**
95 $\quad|\quad return$
96 **end**
97 $endIdx \leftarrow currRequest.node.index + W - 1$
98 $rightNode \leftarrow top.get()$ /* Search for the request from the *top* */
99 $leftNode \leftarrow rightNode.prev$
100 **while** $leftNode.index \neq endIdx$ && $leftNode \neq sentinel$ **do**
101 $\quad|\quad rightNode \leftarrow leftNode$
102 $\quad|\quad leftNode \leftarrow leftNode.prev$
103 **end**
104 **if** $leftNode = sentinel$ **then**
105 $\quad|\quad return$ /* some other thread deleted the nodes */
106 **end**
107 /* Find the target node */
108 $target \leftarrow leftNode$
109 **for** $i=0;\ i < W;\ i++$ **do**
110 $\quad|\quad target \leftarrow target.prev$
111 **end**
112 $rightNode.prev.compareAndSet(leftNode, target)$ /* Perform the CAS operation and delete the nodes */
113 $currRequest.pending \leftarrow$ **false** /* Set the status of the delete request to not pending*/

4   Proof of Correctness

The most popular correctness criteria for a concurrent shared object is *linearizability* [12]. Linearizability ensures that within the execution interval of every operation there is a point, called the linearization point, where the operation seems to take effect instantaneously and the effect of all the operations on the object is consistent with the object's sequential specification. By the property of compositional linearizability, if each method of an object is linearizable we can conclude that the complete object is linearizable. Thus, if we identify the point of linearization for both the push and the pop method in our implementation, we can say that our implementation is linearizable and thus establish its correctness. In our full paper at [5], we show that our implementation is legal and push and pop operations complete in a bounded number of steps.

Theorem 1. *The push and pop operations are linearizable.*

Proof. Let us start out by defining the notion of "pass points". The pass point of a *push* operation is when it successfully updates the *top* pointer in the function *updateTop* (Line 57). The pass point of the *pop* operation, is when it successfully marks a node, or when it throws the *EmtpyStackException*. Let us now try to prove by mathematical induction on the number of requests that it is always possible to construct a linearizable execution that is equivalent to a given execution. In a linearizable execution all the operations are arranged in a sequential order, and if request r_i precedes r_j in the original execution, then r_i precedes r_j in the linearizable execution as well.

Base Case: Let us consider an execution with only one pass point. Since the execution is complete, we can conclude that there was only one request in the system. An equivalent linearizable execution will have a single request. The outcome of the request will be an *EmptyStackException* if it is a *pop* request, otherwise it will push a node to the stack. Our algorithm will do exactly the same in the *pop* and *attachNode* methods respectively. Hence, the executions are equivalent.

Induction Hypothesis: Let us assume that all executions with n requests are equivalent to linearizable executions.

Inductive Step: Let us now prove our hypothesis for executions with $n + 1$ requests. Let us arrange all the requests in an ascending order of the execution times of their pass points. Let us consider the last $((n + 1)^{th})$ request just after the pass point of the nth request. Let the last request be a *push*. If the nth request is also a *push*, then the last request will use the *top* pointer updated by the nth request. Additionally, in this case the nth request will not see any changes made by the last request. It will update *last.next* and the *top* pointer, before the last request updates them. In a similar manner we can prove that no prior *push* request will see the last request. Let us now consider a prior *pop* request. A *pop* request scans all the nodes between the *top* pointer and the sentinel. None of the pop requests will see the updated *top* pointer by the last request because their pass points are before this event. Thus, they have no way of knowing about the existence of the last request. Since the execution of the first n requests is linearizable, an execution with the $(n + 1)^{th}$ push request is also linearizable because it takes effect at the end (and will appear last in the equivalent sequential order).

Let us now consider the last request to be a *pop* operation. A *pop* operation writes to any shared location only after its pass point. Before its pass point, it does not do any writes, and thus all other requests are oblivious of it. Thus, we can remove the last request, and the responses of the first n requests will remain the same. Let us now consider an execution fragment consisting of the first n requests. It is equivalent to a linearizable execution, $\mathcal{E}$. This execution is independent of the $(n + 1)^{th}$ request.

Now, let us try to create a linearizable execution, $\mathcal{E}'$, which has an event corresponding to the last request. Since the linearizable execution is sequential, let us represent the request and response of the last *pop* operation by a single event, R. Let us try to modify $\mathcal{E}$ to create $\mathcal{E}'$. Let the sequential execution corresponding to $\mathcal{E}$ be $\mathcal{S}$.

Now, it is possible that R could have read the *top* pointer long ago, and is somewhere in the middle of the stack. In this case, we cannot assume that R is the last request to execute in the equivalent linearizable execution. Let the state of the stack before the *pop* reads the top pointer be $\mathcal{S}'$. The state $\mathcal{S}'$ is independent of the *pop* request. Also note that, all the operations that have arrived after the *pop* operation have read the *top* pointer, and overlap with the *pop* operation. The basic rule of *linearizability* states that, if any operation R_i precedes R_j

then R_i should precede R_j in the equivalent sequential execution also. Whereas, in case the two operations overlap with each other, then their relative order is undefined and any ordering of these operations is a valid ordering [11].

In this case, we have two possibilities: (I) R returns the node that it had read as the top pointer as an output of its *pop* operation, or (II) it returns some other node.

<u>Case I:</u> In this case, we can consider the point at which R reads the top pointer as the point at which it is *linearized*. R in this case reads the stack top, and pops it.

<u>Case II:</u> In this case, some other request, which is concurrent must have popped the node that R read as the top pointer. Let R return node N_i as its return value. This node must be between the top pointer that it had read (node N_{top}), and the beginning of the stack. Moreover, while traversing the stack from N_{top} to N_i, R must have found all the nodes in the way to be marked. At the end it must have found N_i to be unmarked, or would have found N_i to be the end of the stack (returns exception).

Let us consider the journey for R from N_{top} to N_i. Let N_j be the last node before N_i that has been marked by a concurrent request, R_j. We claim that if R is linearized right after R_j, and the rest of the sequences of events in $\mathcal{E}$ remain the same, we have a linearizable execution ($\mathcal{E}'$).

Let us consider request R_j and its position in the sequential execution, $\mathcal{S}$. At its point of linearization, it reads the top of the stack and returns it (according to $\mathcal{S}$). This node N_j is the successor of N_i. At that point N_i becomes the top of the stack. At this position, if we insert R into S, then it will read and return N_i as the stack top, which is the correct value. Subsequently, we can insert the remaining events in S into the sequential execution. They will still return the same set of values because they are unaffected by R as proved before.

This proof can be trivially extended to take cleanup operations into account.

5   Conclusion

The crux of our algorithm is the *clean* routine, which ensures that the size of the stack never grows beyond a predefined factor, W. This feature allows for a very fast *pop* operation, where we need to find the first entry from the top of the stack that is not marked. This optimization also allows for an increased amount of parallelism, and also decreases write-contention on the *top* pointer because it is not updated by *pop* operations. As a result, the time per *pop* operation is very low. The *push* operation is also designed to be very fast. It simply needs to update the *top* pointer to point to the new data. To provide wait-free guarantees it was necessary to design a *clean* function that is slow. Fortunately, it is not invoked for an average of $W - 1$ out of W invocations of *push* and *pop*. We can tune the frequency of the *clean* operation by varying the parameter, W (to be decided on the basis of the workload).

References

1. Afek, Y., Gafni, E., Morrison, A.: Common2 extended to stacks and unbounded concurrency. Distrib. Comput. **20**(4), 239–252 (2007)
2. Bar-Nissan, G., Hendler, D., Suissa, A.: A dynamic elimination-combining stack algorithm. In: Fernàndez Anta, A., Lipari, G., Roy, M. (eds.) OPODIS 2011. LNCS, vol. 7109, pp. 544–561. Springer, Heidelberg (2011)
3. David, M., Brodsky, A., Fich, F.E.: Restricted stack implementations. In: Fraigniaud, P. (ed.) DISC 2005. LNCS, vol. 3724, pp. 137–151. Springer, Heidelberg (2005)
4. Fatourou, P., Kallimanis, N.D.: A highly-efficient wait-free universal construction. In: SPAA 2011, pp. 325–334. ACM (2011)
5. Goel, S., Aggarwal, P., Sarangi, S.: full paper: "a wait-free stack". http://arxiv.org/abs/1510.00116
6. Hendler, D., Incze, I., Shavit, N., Tzafrir, M.: Flat combining and the synchronization-parallelism tradeoff. In: Proceedings of the 22nd ACM Symposium on Parallelism in Algorithms and Architectures, pp. 355–364. ACM (2010)
7. Hendler, D., Kutten, S.: Constructing shared objects that are both robust and high-throughput. In: Dolev, S. (ed.) DISC 2006. LNCS, vol. 4167, pp. 428–442. Springer, Heidelberg (2006)
8. Hendler, D., Kutten, S., Michalak, E.: An adaptive technique for constructing robust and high-throughput shared objects-technical report (2010)
9. Hendler, D., Shavit, N., Yerushalmi, L.: A scalable lock-free stack algorithm. In: SPAA 2004, pp. 206–215. ACM (2004)
10. Herlihy, M.: Wait-free synchronization. ACM Trans. Program. Lang. Syst. **13**(1), 124–149 (1991)
11. Herlihy, M., Shavit, N.: The Art of Multiprocessor Programming. Elsevier, Burlington (2012)
12. Herlihy, M.P., Wing, J.M.: Linearizability: a correctness condition for concurrent objects. ACM Trans. Program. Lang. Syst. **12**(3), 463–492 (1990)
13. Shavit, N., Zemach, A.: Combining funnels: a dynamic approach to software combining. J. Parallel Distrib. Comput. **60**(11), 1355–1387 (2000)
14. Treiber, R.K.: Systems programming: coping with parallelism. Thomas J. Watson Research Center, International Business Machines Incorporated (1986)

Influential Degree Heuristic for RankedReplace Algorithm in Social Networks

Jatharakonda Mallesham$^{(\boxtimes)}$ and S. Durga Bhavani

School of Computer and Information Sciences, University of Hyderabad,
Hyderabad, India
mallesh537@gmail.com, sdbcs@uohyd.ernet.in

Abstract. Influence maximization is to identify a subset of nodes at which if the information is released, the information spread can be maximized. Faisan and Bhavani [7] proposed incorporating greedy selection in the initialization step of *RankedReplace* algorithm of Charu Aggarwal et al. which would speed up the algorithm. We propose to improve this algorithm further by considering novel heuristic called *influential degree* for selection of the initial set. The experiments are carried out on small as well as large data sets like DBLP and the results show that RRID and its variations perform quite well on all the data sets quite efficiently reducing the time taken and retaining, and in a few cases, obtaining much better influence spread than the original *RankedReplace* algorithm.

1 Introduction

Social networks are represented as graphs in which vertices represent individuals and edges denote interactions or relationships among actors. Some of the challenging problems in social networks relate to information about finding groups that are collaborating together(community discovery) [8], discovering potential new collaborations (link prediction) [12], finding important nodes (influential nodes) [10] and to find good target nodes in the context of marketing [6].

1.1 Problem Definition

Let $\pi(i)$ be the probability that node i contains the information.

Given a social network graph, integer k and information flow model, the problem is to find a set S of k nodes at which information will be released such that it maximizes the aggregate probability of information assimilation over all nodes in the graph.

$$\mathbf{S_k^*} = argmax_{\{\mathbf{S} \subset \mathbf{V}, |\mathbf{S}| = \mathbf{k}\}} \sum_{\mathbf{i} \in \mathbf{V}} \pi(\mathbf{i})$$

2 Related Work

Domingos and Richardson [6] introduced influence maximization problem in marketing context. Kempe et al. [9] proved that the problem of influence

© Springer International Publishing Switzerland 2016
N. Bjørner et al. (Eds.): ICDCIT 2016, LNCS 9581, pp. 56–60, 2016.
DOI: 10.1007/978-3-319-28034-9_7

maximization is NP-Hard. Leskovec et al. [11] applied this problem to placement of sensors in a water distribution network and for the problem of choosing an informative blog. Chen [4,5] proposed two greedy algorithms, one that uses *degree discount* heuristic to reduce time complexity. Narayanam et al. [13] used *shapely value* as a greedy heuristic to ranks the nodes.

Charu Aggarwal et al. [3] proposed a new model, namely *flow authority model*, in which they propose two novel algorithms namely *steady state spread* (SSS) algorithm and *RankedReplace* (RR) algorithm for *flow authority model (FAM)*. Steady state spread algorithm calculates aggregate spread for a given set of nodes.

3 Proposed Approach: Modified RankedReplace Algorithm

In the proposed modification to *RankedReplace* algorithm, in the initialization step, the top k nodes ranked by the influential degree heuristic are stored in the set S in ascending order and remaining nodes are ordered in the descending order of influential degree in R. Now the first node in S is replaced with the top node from R and checked if the total spread increases with the change. If yes, the node will be replaced. The algorithm is repeated until r consecutive unsuccessful replacement attempts. The algorithm returns the final S as the top k influential nodes.

3.1 Influential Degree (ID) and Influential Degree Discount (IDD) Heuristics

For each node, consider the number of edges (directed outward) whose weight is greater than or equal to a predefined threshold value θ. We set the threshold θ on weights of edges so that $X\%$ of total edges of the graph can be considered for degree calculation. This count called as *influential degree (ID)* is a kind of modified out-degree based on weight. And in the process of calculating degree of a node, say u is a neighbor of v, if v has been selected in degree calculation of u, that is, edge (u, v) has been considered once then the same edge is disabled and cannot be considered as (v, u) for degree of v.

4 Experimentation and Results

The modified RankedReplace algorithm is carried out with six different heuristics: two standard heuristics: *MaxDegree, DegreeDiscount*; and the proposed heuristics of Influential Degree (ID) and InfluentialDegree Discount (IDD) each with two different thresholds θ_1 and θ_2; and of course compared with the regular RankedReplace algorithm. Hence seven experimental settings are carried out. It is to be noted that the experimentation reported by Faisan and Bhavani [7] is limited to small data sets.

4.1 Data Sets

For analysis purpose we considered three collaboration graphs: Astrophyics, condmat2003 (medium) and DBLP. In order to apply FAM model to collaboration graphs, weights have been normalized w.r.t the maximum number of contributions between any two authors. We consider two threshold values for influential degree θ_1 and θ_2 and the details are given in Table 1.

Table 1. Data sets

Data Set	# of Nodes	# of Edges	θ_1 (33 % Edges)	θ_2 (50 % Edges)
Astrophysics [1]	16046	121251	0.0142	0.00758
Condmat2003 [1]	27519	116181	0.014	0.007
DBLP [2]	684911	2284991	0.0005	-

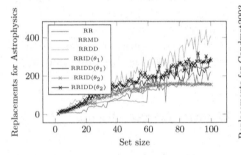

Fig. 1. Replacement analysis for Astrophysics

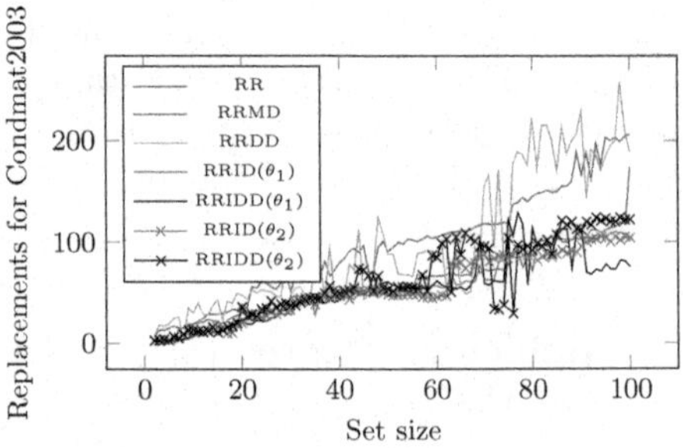

Fig. 2. Replacement analysis for condmat2003

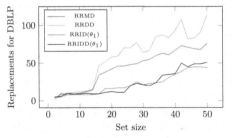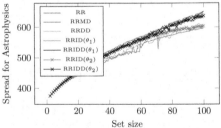

Fig. 3. Replacement analysis for DBLP

Fig. 4. Spread analysis for Astrophysics data set.

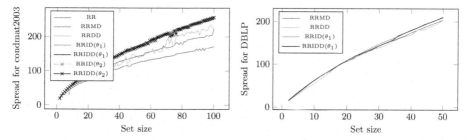

Fig. 5. Spread analysis for Condmat2003 data set. **Fig. 6.** Spread analysis for DBLP data set.

5 Conclusion

The initial step of RankReplace algorithm of Charu Aggarwal et al. is modified by incorporating the proposed influential degree heuristics. These algorithms are implemented on medium and large data sets, namely Condmat2003, Astrophysics and DBLP respectively. It can be seen in Figs. 1, 2, 3, 4, 5 and 6 that heuristics based on RRID and RRIDD yield low number of replacements and obtain high total spread or at least values on par with RR. In all the cases the influential degree heuristic algorithms are performing much better than the standard heuristics.

References

1. http://www-personal.umich.edu/~mejn/netdata/
2. http://people.inf.ethz.ch/khana/dataset.html
3. Aggarwal, C.C., Khan, A., Yan, X.: On flow authority discovery in social networks. In: Proceedings of the Eleventh SIAM International Conference on Data Mining, SDM, pp. 522–533 (2011)
4. Chen, W., Wang, C., Wang, Y.: Scalable influence maximization for prevalent viral marketing in large scale social networks. In: Proceedings of the ACM SIGKDD Conference on Knowledge Discovery and Data Mining, pp. 1029–1038. ACM Press (2010)
5. Chen, W., Wang, Y., Yang, S.: Efficient influence maximization in social networks. In: Proceedings of the 15th ACM SIGKDD International Conference on Knowledge Discovery and Data Mining, pp. 199–208 (2009)
6. Domingos, P., Richardson, M.: Mining the network value of customers. In: Proceedings of Seventh ACM SIGKDD International Conference on Knowledge Discovery and Datamining, pp. 57–66 (2001)
7. Faisan, M.M., Bhavani, S.D.: Maximizing information or influence spread using flow authority model in social networks. In: Natarajan, R. (ed.) ICDCIT 2014. LNCS, vol. 8337, pp. 233–238. Springer, Heidelberg (2014)
8. Girvan, M., Newman, M.E.J.: Community structure in social and biological networks. Proc. Nat. Acad. Sci. **99**(12), 7821–7826 (2002)

9. Kempe, D., Kleinberg, J., Tardos, E.: Maximizing the spread of influence through a social network. In: Proceedings of the Ninth ACM SIGKDD International Conference on Knowledge Discovery and Data Mining, pp. 137–146 (2003)
10. Kleinberg, J.: Authoritative sources in a hyperlinked environment. J. ACM **46**(5), 604–632 (1999)
11. Leskovec, J., Krause, A., Guestrin, C., Faloutsos, C., VanBriesen, J.M., Glance, N.S.: Cost-effective outbreak detection in networks. In: Proceedings of the 13th ACM SIGKDD International Conference on Knowledge Discovery and Data Mining, pp. 420–429 (2007)
12. Liben-Nowell, D., Kleinberg, J.: The link-prediction problem for social networks. J. Am. Soc. Inf. Sci. Technol. **58**(7), 1019–1031 (2007). doi:10.1002/asi.v58:7
13. Narayanam, R., Narahari, Y.: A shapley value-based approach to discover influential nodes in social networks. IEEE Trans. Autom. Sci. Eng. **8**(1), 130–147 (2011)

An Efficient Task Consolidation Algorithm for Cloud Computing Systems

Sanjaya K. Panda[1(✉)] and Prasanta K. Jana[2]

[1] Department of Computer Science and Engineering
and Information Technology, Veer Surendra Sai University of Technology,
Burla 768018, India
sanjayauce@gmail.com
[2] Department of Computer Science and Engineering, Indian School of Mines,
Dhanbad 826004, India
prasantajana@yahoo.co.in

Abstract. With the increasing demand of cloud computing, energy consumption has drawn enormous attention in business and research community. This is also due to the amount of carbon footprints generated from the information and communication technology resources such as server, network and storage. Therefore, the first and foremost goal is to minimize the energy consumption without compromising the customer demands or tasks. On the other hand, task consolidation is a process to minimize the total number of resource usage by improving the utilization of the active resources. Recent studies reported that the tasks are assigned to the virtual machines (VMs) based on their utilization value on VMs without any major concern on the processing time of the tasks. However, task processing time is also equal important criteria. In this paper, we propose a multi-criteria based task consolidation algorithm that assigns the tasks to VMs by considering both processing time of the tasks and the utilization of VMs. We perform rigorous simulations on the proposed algorithm using some randomly generated datasets and compare the results with two recent energy-conscious task consolidation algorithms, namely random and MaxUtil. The proposed algorithm improves about 10 % of energy consumption than the random algorithm and about 5 % than the MaxUtil algorithm.

Keywords: Cloud computing · Task consolidation · Energy consumption · Virtual machine · Resource utilization

1 Introduction

Cloud computing is extensively adopted in various communities for its variety of services, namely infrastructure as a service (IaaS), platform as a service (PaaS) and software as a service (SaaS) [1]. It makes tremendous growth in startups and small-to-medium businesses as the services of cloud are delivered with no upfront commitments. As the demands of cloud computing rapidly grow, it is very much essential to manage the resources and properly utilize them. However, efficient resource utilization does not imply to energy efficiency [2]. Therefore, the current research interest is to reduce the energy consumption and minimize the total number of resource usage by enhancing the

© Springer International Publishing Switzerland 2016
N. Bjørner et al. (Eds.): ICDCIT 2016, LNCS 9581, pp. 61–74, 2016.
DOI: 10.1007/978-3-319-28034-9_8

resource utilization of the active resources. The increasing demand for information and communication technology (ICT) resources make the service providers to re-think about the energy consumption as ICT is responsible for a vast amount of CO_2 emissions. For instance, ICT resources consume about 8 % of the total energy consumption in the United States each year and it is expected to reach about 50 % in the next decade [3, 4]. It is reported that 66 % of the electricity in the United States is generated using coal and natural gas [3]. As a result, some practitioners' objective is to maximize the resource utilization [5, 6] whereas others objective is to minimize the energy consumption [7, 8]. Most of the current research works [2, 9, 10] focus on both objectives by assigning the customer tasks to that virtual machine (VM) which results in maximum resource utilization. Moreover, it turned off the unused VMs to save the energy. Note that these works are minimizing the energy only by considering the utilization of the VMs without processing time of the tasks. This phenomenon inspires the idea of considering both criteria, i.e., processing time and utilization in the form of a multi-criteria function to save a substantial amount of energy. Therefore, we propose a multi-criteria based task consolidation (MTC) algorithm that minimizes energy consumption.

The key idea of MTC is to consider the linear combination (referred as fitness value) of processing time and utilization of the tasks. For this, it assigns a weight value to the processing time as well as the utilization. Then it sorts the tasks in the ascending order of their fitness value. Finally, it assigns the tasks to that VM where it achieves maximum utilization value. It makes the unused resources to be turned off. Thus the main contributions of this paper are as follows. (1) We propose a multi-criteria function to find the ordering of task execution. (2) We present how MTC can reduce energy consumption by consolidating the tasks in cloud systems. (3) We compare our simulation results with two well-known algorithms using some randomly generated datasets.

The rest of this paper is organized as follows: Sect. 2 discusses the state-of-the-art in task consolidation. Section 3 presents the cloud and energy models followed by task consolidation problem. Section 4 introduces the proposed algorithm with an illustrative example. The simulation results of the proposed algorithm and its comparison with two well-known task consolidation algorithms are presented in Sect. 5. We conclude with brief remarks in Sect. 6.

2   Related Work

As the ICT devices are drawing the significant amount of power, energy consumption is a crucial issue in the field of cloud computing. Many researchers [2, 7–11] have proposed energy efficient algorithms to reduce the consumption of energy. One of the possible solutions is to reduce the energy by transferring some of the customer tasks from least loaded resources to the active resources and make the least loaded resources in turn off mode. Chen et al. [12] have proposed a software-based approach that includes two techniques, namely dynamic provisioning and load dispatching. The first one aims to switch on the minimum number of resources, whereas the second aims to share the loads among the active resources. However, frequent on and off resources may cause a major overhead in this approach. Srikantaiah et al. [13] have presented the consolidation problem as a modified bin packing problem. However, the problem is considered only in terms of CPU and disk resources. Tesfatsion et al. [14] have combined three techniques such as the number of VMs, the number of cores and the CPU frequencies to minimize the energy consumption. They have used a feedback controller to determine the optimal configuration. Chen et al. [15] have presented proactive and reactive scheduling methods for real-time tasks in cloud computing. Furthermore, they propose three scaling strategies to improve the energy consumption. Hsu et al. [2] have proposed an energy-aware task consolidation by restricting the CPU use below a threshold value. However, the threshold is set manually without considering the dynamic nature of the cloud environment. Lee et al. [9] have introduced two energy efficient task consolidation algorithms for minimizing the energy consumption implicitly or explicitly. The algorithms are purely based on the cost functions that select a VM for a ready task. However, the frequent arrival of the tasks at any given time is not considered in these algorithms.

The algorithm proposed in this paper is different from that of [2, 9] with respect to following novel concepts. (1) Our algorithm takes advantage by considering a multi-criteria function instead of single criterion function as used by [2, 9]. (2) The algorithm reduces the substantial amount of energy in contrast to [9] by assigning the tasks in ascending order of fitness value. (3) We evaluate the performance of our proposed algorithm with a large set of tasks and VMs in compare to [2, 9]. Comparison results show the efficacy of the proposed algorithm over random [9] and MaxUtil [9] algorithms with respect to energy consumption.

3 Models and Problem Statement

3.1 Cloud and Energy Models

The cloud system consists of a set of physical servers that are connected to a network. In order to meet the customer demands or tasks, VMs are created on the physical servers. However, we assume that these VMs are homogeneous in terms of the computational power, memory and storage. It is also assumed that the VM utilization of the customer demands is determined before the task assignment takes place [9, 11]. A VM may be present in one of the following states: idle, active or sleep/awake. They are briefly described as follows. (1) Idle: A VM is yet to receive a task. (2) Active: A VM is currently executing a task. (3) Sleep/Awake: A VM is turned off. However, in this paper, we assume only idle and active states. Upon receiving a task, a VM changes its state from idle to active. It again returns to the idle state after the completion of the assigned task. The energy model assumes that the VM utilization is a linear one with the energy consumption. Alternatively, the energy consumption of a VM is increased if the VM utilization is also increased. The utilization of the VM i at any given time j (denoted as UV_i^j) is defined as the sum of the VM usage of all the tasks at any given time j (denoted as UT_o^j). Mathematically,

$$UV_i^j = \sum_{o=1}^{n} UT_o^j \times F_o^j \tag{1}$$

where

$$F_o^j = \begin{cases} 1 & \text{if task } o \text{ is assigned at any given time } j \\ 0 & \text{Otherwise} \end{cases} \qquad (2)$$

and n = the total number of tasks. Therefore, the average utilization of all the VMs at any given time j (i.e., UV^j) is mathematically expressed as follows.

$$UV^j = \frac{1}{m} \sum_{i=1}^{m} UV_i^j \qquad (3)$$

where m = the total number of VMs. The energy consumption of the VM i at any given time j (i.e., E_i^j) is mathematically defined as follows [9].

$$E_i^j = (p_{\max} - p_{\min}) \times UV_i^j + p_{\min} \qquad (4)$$

where p_{max} and p_{min} are the power consumption at the peak and the active load respectively. Therefore, the energy consumption of all the VMs at any given time j (i.e., E^j) is mathematically presented as follows.

$$E^j = \sum_{i=1}^{m} E_i^j \qquad (5)$$

The above model is similar to the cloud and energy models as used in [9] and our earlier work [10].

3.2 Task Consolidation Problem

Given a set of n independent tasks and a set of m identical virtual machines in which each task T_i, $1 \leq i \leq n$ is a quintuple, {ID, AT, PT, FT, U} where ID denotes the task identification number, AT is the arrival time (also the start time), PT is the processing time, FT is the finish time and U is the utilization. Note that $FT = AT + PT$. The utilization value of a task T_i, $1 \leq i \leq n$ denotes how much time this task makes the VM busy in a higher end. The problem is to assign the tasks to the VMs such that the energy consumption is minimized. This problem is subjected to following scheduling constraints. (1) The time constraints of a task T_i, $1 \leq i \leq n$ such as start and processing times are fixed. (2) A task T_i, $1 \leq i \leq n$ is assigned before a task T_j, $1 \leq j \leq n$, $i \neq j$ iff the arrival time of the task T_i, denoted as $AT(T_i)$, is less than the arrival time of the task T_j (i.e., $AT(T_j)$). Mathematically, $AT(T_i) < AT(T_j)$. However, if the arrival time of two different tasks is same, then they are assigned in any order. (3) A task T_i, $1 \leq i \leq n$ is not assigned to a virtual machine VM_j, $1 \leq j \leq m$ iff the sum of the utilization of the task and the utilization of the VM at a requested period exceeds 100 %. (4) A task T_i, $1 \leq i \leq n$ cannot be preempted, migrated and/or split at any cost.

4   Proposed Algorithm

4.1   Multi-criteria Based Task Consolidation

The multi-criteria based task consolidation (MTC) is a two-phase task consolidation algorithm. In the first phase, it makes a decision on the ordering of tasks that arrives at the same time. For this, it normalizes the processing time and the utilization of each task based on the maximum processing time and maximum utilization respectively. Then it calculates the fitness value F for each task as follows.

$$F = \lambda \times (normalized\ processing\ time) + (1 - \lambda) \times (normalized\ utilization) \quad (6)$$

where $0 < \lambda < 1$. Subsequently, it sorts the tasks in the ascending order of their fitness value. This completes the first phase. The rationality behind the first phase is that the task with low fitness value is ordered before higher ones as it increases the VM utilization in compare to the chronological order as used in [9]. Note that it is possible if and only if two or more tasks are arriving at the same time.

Remark 4.1. The process of normalization is essential as it makes the value in the range of 0 to 1. Otherwise, one high value may dominate the others.

In the second phase, the sorted tasks are assigned one after another to one of the VMs where it achieves maximum cost value. The cost value of a VM_i (i.e., CO_i) is defined as follows [9].

$$CO_i = \frac{1}{p} \sum_{j=1}^{p} UV_i^j \quad (7)$$

where p is the processing time of the task.

4.2   Algorithm Description

We use the following terminologies (Table 1) for the pseudo code of the proposed MTC which is shown in Fig. 1.

MTC places the customer tasks in the ascending order of their arrival time in Q (Line 1) and the quintuple of the tasks are placed in the TC matrix where each row denotes a task i and the columns denote the task identification number (i.e., $TC(i, 1)$), arrival time ($TC(i, 2)$), processing time ($TC(i, 3)$), finish time ($TC(i, 4)$) and utilization ($TC(i, 5)$) respectively. Next it initializes the weight value based on the various factors such as energy consumption, processing cost and utilization cost (Line 2). Then it calculates the $|Q|$ (Line 3). Note that the tasks in the Q may have same arrival time. MTC begins its first phase by normalizing the processing time and the utilization of the tasks in Q (Line 4–10). For this, it needs to find the maximum processing time and the maximum utilization of the tasks in Q (Line 4–5). Then it divides each processing time by the maximum processing time (Line 7) and each utilization by the maximum

Table 1. Notations and their definitions.

Notation	Definition
Q	Queue of all the tasks
λ	Weight value, $\lambda \in [0 \sim 1]$
$|Q|$	Total number of tasks in the queue Q
max	A function to find the maximum
TC	Task consolidation matrix
NTC	Normalized task consolidation matrix
UT_i^j	Utilization of task i at any given time j
UV_k^j	Utilization of VM k at any given time j

utilization (Line 8) to normalize these values in the range of $(0 \sim 1]$. Next it calculates the fitness value of the tasks using the normalized processing time, normalized utilization and weight value respectively (Line 9). Finally, it sorts the tasks in the ascending order of their fitness value and accordingly sort the Q and TC respectively (Line 11).

Algorithm: MTC
1. **while** $Q \neq NULL$
2.   Initialize λ
3.   Find $|Q|$
4.   Find $max\_p = \max_{k}(TC(k,3)), 1 \leq k \leq |Q|$
5.   Find $max\_u = \max_{k}(TC(k,5)), 1 \leq k \leq |Q|$
6.   **for** $k = 1, 2, 3, \ldots, |Q|$
7. $NTC(k,1) = \dfrac{TC(k,3)}{max\_p}$
8. $NTC(k,2) = \dfrac{TC(k,5)}{max\_u}$
9. $F(k) = \lambda \times NTC(k, 1) + (1 - \lambda) \times NTC(k, 2)$
10.   **endfor**
11.   Sort the tasks in the ascending order of their F value and update Q and TC
12.   Call $SCHEDULE\text{-}BY\text{-}MULTI\text{-}CRITERIA(TC, |Q|)$
13. **endwhile**

Fig. 1. Pseudo code for MTC algorithm

Lemma 4.1. The time complexity of the process of normalization is $O(kn)$.

Proof: Let n' be the number of tasks that are ready at time $t = 1$, n is the total number of tasks, $n' << n$ and k is the total number of iterations. To find the maximum processing time and the maximum utilization at $t = 1$, Steps 4 and 5 require $O(n')$ time. Again, the for loop of Steps 6 to 10 require $O(n')$ time. Therefore, the normalization process of n' tasks requires $O(n')$ time. In the similar fashion, $O(n'')$ time is required to normalize n''

tasks that are ready at time $t = 2$ and $O(n''')$ time is required for n''' tasks that are ready at time $t = k$. Therefore, the time complexity of the process of normalization is $O(kn)$ by assuming $n = max(n', n'',\ldots, n''')$.

MTC calls the Procedure 1 (*SCHEDULE-BY-MULTI-CRITERIA*) to assign the sorted tasks one after another to one of the VMs. First, it finds the sum of the VM utilization and the task utilization in the requested period (Line 5). If it is not exceeding 100, then it increases the count value by one (Line 6) and updates the estimated value (Line 7). Next it checks the count value is same as the requested period or not (Line 10). If not, it fixes the estimated utilization value to zero (Line 13). Otherwise, it stores the estimated value (Line 11). Note that the estimated utilization is fixed to zero as the VM should not satisfy the task requirements. The maximum estimated utilization is determined to assign the task to the VM (Line 16). Then it finds the VM where the maximum estimated utilization is achieved (Line 17–18). Subsequently, it assigns the task to the VM (Line 19) and updates the VM utilization for the requested period of the task (Line 20–22). The above process is repeated for all the tasks in Q (Line 1–25) (Fig. 2).

Remark 4.2. The count value should not equal to the requested period if and only if one or more requested period exceeds 100.

Procedure 1: *SCHEDULE-BY-MULTI-CRITERIA(TC, |Q|)*
1. **for** $k = 1, 2, 3,\ldots, |Q|$
2.   **for** $i = 1, 2, 3,\ldots, m$
3.   Set $count = 0$ and $est = 0$
4.   **for** $j = TC(k, 2)$ to $TC(k, 4)$
5.   **if** $UV_i^j + UT_k^j \leq 100$
6. $count = count + 1$
7. $est = est + UV_i^j + UT_k^j$
8.   **endif**
9.   **endfor**
10.   **if** $count == (TC(k, 4) - TC(k, 2))$
11. $est\_util(i) = est$
12.   **else**
13. $est\_util(i) = 0$
14.   **endif**
15.   **endfor**
16. $max\_est\_util = \max_i(est\_util(i)), 1 \leq i \leq m$
17.   **for** $i = 1, 2, 3,\ldots, m$
18.   **if** $est\_util(i) == max\_est\_util$
19.   Assign task T_k to VM V_i
20.   **for** $j = TC(k, 2)$ to $TC(k, 4)$
21. $UV_i^j = UV_i^j + UT_k^j$
22.   **endfor**
23.   **endif**
24.   **endfor**
25. **endfor**

Fig. 2. Pseudo code for schedule the tasks

***Lemma* 4.2.** *The time complexity of finding the utilization of VMs are $O(mp)$.*

Proof: Let m be the total number of VMs and p is the maximum processing time of all the tasks. The inner for loop of the Procedure 1 iterates p times in the worst case (Steps 4 to 9). Hence, it takes $O(p)$ time. Steps 10 to 14 require $O(1)$ time. However, Steps 2 to 15 iterate m times. Therefore, the time complexity of finding the utilization of VMs are $O(mp)$ time.

***Lemma* 4.3.** *The time complexity of finding the VM for a task and assigning that task to the VM is $O(mp)$.*

Proof: To assign a task to the VM that gives maximum utilization, Steps 20 to 22 requires $O(p)$ time. To find the VM that gives maximum utilization for a task, it requires $O(m)$ time. However, Steps 17 to 24 requires $O(mp)$ time. Therefore, the time complexity is $O(mp)$ time.

***Lemma* 4.4.** *The time complexity of Procedure 1 is $O(nmp)$.*

Proof: Like Lemma 4.1, for n' tasks, Steps 1 to 25 requires $O(n'mp)$ time as Steps 2 to 15 requires $O(mp)$ time (Lemma 4.2), Steps 16 requires $O(m)$ time and Steps 17 to 24 requires $O(mp)$ time (Lemma 4.3). Similarly, for n'' tasks at $t = 2$, Steps 1 to 15 requires $O(n''mp)$ time and $O(n'''mp)$ time for n''' tasks at $t = k$. As a result, the time complexity of Procedure 1 is $O(nmp)$ by assuming $n = max(n', n'',\ldots, n''')$.

***Theorem* 4.1.** *The time complexity of proposed algorithm MTC is $O(knmp)$.*

Proof: The MTC algorithm iterates k times for $n', n'',\ldots, n'''$ tasks respectively. For n' tasks, Steps 2 to 3 require $O(1)$ time, the process of normalization takes $O(n')$ time, Step 11 takes $O(n')$ time and Procedure 1 takes $O(n'mp)$ time. Hence, the time complexity to execute n' tasks require $O(n'mp)$ time as Procedure 1 dominates others. Similarly, for n'' tasks, it requires $O(n''mp)$ time and $O(n'''mp)$ time for n''' tasks. Therefore, the time complexity of proposed algorithm MTC is $O(knmp)$ by assuming $n = max(n', n'',\ldots, n''')$.

***Lemma* 4.5.** *MTC behaves like MaxUtil if the ordering of the tasks after the first phase remains intact with the arrival sequence of the tasks.*

Proof: Let the ordering of the tasks is $T_i, T_{i+1}, \ldots, T_n$ and it is same as the arrival of the tasks. In this case, both MaxUtil and MTC assign tasks in the chronological order. As stated earlier, the second phase of the MTC is inherited from MaxUtil. As a result, both algorithms assign the tasks to the VMs that gives the maximum VM utilization. Therefore, this is a typical case where MTC behaves like MaxUtil.

4.3   An Illustration

Let us consider an example that consists of ten tasks as shown in Table 2. These tasks are assigned to three VMs as per their arrival time.

Table 2. Task consolidation (TC) matrix.

ID	AT	PT	FT	U
T_1	1	25	26	30
T_2	1	29	30	31
T_3	1	23	24	32
T_4	2	32	34	24
T_5	2	24	26	30
T_6	2	28	30	30
T_7	2	31	33	22
T_8	3	34	37	21
T_9	3	35	38	27
T_{10}	3	28	31	35

At $t = 1$, three tasks arrive into the cloud system. The proposed MTC algorithm calculates the fitness value of these tasks by assuming $\lambda = 0.5$ and they are 0.8998 (i.e., $0.5 \times (25/29) + 0.5 \times (30/32)$), 0.9844 and 0.8966 respectively. As a result, it assigns the tasks in the following order: T_3, T_1 and T_2 respectively (Fig. 3). At $t = 2$, another four tasks arrive and their fitness value is 0.9, 0.875, 0.9375 and 0.8510 respectively. Therefore, they are assigned in the following order: T_7, T_5, T_4 and T_6 respectively. However, task 6 requires 30 % utilization that is not satisfied by both virtual machines (Fig. 4). Hence, it is assigned to a new VM_3 (Fig. 5). At $t = 3$, three more tasks arrive and their processing order is T_8, T_9 and T_{10} respectively (Fig. 5).

VM_1	1~32	32~62	62~93	93~100
1~24	T_3	T_1		*
24~26	*		T_2	*
26~30	*	*		*
30~38	*	*	*	*

Fig. 3. Gantt chart for VM_1 using MTC

VM_2	1~22	22~52	52~76	76~97	97~100
2~3				*	*
3~26	T_7	T_5			*
26~33		*	T_4	T_8	
33~34	*	*			*
34~37	*	*	*		
37~38	*	*	*	*	*

Fig. 4. Gantt chart for VM_2 using MTC

In Fig. 4, task 8 is assigned to VM_2 based on the higher utilization (i.e., $(97 \times 31 + 21 \times 3)/34 = 90.29$) whereas the utilization is 44.82 in VM_3. The energy consumption is 115140 units of energy by assuming p_{max} and p_{min} value as 30 and 20 respectively.

VM3	1~30	30~57	57~92	92~100
2~3	T6	*	*	*
3~30			T10	*
30~31	*	T9		*
31~38	*		*	*

Fig. 5. Gantt chart for VM_3 using MTC

We also produce the Gantt charts of the existing MaxUtil in Figs. 6 , 7, 8 and 9 and existing random in Figs. 10, 11, 12 and 13 respectively. Note that these algorithms require four VMs to execute the same ten tasks. If we have only three VMs, then these algorithms execute all the tasks except task 10 with an energy consumption of 115140 units of energy. However, it takes 153520 in four VMs, i.e., 34 % (approx.) more energy consumption than the proposed algorithm. The illustration shows that the proposed algorithm performs better than the existing algorithms in terms of energy consumption.

VM1	1~30	30~61	61~93	93~100
1~24	T1		T3	*
24~26		T2	*	*
26~30	*		*	*
30~38	*	*	*	*

Fig. 6. Gantt chart for VM_1 using MaxUtil

VM2	1~24	24~54	54~84	84~100
2~26	T4	T5	T6	*
26~30		*		*
30~34		*	*	*
34~38	*	*	*	*

Fig. 7. Gantt chart for VM_2 using MaxUtil

VM3	1~22	22~43	43~70	70~100
2~3		*	*	*
3~4	T7			*
4~33		T8	T9	*
33~37				*
37~38	*	*		*

Fig. 8. Gantt chart for VM_3 using MaxUtil

VM4	1~35	70~100
3~31	T10	*
31~38	*	*

Fig. 9. Gantt chart for VM_4 using MaxUtil

VM1	1~32	32~62	62~89	89~100
1~2		*	*	*
2~3	T3		*	*
3~24		T5		*
24~26	*		T9	*
26~38	*	*		

Fig. 10. Gantt chart for VM_1 using random

VM2	1~30	30~61	61~85	85~100
1~2			*	*
2~26	T1	T2		*
26~30	*		T4	*
33~34	*	*		*
34~38	*	*	*	*

Fig. 11. Gantt chart for VM_2 using random

VM_3	1~30	30~52	52~73	73~100
2~3	T_6		*	*
3~30		T_7		*
30~33	*		T_8	*
33~37	*	*		*
37~38	*	*	*	*

VM_4	1~35	70~100
3~31	T_{10}	*
31~38	*	*

Fig. 12. Gantt chart for VM_3 using random   **Fig. 13.** Gantt chart for VM_4 using random

5   Simulation Results

5.1   Simulation Setups and Datasets

We carried out the simulations using MATLAB R2014a version 8.3.0.532 on an Intel (R) Core (TM) i3-2330M CPU @ 2.20 GHz 2.20 GHz CPU and 4 GB RAM running on Microsoft Windows 7. We evaluate the performance of the proposed algorithm through simulation run with some randomly generated datasets. In each simulation run, we took an instance of the dataset whose general structure is t_ix_yy. Here, t denotes the total number of tasks that are assigned to the yy number of VMs and ix denotes the instance ID. We select the diverse set of tasks such as 100, 500, 1000, 5000 and 10000. We choose the different number of VMs such as 10, 20, 30, 40 and 50. In each task and VM type, we prepare five different instances as shown in the even column of Table 4. These instances are generated using the MATLAB random function with various constraints as shown in Table 3.

Table 3. Dataset parameters and their lower and upper limits.

Parameter	100_ix_10	500_ix_20	1000_ix_30	5000_ix_40	10000_ix_50
Arrival time	[1 ~ 15]	[1 ~ 100]	[1 ~ 250]	[1 ~ 1000]	[1 ~ 2000]
Processing time	[5 ~ 20]	[5 ~ 25]	[5 ~ 35]	[5 ~ 40]	[5 ~ 50]
Utilization	[5 ~ 20]	[5 ~ 25]	[5 ~ 35]	[5 ~ 40]	[5 ~ 50]

5.2   Results and Discussion

We ran 25 instances for random, MaxUtil and the proposed MTC algorithms and their energy consumptions are calculated by taking $p_{max} = 30$ and $p_{min} = 20$ as used in [9].

Table 4. Comparison of energy consumption for random, MaxUtil and MTC algorithms.

Algorithm	Dataset	Units of energy	Dataset	Units of energy	Dataset	Units of energy	Dataset	Units of energy	Dataset	Units of energy
Random	100	336330	500	1476620	1000	7634590	5000	32337170	10000	112145350
MaxUtil	_$i1$_	323200	_$i1$_	1373600	_$i1$_	7097270	_$i1$_	30211120	_$i1$_	104561260
MTC	10	316130	20	1366530	30	7079090	40	29714200	50	104396630
Random	100	329260	500	1420060	1000	7618430	5000	31616030	10000	113617930
MaxUtil	_$i2$_	328250	_$i2$_	1329160	_$i2$_	7264930	_$i2$_	29223340	_$i2$_	105936880

(Continued)

Table 4. (*Continued*)

Algorithm	Dataset	Units of energy	Dataset	Units of energy	Dataset	Units of energy	Dataset	Units of energy	Dataset	Units of energy
MTC	10	314110	20	1318050	30	7162920	40	29182940	50	105881330
Random	100	290880	500	1402890	1000	7570960	5000	42040240	10000	111902950
MaxUtil	_i3_	278760	_i3_	1287750	_i3_	7219480	_i3_	39556650	_i3_	104643070
MTC	10	269670	20	1284720	30	7104340	40	39519280	50	104395620
Random	100	309060	500	1990710	1000	7658830	5000	41821070	10000	112549350
MaxUtil	_i4_	305020	_i4_	1852340	_i4_	7251800	_i4_	38994080	_i4_	105402590
MTC	10	300980	20	1823050	30	7203320	40	38933480	50	105297550
Random	100	313100	500	1947280	1000	7714380	5000	41504940	10000	112241300
MaxUtil	_i5_	304010	_i5_	1822040	_i5_	7339670	_i5_	38693100	_i5_	104742050
MTC	10	296940	20	1788710	30	7257860	40	38612300	50	104711750

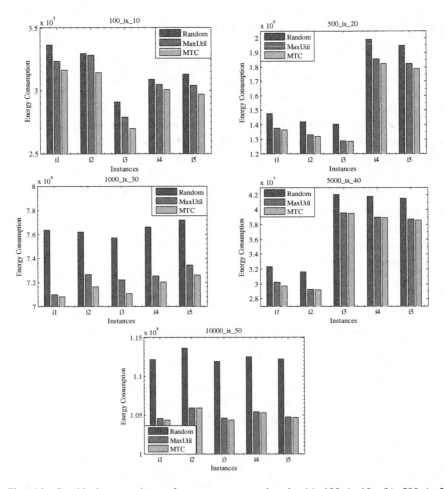

Fig. 14. Graphical comparison of energy consumption in (a) 100_*ix*_10, (b) 500_*ix*_20, (c) 1000_*ix*_30, (d) 5000_*ix*_40 and (e) 10000_*ix*_50 datasets

The comparison of energy consumption for these algorithms is shown in Table 4. For the sake of easy visualization, we also present the graphical comparison as shown in Fig. 14(a)–(e). The results clearly conclude that 25 out of 25 instances (i.e., 100 %) give better energy consumption for the proposed algorithm MTC than the random and MaxUtil algorithms. Note that we have not shown the resource utilization of the VMs as it is already associated with energy consumption. It is important to note that the proposed MTC improves about 10 % energy consumption over the random and about 5 % over the MaxUtil task consolidation algorithm.

6 Conclusion

We have presented a task consolidation algorithm MTC for cloud computing systems. The algorithm has been shown to require $O(knmp)$ time. It was simulated on various datasets and evaluated in terms of energy consumption. The results show that the proposed algorithm reduces about 10 % energy consumption than random algorithm and about 5 % than MaxUtil algorithm in the generated datasets.

References

1. Buyya, R., Yeo, C.S., Venugopal, S., Broberg, J., Brandic, I.: Cloud computing and emerging it platforms: vision, hype and reality for delivering computing as the 5th utility. Future Gener. Comput. Syst. **25**, 599–616 (2009). Elsevier
2. Hsu, C., Slagter, K.D., Chen, S., Chung, Y.: Optimizing energy consumption with task consolidation in clouds. Inf. Sci. **258**, 452–462 (2014). Elsevier
3. Mills, M.P.: The Cloud Begins with Coal: Big Data, Big Networks, Big Infrastructure and Big Power. Technical report, National Mining Association, American Coalition for Clean Coal Electricity (2013)
4. Hohnerlein, J., Duan, L.: Characterizing cloud datacenters in energy efficiency, performance and quality of service. In: ASEE Gulf-Southwest Annual Conference, The University of Texas, San Antonio, American Society for Engineering Education (2015)
5. Panda, S.K., Jana, P.K.: Efficient task scheduling algorithms for heterogeneous multi-cloud environment. J. Supercomputing **71**, 1505–1533 (2015). Springer
6. Li, J., Qiu, M., Ming, Z., Quan, G., Qin, X., Gu, Z.: Online optimization for scheduling preemptable tasks on iaas cloud system. J. Parallel Distrib. Comput. **72**, 666–677 (2012). Elsevier
7. Friese, R., Khemka, B., Maciejewski, A.A., Siegel, H.J., Koenig, G.A., Powers, S., Hilton, M., Rambharos, J., Okonski, G., Poole, S.W.: An analysis framework for investigating the trade-offs between system performance and energy consumption in a heterogeneous computing environment. In: 27th IEEE International Symposium on Parallel and Distributed Processing Workshops and Ph.D. Forum, pp. 19–30 (2013)
8. Khemka, B., Friese, R., Pasricha, S., Maciejewski, A.A., Siegel, H.J., Koenig, G.A., Powers, S., Hilton, M., Rambharos, R., Poole, S.: Utility driven dynamic resource management in an oversubscribed energy-constrained heterogeneous system. In: 28th IEEE International Parallel and Distributed Processing Symposium Workshops, pp. 58–67 (2014)

9. Lee, Y.C., Zomaya, A.Y.: Energy efficient utilization of resources in cloud computing systems. J. Supercomputing **60**, 268–280 (2012). Springer
10. Panda, S.K., Jana, P.K.: An efficient energy saving task consolidation algorithm for cloud computing. In: Third IEEE International Conference on Parallel, Distributed and Grid Computing, pp. 262–267 (2014)
11. Fan, X., Weber, W., Barroso, L.A.: Power provisioning for a warehouse-sized computer. In: The 34th Annual International Symposium on Computer Architecture, pp. 13–23. ACM (2007)
12. Chen, G., He, W., Liu, J., Nath, S., Rigas, L., Xiao, L., Zhao, F.: Energy-aware server provisioning and load dispatching for connection-intensive internet services. In: 5th USENIX Symposium on Networked Systems Design and Implementation, pp. 337–350 (2008)
13. Srikantaiah, S., Kansal, A., Zhao, F.: Energy aware consolidation for cloud computing. In: International Conference on Power Aware Computing and Systems, pp. 1–5 (2008)
14. Tesfatsion, S.K., Wadbro, E., Tordsson, J.: A combined frequency scaling and application elasticity approach for energy-efficient cloud computing. Sustain. Comput. Inf. Syst. **4**, 205–214 (2014). Elsevier
15. Chen, H., Zhu, X., Guo, H., Zhu, J., Qin, X., Wu, J.: Towards energy-efficient scheduling for real-time tasks under uncertain cloud environment. J. Syst. Softw. **99**, 20–35 (2015). Elsevier

Storage Load Control Through Meta-Scheduler Using Predictive Analytics

Kumar Dheenadayalan$^{(\boxtimes)}$, V.N. Muralidhara,
and Gopalakrishnan Srinivasaraghavan

International Institute of Information Technology, Bangalore, India
d.kumar@iiitb.org, {murali,gsr}@iiitb.ac.in

Abstract. The gap between computing capability of servers and storage systems is ever increasing. Genesis of I/O intensive applications capable of generating Gigabytes to Exabytes of data has led to saturation of I/O performance on the storage system. This paper provides an insight on the load controlling capability on the storage system through learning algorithms in a Grid Computing environment. Storage load control driven by meta schedulers and the effects of load control on the popular scheduling schemes of a meta-scheduler are presented here. Random Forest regression is used to predict the current response state of the storage system and Auto Regression is used to forecast the future response behavior. Based on the forecast, time-sharing of I/O intensive jobs is used to take proactive decision and prevent overloading of individual volumes on the storage system. Time-sharing between multiple synthetic and industry specific I/O intensive jobs have shown to have superior total completion time and total flow time compared to traditional approaches like FCFS and Backfilling. Proposed scheme prevented any down time when implemented with a live NetApp storage system.

Keywords: Storage response time · Storage filer · Random forest regression · Time-sharing · Storage load controller

1 Introduction

Large scale systems like the Grid Computing environment [7] has tremendous computing power. Storage technology has been evolving continuously to keep up with the growth in computing power. Even though storage technology has advanced considerably, it still forms the bottleneck in delivering high performance in a distributed environment. As more applications are becoming data intensive, there is continuous growth in data access intensity, imposing greater load on the storage systems. For instance, CERN lab generates around 1 Petabyte (PB) of data per day [3] with peak load reaching up to 10 Gigabytes (GB) per second. This generates huge I/O operations capable of clogging the I/O bandwidth resulting in unresponsiveness and sometimes leading to job failure [5,9].

© Springer International Publishing Switzerland 2016
N. Bjørner et al. (Eds.): ICDCIT 2016, LNCS 9581, pp. 75–86, 2016.
DOI: 10.1007/978-3-319-28034-9_9

Grid Computing Environment can handle different type of jobs with different run lengths. With storage being an important resource in Grid Computing system, it's important to consider the performance of the storage system while scheduling jobs. Storage as a resource has found limited consideration while scheduling a job. Past research was focused on decoupling problems of storage and the performance of a scheduler. Finding the right balance between controlling the load on the filer and maintain good performance of the scheduler is attempted here. Not much of research has gone into controlling I/O load through a scheduler that is actually controlling the sequence of jobs responsible for I/O load generation. Meta-Schedulers are used in large scale Grid computing environments to manage millions of jobs. A meta-scheduler driven storage load controller that maintains the performance at optimal levels and enhancing the productivity of the meta-scheduler and Grid environment on the whole is achieved in the paper. This can eliminate the need to have a storage oriented load balancing mechanism.

A filer is a specialized file server capable of providing fast data access. A modern storage filer supports various specialized hardware to handle high I/O load. Performance of a storage filer depends on a number of parameters. Monitoring a single filer performance parameter like CPU or memory utilization or I/O latency on a filer with multiple individual components is not the wisest approach to find the response state. Identifying the different combination of the parameters that are ideally suited for accurately deciding the response state is a difficult task. Machine learning approach to identify and predict current response state and forecast future response was proven to be successful in [6]. We build on the ideas presented in [6] and provide a simpler solution to identify the current state of the filer and its individual logical entity called volume. The time required by the filer (in its current state) to write benchmark units of data on an individual volume is predicted. We also extend the idea to provide a simplistic solution to forecast the future response time of the volumes in the next t minutes. If the forecasted response time is beyond a threshold $r_{threshold}$, informed time-sharing of I/O intensive jobs is enforced to minimize the load on the individual volumes that are being accessed by jobs.

As the set of candidate jobs for time-sharing is derived from the information provided by the meta-scheduler the need to have a storage oriented load balancing mechanism is eliminated. Total completion time and Total Flow time are couple of key criterion used to measure the success of a schedule [1]. Completion time is defined as the difference between job processing start time and job finish time. Total completion time is measured as the sum of completion times of individual jobs submitted to the Grid environment in a schedule. We define Flow completion time as the difference between the job submit time and the job finish time. Flow completion time includes the time spent by the job waiting for a slot to be scheduled plus the completion time.

Next section talks about the past literature followed by an overview and analysis of the proposed Storage Load Controller in Sect. 3. Modeling and implementation details are discussed in Sect. 4. Model is validated and the results are presented in Sect. 5 followed by the conclusion in Sect. 6.

2   Literature Survey

There is considerable amount of research in the field of storage load balancing in the past [8,12]. But the action of load balancing is derived based on individual or a small subset of storage performance parameters. Data migration based on deterministic analysis of the individual filer performance parameters is one of the popular techniques in load balancing [12,13,15] The performance impact on the storage system during the process of load balancing is not negligible. The need for migration which has been used in traditional approaches of load balancing is completely eliminated in this paper.

NetApp is a popular storage vendor which provides a solution to control the load on a storage filer [5,9]. The process of identifying the filer performance parameters to be monitored and defining the threshold for individual filer performance parameters in [5,9] are left to the administrators. This can be a big problem as the parameter subset and their thresholds vary based on the filer configuration and workload generating the I/O. It also has a hierarchical method of deciding the state of each volume (logical entity of a filer). The process of manually identifying parameters and their associated threshold values is eliminated by using Random Forest Regression with windowing scheme is proposed in this paper. Existing NetApp Solution forces all the jobs accessing a loaded volume to be in *PEND*ing state till the filer parameters go below the thresholds defined by the administrator. This is detrimental to the overall compute efficiency as short jobs are bound to suffer in that scenario. Time-sharing among I/O intensive jobs accessing the filer with high load may help short jobs to get access to the filer for short periods of time. This allows shorter jobs to complete their task instead of starving for I/O bandwidth. [11,19,20] propose data-aware schedulers with emphasis on the data requirement of the jobs. Knowing data requirements of the job is a difficult task and it depends on the information provided by user while launching jobs. Estimating the size of the output generated by the job is not easy. [11] also assumes that the data request sequence is known to the scheduler which is not always true. The proposed solution makes no such assumptions.

Our past work in [6] uses Random Forest, a decision tree based algorithm to identify multiple rules that help the framework to decide the current state of the filer. This offers a major advantage compared to [5,9] and helps in developing an efficient self-learning system. [6] forecasts the future response class by forecasting the individual parameters of a filer and these forecasts are provided to the classifier. The idea of forecasting individual parameters lead to higher error rates as forecasting hundreds of filer parameters comes with individual error rates. The cumulatively error rate of forecasting hundreds of parameters will decrease the overall accuracy of response class. Random Forest Regression [14] is used in the current work instead of Random Forest Classification [2] to get the instantaneous response time of the filer. The predicted response time trends are treated as time series data to forecast the future response times using Auto Regression model. This modification proves to be 7 %

more accurate over a forecasting period of 10 min compared to the forecasting proposed in [6].

Knowing the state of the filer can be used to efficiently share I/O bandwidth between multiple jobs accessing the same volume. Controlling the load on the filer can help in achieving faster completion time leading to earlier execution starts for other jobs. [4] illustrates how time sharing has been useful in enhancing the throughput of the system.

3   Storage Load Controller

Storage Load Controller is an independent component developed to control load and optimize the completion times for all I/O jobs. Load Sharing Facility (LSF) [17] is a popular, commercially available meta-scheduler from International Business Machines (IBM), widely used in various industries, especially in Electronic Design and Automation (EDA) industry. We integrate the Storage Load Controller with LSF meta-scheduler for Grid Computing Environment. Three important states of a job handled by LSF are PEND (new job waiting for a slot/server to begin execution), USUSP (job suspended by user or forced preemption) and RUN state. Storage Load Controller has the capability to interact with filers, compute servers and meta-schedulers. It also has the ability to suspend and resume jobs managed by the meta-scheduler. Suspending a job on LSF will put the processes of the job to USUSP state but the slot occupied by the job is retained. No pending job in the meta-scheduler will be able to get access to a slot occupied by a suspended job. Hence, the Load Controller has to effectively time-share the I/O jobs and move them between USUSP and RUN state to ensure early finish of jobs.

The core idea of Storage Load Controller is to monitor, predict and forecast the load on individual volumes of the filer. When the load on an individual volume is above the threshold defined by the Grid administrator, all the I/O intensive jobs accessing the volume except the oldest job are forced to share I/O bandwidth in a Round Robin fashion. In the proposed scheme none of the CPU intensive jobs are involved in time-sharing. The idea here is to allow the oldest I/O intensive job that entered the Grid setup to run to completion without being hampered by load generated by other jobs. Time-sharing also helps the completion of I/O intensive jobs that have enough compute resource but their progress is hampered by slow I/O response.

We focus our analysis on the time required to process a job at a load of η as defined in Eq. (1) where r_{normal} is the response time at normal load or no load on the filer. The worst case scenario for a Grid setup is when all jobs experience high I/O load when they enter the system. We assume that the jobs follow Poisson's arrival with ρ being the utilization factor of Poisson's distribution. We also assume a hyper-exponential service time distribution. Let n_i be the number of jobs required to breach the threshold factor η for i^{th} volume, vol_i. It is assumed that till a point where a volume has $(n_i - 1)$ jobs accessing it, the load on the filer will be under control. The worst case processing time T_q of job q at load η is given by Eq. (2).

$$\eta = \frac{r_{threshold}}{r_{normal}} \tag{1}$$

$$T_q = \sum_{r<q} T_r + Remaining\ Processing\ time\ of\ q. \tag{2}$$

The amount of time a job spends in a Round Robin scheme and the amount of time a job gets uninterrupted storage access are given by $\sum\limits_{r<q} T_r$ and $T_q - \sum\limits_{r<q} T_r$ respectively. As soon as all the 'r' older jobs complete their execution, job_q will get continuous I/O access till completion without being suspended. The fact that one job will go to completion under controlled filer load enhances the completion time for that individual job. [18,21] uses Pollaczek-Khinchin (P-K) Formula to show that expected time for completion of jobs in FCFS scheme is directly proportional to the variability of the service times of the jobs. When coefficient of variability of service time is much greater than 1, Round Robin implementation is superior [18]. Large-scale Grid environments are known to have large variance in service time. We do not use classical Round Robin algorithm because there will be loss of throughput and underutilization of storage resource due to which at least one job will get uninterrupted access.

When the number of I/O jobs accessing a volume are less than n_i, the response time is less than $r_{threshold}$. Hence Storage Load Controller will work like FCFS as the response time is maintained below $r_{threshold}$. If the number of I/O jobs accessing a volume are greater than or equal to n_i, Storage Load Controller will share the I/O subsystem among n - 1 jobs. Let δ be the length of the time slice and $N(\delta)$ be the number of time slices required for job_q to complete in a classical Round Robin Scheduling scheme. Let $l = \sum\limits_{r<q} T_r$ which is the time spent by job_q in the Round Robin scheme of the proposed Storage Load Controller. We calculate the remaining processing time for a job after it becomes the oldest job as $R_q = (N(\delta) * \delta) - l$. If Round Robin scheme was continued after R_q duration, then the number of time slices remaining is given by Eq. (3).

$$R_{RR_q} = \frac{(N(\delta) * \delta) - l}{(1 - \rho)} \tag{3}$$

$$((N(\delta) * \delta) - l) < \frac{(N(\delta) * \delta) - l}{(1 - \rho)} \tag{4}$$

It is clear that $R_q < R_{RR_q}$. Equation (4) holds true whenever there are n_i or more jobs accessing a volume which has necessitated the need for time sharing. As soon as the load factor is below η Eq. (4) fails and hence FCFS is enforced by the Storage Load Controller. The number of I/O intensive jobs required to load a volume depends on multiple factors. n_i will gradually decrease as more volumes are loaded for the same filer. This is because, all physical entities of a filer are shared among the logical entities (vol_i). Hence, $n_i > \ldots > n_j$ for $vol_i \ldots vol_j$, where vol_i is the first volume loaded.

4   Modeling and Implementation

4.1   Data Extractor

The data extractor is responsible for collecting live storage filer performance parameters at a pre-defined interval 'd', which will be used for response prediction. Data extractor is also responsible to collect information about all jobs that are executing in the Grid Environment. A job can launch multiple processes and each process can access multiple files. It's important to identify candidate jobs for time-sharing that are actually involved in I/O to cause prolonged load on the filer. A naive way of achieving this is to keep track of all the file descriptors opened by the job and its processes along with the size and time stamps. This will be used to identify the jobs, which are most probable candidates for generating the load on the filer and hence be a candidate to share the I/O bandwidth. A job involved in continuous change in the file size or continuous modification of large files can be a typical candidate. Data extractor communicates directly with meta-schedulers like LSF to gather job related information and store the same in a structured form called the *jobDetails* structure. The key information collected are: *jobID, serverName, jobStartTime, allFileDetails* → [*processIDs, fileDescriptors, filerName, volumeName, size, accessTime, modifyTime*].

allFileDetails is used to store multiple file descriptors which are actively being accessed by the job on the filer. There is no overhead generated by data extractor in this process as all the necessary information except file statistics are already available with LSF. Filer performance parameters are also collected by Data Extractor. Each request to fetch a set of filer performance parameter (V) provides a set of volume parameters (V_{vol_i}) and system (network, protocol, other subsystem and statistics) related parameters (V_{sys}). Volume parameters will be unique to each volume but rest of the system parameters will have the same impact on the load of a filer. Hence, we decompose the data collected into volume parameters and non-volume system parameters. Each row in the data set will be of the form:

$$D_j = V_{sys} + V_{vol_i}$$

The above equation has essentially created x data instances for x volumes through a single data request from the filer as a result of decomposition.

4.2   Response Forecaster

Forecasting the response time is important as rescheduling is based on the forecast of response states for each filer/volume. Identifying the continuous high load period is important for time-sharing among I/O intensive jobs to be effective. The entire data collection and data aggregation phase is explained in great detail in [6]. I/O load is generated through real world or synthetic workload and parallely traning data is collected for a prolonged period of time. Training data essentially contains the set of filer performance parameters while writing benchmark data. When the I/O load is being generated time taken to write benchmark data and the performance parameters recorded during this write operation forms the dataset. Training data is pre-processed to identify the filer parameters having high correlation with the response times. All parameters above a *correlation_threshold* will be used as features in Random Forest Regression to build a model with smallest Out Of Bag (OOB) error rate [14]. Once the model is successfully generated in the training phase, every new data instance generated in a live filer will be sent as input to the Random Forest Regression model. The model will predict the possible response time, r_{out}.

$$\beta = ws.\frac{60}{d} \tag{5}$$

$$\phi(\beta) = \begin{cases} -\left\lfloor \frac{\beta}{3} \right\rfloor & \text{if } r_{out} < r_{threshold} \\ 1 & \text{if } r_{out} > r_{threshold} \end{cases} \tag{6}$$

A high response time threshold, $r_{threshold}$, will be used to predict a positive value indicating high response time and a negative penalty if low response is predicted as shown by the penalty function, $\phi(\beta)$. The values returned from the penalty function, $\phi(\beta)$ is stored in a separate array for each volume, which represents the window (w) with window size β. ws is the number of minutes to be considered by the moving window. Any negative class prediction will have its impact for 33 % of β instances as indicated by the penalty function. The value of 33 % was arrived purely on the basis of experience and there is no theoretical explanation for the same. The decay function defined by $\psi(i)$ makes sure that the most recent filer load is given higher preference. With every new instance, the older negative predictions decay by a factor of 1. It is assured that the negative prediction loses its weight after $\frac{\beta}{3}$ data instances. A decision on the overall state of the volume can be concluded using the function (8).

$$\psi(i) = \begin{cases} \psi(i-1) + 1 & \text{if } \psi(i-1) < 0 \\ \psi(i-1) & \text{otherwise} \end{cases} \tag{7}$$

$$S(\alpha, \beta) = \begin{cases} 1 & \text{if } \frac{\sum_{i=n}^{n-\beta} w_i}{\beta} \geq \alpha \\ 0 & \text{otherwise} \end{cases} \tag{8}$$

$S(\alpha, \beta)$ evaluates to see if at least α of the past β data instances of a volume has high load predicted by $\phi(\beta)$. If the function $S(\alpha, \beta)$ returns a 1, the algorithm concludes that the volume is loaded for the past ws minutes. Response time (r_{out}) predicted by the model is treated as a time series data. Every minute, a short term response time forecast is carried out using $AR(q)$ autoregression model. The duration of the forecast t, should be of the order of few minutes as this will determine the number of minutes a suspended job will wait before a rescheduling cycle (suspension/resumption of jobs) might restart. One of the criteria used by the meta-scheduler to choose the best machine available to run a job is the load on each server for 15 min (r15m). The windowing scheme helps to replicate the same for *ws* minutes by considering the current response behavior along with the recent response trend to conclude the load on the filer.

4.3   Job State Handler

Job state handler manages the state changes of all the jobs that have started their execution and might be causing the load on the individual volumes of a filer. A virtual queue is created for each individual volume of a filer to provide a time-sharing system for all jobs accessing a loaded volume/filer. Each job will have multiple processes associated with it and any of these processes can be involved in some I/O operation. *'jobDetail'* structure is extracted from Data Extractor to build a structure called *'runList'*. A *'runList'* structure per volume helps maintain details of all jobs actively accessing or generating load on the volume. *runList* is a hashtable data structure with filerName:volumeName as key and a reference to stack data structure as the value. Each element of the stack points to *jobDetail* structure. This stack maintains the list of jobs that are in RUN state and accessing the volume to which the *runList* is associated. Stack data structure is used to pick the most recent job (execution start time) as a possible candidate for suspension.

List of suspended jobs are maintained in a separate hash called *suspendList*. The *suspendList* structure is similar to *runList* except for the fact that a Queue data structure is maintained for each filerName:volumeName key. Using queue data structure facilitates implementing different SLA based priority schemes for resuming jobs. The criterion for selecting the jobs for time-sharing by Storage Load Controller can vary based on the understanding of the workload and the Grid setup. Possible checks to identify if the running job is a candidate for rescheduling are: (1) If the file was accessed or modified in the last 60 s to ensure that we don't choose a job for suspension that is not generating any I/O on the volume. (2) A check on the size of the file to ensure that short jobs accessing files of size less than ω can be ignored. (3) The number of open files is also important (Load can also be generated when millions of small files are accessed creating huge number of metadata operations [10]). (4) If the file size is not varying or not being accessed continuously, then jobs associated with such files are ignored. Every volume is monitored and $S(\alpha, \beta)$ is evaluated at the beginning of a rescheduling cycle. If $S(\alpha, \beta)$ returns 1 for any volume, then a job is popped from the stack in *runlist*, pushed onto the queue of the *suspendList* and a suspension request for this job is sent to the meta-scheduler. This ensures that the oldest job that started accessing the volume will never be suspended. If $S(\alpha, \beta)$ returns 0 for any volume, then a job from *suspendList* is pulled and pushed onto the stack of the *runlist* and resume request is sent to the meta-scheduler. It must be noted that, suspension is called only if there is more than one job associated with each volume.

If any job job_q is suspended for accessing volume vol_i, then no job related to vol_i will be resumed in the same rescheduling cycle. It helps to see the effect of suspending job_q. Once the rescheduling cycle is completed, sleep signal is issued for a time interval identified by $\Psi(r_{forecast_{ij}})$.

$$\Psi(r_{forecast_{ij}}) = \begin{cases} t & \text{if } \exists r_{forecast_{ij}} \geq r_{threshold}, \forall i, j \\ 1 & \text{otherwise} \end{cases} \quad (9)$$

If the forecast for any vol_i is high for next t minutes, then the rescheduling cycle will start after t minutes. If the forecast indicates that the volume load for any volume is going to reduce over a period of next t minutes, then the rescheduling cycle will start after 1 min. $\Psi(r_{forecast_{ij}})$ makes sure that the suspended jobs don't spend their time in suspended state even after the load on the volume has come down.

5 Results

Storage Load Controller was developed using C programming language for job state handler, PERL for Data Extractor and R statistical package for Response Forecaster. The test setup includes a NetApp ONTAP 8 filer with Dual 2.8 GHz Intel P4 Xeon MP processor, 2 MB L3 cache, 8 GB of main memory and 512 MB NVRAM. Three servers with quad core processors and 4 GB of RAM as execution hosts. One single core machine is used to run the proposed Storage Load Controller. LSF version 9.1 was used as the meta-scheduler with its default FCFS scheduling algorithm enabled. A new queue was defined to test Backfilling algorithm. Total of 12 slots were configured with each core taking up one slot. We present the results obtained by executing two different workloads with/without Storage Load Controller in action. DS1, DS2 and DS3 are the identifiers for the datasets used in our experiments. DS1 consists of 6 jobs having 2 CPU intensive jobs and 4 I/O intensive jobs. Table 1 gives details of the type of jobs in each dataset. The ratio of CPU intensive versus I/O intensive jobs was chosen based on the trend observed in EDA industry workload. I/O intensive jobs had a combination of EDA workload (20 jobs), metadata intensive jobs generated using PostMark (12 jobs) [10], I/O benchmark applications like IOZONE (16 jobs) [16]. DS2 follows Poisson's arrival distribution with hyper-exponential service time distribution. DS3 was generated by using DS2 as the population and random sampling was carried out with no bias towards any type of job.

Different types of I/O operations were tested specially using the industry workload and IOZONE tool. PostMark was used to test the behaviour of the storage filer towards jobs working with 10,000 to 10 million short files of less than 256 KB. The amount of data by non-PostMark jobs ranged from 10 GB to 100 GB each. Storage Load Controller is combined with FCFS and Backfilling separately and we compare the results in Table 1. The values of various parameters set for the experiments carried out are: $d \rightarrow 10$ s; $r_{threshold} \rightarrow 60$ s; $\beta \rightarrow 18$; $ws \rightarrow 3$ min; $\alpha \rightarrow 0.75$; $t \rightarrow 3$ min; $p \rightarrow 1$ GB; $\omega \rightarrow 4000$ MB; The key parameters that have a major impact on the success of Storage Load Controller are the values of $r_{threshold}$ and t. Setting a low value for $r_{threshold}$ and t will force frequent job suspensions which is detrimental to the performance of the Storage Load Controller. DS2 considered in the current experiment were run with four different values of t. For $t = 1$ and 5 min, Storage Load Controller performed

Table 1. Performance Measure (unit - hh:mm:ss)

Dataset ID	Size	CPU Jobs	I/O Jobs	Prediction (%) for t mins	Total Completion Time		Total Flow Time	
					FCFS	**Controller**	**FCFS**	**Controller**
DS1	6	2	4	94.2 %	15:35:27	12:51:16	15:35:34	12:51:23
DS2	152	104	48	92.0 %	256:06:14	235:57:28	298:28:12	274:24:14
DS3	21	13	8	93.4 %	63:26:42	57:58:39	67:11:32	61:03:05
					Backfill	**Controller**	**Backfill**	**Controller**
DS2	152	104	48	91.1 %	314:12:18	295:16:17	345:33:11	323:02:10
DS3	21	13	8	92.3 %	65:12:12	60:14:55	69:03:22	62:33:54

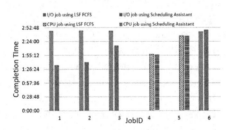

Fig. 1. Gantt chart for time-sharing process

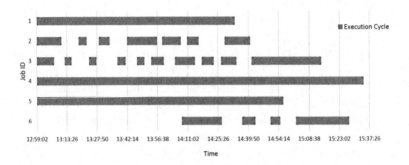

Fig. 2. Completion Time for LSF FCFS with/without Storage Load Controller

worse than LSF scheduling by 2.4 % and 6.4 % respectively. For $t = 2$ and 3 min, Storage Load Controller performed better than LSF scheduling by 5.7 % and 7.8 % respectively. t should be set to high values (2 to 5 min) when I/O intensive jobs are expected to have a runtime of few hours. Short I/O intensive jobs might run to completion with limited effect on the completion time of the job.

To show the importance of time-sharing, a Gantt chart is presented in Fig. 1. It shows the suspension and resume cycles of individual jobs which share I/O bandwidth among themselves. Jobs 4 and 5 are CPU intensive jobs, which do not access any files on the filer. Jobs 1–3 and 6 are I/O intensive jobs, involved in read, write, reread and rewrite operations of various file sizes ranging from 10 GB to 100 GB. Job 1 is the first I/O intensive job to get a slot and it executes to completion because start time is used as the measure of priority. Other jobs are time shared till they become the oldest running jobs accessing the volume on the filer. Other forms of priority can also be used to change the suspension order based on the SLA that needs to be implemented. Figure 2 shows the completion time comparison of FCFS with/without Storage Load Controller. It is evident that Storage Load Controller affects no CPU intensive job but completion of I/O intensive jobs has improved.

Table 1 shows the performance comparison in terms of Total Completion Time and Total Flow Time for FCFS, Backfill, FCFS with Load Controller and Backfill with Load Controller. Early completion of I/O jobs has a direct effect on the total flow time of all jobs. Storage Load Controller is able to complete the tasks much earlier than FCFS/Backfill scheme. As more I/O jobs complete early, it enables early start for other waiting jobs. For DS2, more than 20+ h of compute time is gained by Storage Load Controller when compared to FCFS and an average gain of 25 min per I/O intensive job. 18+ h of compute time gain with an average gain of 22 min was observed for the same dataset was observed for Backfilling algorithm with Storage Load Controller. Storage Load Controller doesn't have any dependency on the order of job submission. As the framework tries to control the load generated by running jobs, we continue to see improvements in the job completion times and flow times. Since we have specific checks in Job State Handler to omit CPU intensive and small I/O jobs, the system is able to take all CPU intensive jobs to completion without affecting other I/O intensive jobs.

6 Conclusion

The major objective of maintaining the load on the storage system is achieved through Storage Load Controller. Response time to write benchmark data is kept under $r_{threshold}$ throughout the schedule. This leads to faster overall completion times and hence the faster flow times. Storage Load Controller being at a level above the meta-scheduler can be integrated with any meta-scheduler that is using a variety of algorithms. Our work presents the results for FCFS and Backfill but the same can be extended to any scheduling algorithm. Order of job suspension can be improved for Backfilling as the runtime is provided in advance which will be part of our future work. The Suspend and Resume order in the Job State Handler module can be changed by implementing various priority schemes which gives the framework a better chance to succeed in various environments.

References

1. Avrahami, N., Azar, Y.: Minimizing total flow time and total completion time with immediate dispatching. Algorithmica **47**(3), 253–268 (2007)
2. Breiman, L.: Random forests. Mach. Learn. **45**(1), 5–32 (2001)
3. CERN: European Laboratory for Particle Physics (2014). http://home.web.cern. ch/about/computing. Accessed 30 September 2014

4. Chen, J., Zhou, B.B., Wang, C., Lu, P., Wang, P., Zomaya, A.: Throughput enhancement through selective time sharing and dynamic grouping. In: 2013 IEEE 27th International Symposium on Parallel Distributed Processing (IPDPS), pp. 1183–1192 (2013)
5. Choudhury, B.R.: IBM Platform Load Sharing Facility (LSF) Integration with Netapp Storage. Technical report (2013)
6. Dheenadayalan, K., Muralidhara, V., Datla, P., Srinivasaraghavan, G., Shah, M.: Premonition of storage response class using skyline ranked ensemble method. In: 2014 21st International Conference on High Performance Computing (HiPC), pp. 1–10, December 2014
7. Foster, I., Kesselman, C.: The grid: blueprint for a new computing infrastructure. Morgan Kaufmann Publishers Inc., San Francisco (1999)
8. Gulati, A., Kumar, C., Ahmad, I., Kumar, K.: BASIL: Automated IO load balancing across storage devices. In: Proceedings of the 8th USENIX Conference on File and Storage Technologies, FAST 2010, p. 13. USENIX Association, Berkeley (2010)
9. Hameed, S.: Integrating lsf storage-aware plug-in with operations manager. Technical report (2011)
10. Katcher, J.: PostMark: A New File System Benchmark. Technical report (1997)
11. Kosar, T.: A new paradigm in data intensive computing: stork and the data-aware schedulers. In: 2006 IEEE Challenges of Large Applications in Distributed Environments, pp. 5–12 (2006)
12. Kunkle, D., Schindler, J.: A load balancing framework for clustered storage systems. In: Sadayappan, P., Parashar, M., Badrinath, R., Prasanna, V.K. (eds.) HiPC 2008. LNCS, vol. 5374, pp. 57–72. Springer, Heidelberg (2008)
13. Liang, H., Faner, M., Ming, H.: A dynamic load balancing system based on data migration. In: Proceedings of the 8th International Conference on Computer Supported Cooperative Work in Design, vol. 1, pp. 493–499, May 2004
14. Liaw, A., Wiener, M.: Classification and regression by randomforest. R News **2**(3), 18–22 (2002)
15. Mondal, A., Goda, K., Kitsuregawa, M.: Effective load-balancing via migration and replication in spatial grids. In: Mařík, V., Štěpánková, O., Retschitzegger, W. (eds.) DEXA 2003. LNCS, vol. 2736, pp. 202–211. Springer, Heidelberg (2003)
16. Norcott, W., Capps, D.: IOzone file system benchmark. Technical report (2006)
17. Quintero, D., Denham, S., Garcia da Silva, R., Ortiz, A., Guedes Pinto, A., Sasaki, A., Tucker, R., Wong, J., Ramos, E.: IBM Platform Computing Solutions (IBM Redbooks). IBM Press (2012)
18. Thompson, S., Lipsky, L., Tasneem, S., Zhang, F.: Analysis of round-robin implementations of processor sharing, including overhead. In: Eighth IEEE International Symposium on Network Computing and Applications, NCA 2009, pp. 60–65 (2009)
19. Venkataraman, S., Panda, A., Ananthanarayanan, G., Franklin, M.J., Stoica, I.: The power of choice in data-aware cluster scheduling. In: Proceedings of the 11th USENIX Conference on Operating Systems Design and Implementation, OSDI 2014, pp. 301–316. USENIX Association, Berkeley (2014)
20. Wei, X., Li, W.W., Tatebe, O., Xu, G., Hu, L., Ju, J.: Implementing data aware scheduling in Gfarm(r) using LSF^{TM} scheduler plugin mechanism. In: Arabnia, H.R., Ni, J. (eds.) GCA, pp. 3–10. CSREA Press (2005)
21. Zhang, F., Tasneem, S., Lipsky, L., Thompson, S.: Analysis of round-robin variants: favoring newly arrived jobs. In: Proceedings of the 2009 Spring Simulation Multiconference, SpringSim 2009 (2009)

A Distributed Approach Based on Maximal Far-Flung Scalar Premier Selection for Camera Actuation

Sushree Bibhuprada B. Priyadarshini and Suvasini Panigrahi[✉]

Veer Surendra Sai University of Technology, Burla, Sambalpur, India
bimalabibhuprada@gmail.com, spanigrahi_cse@vssut.ac.in

Abstract. The article proposes a distributed approach inspired by maximal far-flung scalar premier selection for actuation of cameras. This manner of scalar premier selection reduces the possible overlapping among the field of views of cameras, thereby minimizing the amount of redundant data transmission due to it. The scalar premiers communicate their corresponding cameras regarding the occurring event information and the cameras collaboratively decide which among them are to be actuated. Experimental results obtained from the investigation validate the significance of our proposed algorithm as compared to three other methods proposed in the literature.

Keywords: Scalar premier · Field of view · Depth of field · Sub-compartment · Far-flung

1 Introduction

In this advanced era of rapid technological proliferation, the popularity of sensor networks is predominantly due to their diversified spectrum of applications resulting in several challenges. The principal challenge in sensor network is how to have an adequate coverage of the monitored region, while minimizing the amount of redundant data transmission. This redundant data transmission takes place due to overlapping of *Field of View (FOV)* angles of cameras [1]. The scalars present at the overlapping regions communicate the same event information to cameras, resulting in redundant transmission. Generally, cameras are kept in off state whereas the scalars are kept in on condition. The cameras are turned on; whenever an event is detected by them. In *"Distributed collaborative camera actuation based on scalar count (DCA-SC)* the cameras collaboratively decide which among them are to be actuated [1]. Further, another work called *Distributed collaborative camera actuation scheme based on sensing region management (DCCA-SM)* given in [2] activates the cameras based on their remaining energy. A Non-heuristic (N-H) approach [3] keeps the cameras which are activated due to sensing of event in off condition. The idea of cover-set in [4] helps in monitoring all the targets in an area.

© Springer International Publishing Switzerland 2016
N. Bjørner et al. (Eds.): ICDCIT 2016, LNCS 9581, pp. 87–91, 2016.
DOI: 10.1007/978-3-319-28034-9_10

2   Problem Analysis and Proposed Approach

Although several approaches have been devised, but always a tradeoff exists between the portions of area covered by activated cameras and the amount of redundant transmission. Hence, our objective is to activate minimum number of cameras to provide improved coverage of event region, while minimizing the amount of redundant data transmission. In this paper, we have devised a distributed algorithm called *Maximal Far-Flung Scalar Premier Selection for Camera Actuation (MFSPS-CA)* that actuates reduced number of cameras, which are required to afford better coverage of the occurring event while minimizing the amount of redundant data transmission. This is achieved by the selection of maximal *far-flung scalar premiers (SPs)* for camera activation. Such selection of *SPs* is done in such a way that the cameras activated can cover more distinct portions of the occurring event region.

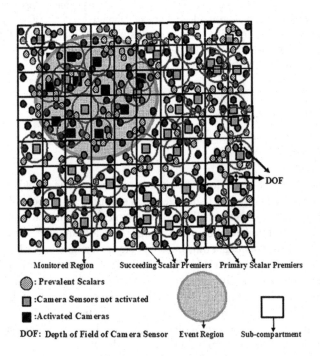

Fig. 1. Event detection and camera actuation

Initially, all the sensors are randomly sprinkled. Each scalar and camera broadcast *My Scalar Information Message (MSIM)* and *My Camera Information Message (MCIM)* respectively. These messages contain the id and location information of concerned sensors. Afterwards, the sensors calculate the *Euclidian distance (ED)* between itself and other sensors individually. If the *ED* value for a scalar and a camera is less than the *depth of field (DOF)* of the camera then the scalar lies within the purview of camera.

Subsequently, the monitored region is divided into a number of sub-compartments in such a manner that the side length of each sub-compartment is one tenth of the length of monitored region (500 m in our context). In each of the sub-compartments a scalar premier called *Primary Scalar Premier (PSP)* is selected so that it has the minimal mean distance among all the scalars belonging to that sub-compartment. The scalar having maximum distance from the *PSP* is then chosen as the *Succeeding Scalar Premier (SSP)* of concerned sub-compartment.

Whenever, any event takes place, *SPs* detect the event and they broadcast *Detect Message (DM)* containing event information and their respective ids. All the cameras maintain their respective event detecting *SP* ids in a list called *Event Reporting Scalar Premier List (ERSPL)*. Each camera calculates the sum of event reporting *SPs* present within their *FOVs* called *event reporting scalar premier sum (ER-SPS)* value. If ER-SPS = 1, then add camera id to *Single Premier Camera List (SPCL)*, otherwise add id of camera to *Multi Premier Camera List (MPCL)*. Initially, the camera that comes first in *MPCL* is activated first and its id is added to *ACTIVATION* list. The activated camera broadcasts *Update Scalar Premier (USP)* message containing the ids of *SPs* present within its *DOF* [1]. The ids of *SPs* present in *USP* message of activated camera is added to *Update Message id List (UM-IDL)*. Rest of the cameras present in *MPCL* make decision for actuation by comparing the *SP* ids present in their *ERSPL* list with *SP* ids present in *USP* message (s) sent by activated camera (s). If at least a single mismatch is found concerned camera is to be activated. Afterwards, the cameras present in *SPCL* compare their *SP* ids present in their *ERSPL list* with *SP* ids present in updated *UM-IDL* list. If a mismatch is noticed concerned camera is activated. The updated *ACTIVATION* list contains the ids of activated cameras. A scenario of scalar premier selection and camera actuation is portrayed in Fig. 1.

3   Implementation and Performance Evaluation

The *MFSPS-CA* approach has been compared with three approaches namely: *DCA-SC* [1], *DCCA-SM* [2] and *N-H* [3]. We have varied the number of cameras (noc) and observed its effect on the four parameters: (a) number of cameras activated (noca) (b) coverage ratio (cr) [1] (c) redundancy ratio (rr): rr is the ratio of total portions of over-lapping areas of *FOVs* of activated cameras covering the event region to the total unique portions of the occurring event region (d) power consumption for camera activation (pcca). It is evident from Fig. 2(a) that with an increasing noc the noca increases in all the approaches and it is minimum in *MFSPS-CA*. Hence, pcca is lowest in our case as shown in Fig. 2(b). Similarly, rr and cr are obtained as minimum and maximum in *MFSPS-CA* as shown in Fig. 3(a) and (b) respectively.

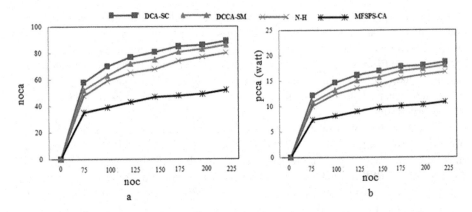

Fig. 2. Effect of varying number of cameras (noc) on (a) noca (b) pcca (watt)

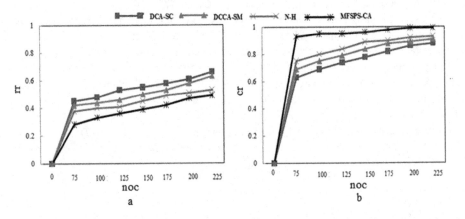

Fig. 3. Effect of varying number of cameras (noc) on (a) rr (b) cr

4   Conclusions

The results obtained from the investigation justifies the effectiveness of our proposed MFSPS-CA approach in terms of reduced camera activation, minimized redundancy ratio, increased coverage ratio as well as lesser power consumption in case of proposed approach.

References

1. Newell, A., Akkaya, K.: Distributed collaborative camera actuation for redundant data elimination in wireless multimedia sensor networks. Ad Hoc Netw. **9**(4), 514–527 (2011). Elsevier
2. Luo, W., Lu, Q., Xiao, J.: Distributed collaborative camera actuation scheme based on sensing-region management for wireless multimedia sensor networks. International Journal of Distributed Sensor Networks **2012**, Article ID 486163 (2012). doi:10.1155/2012/486163, Hindawi Publishing Corporation

3. Priyadarshini, S.B.B., Panigrahi, S.: A non-heuristic approach for minimizing the energy and power consumption in wireless multimedia sensor networks. In: International Conference on Computational Intelligence and Networks (CINE), Bhubaneswar, 12-13 January 2015, pp. 104–109. IEEE (2015). doi:10.1109/CINE.2015.29
4. Zorbas, D., Glynos, D., Kotzanikolaou, P., Douligeris, C.: Solving coverage problems in wireless sensor networks using cover sets. Ad Hoc Netw. **8**(4), 400–415 (2010). Elsevier Science Publishers

An Extension to UDDI for the Discovery of User Driven Web Services

Anu Saini[✉]

Maharaja Surajmal Institute of Technology, New Delhi, India
drsainianu@gmail.com

Abstract. Service registries are used by web service providers to publish services and registries are used by requestors to find them in an SOA (Service Oriented Architecture). The following drawbacks are presented in the main existing service registry specifications, UDDI (Universal Description, Discovery and Integration). First, only abstract, unscalable and inefficient definition of the web services publications is present in all UBR (Universal Business Registry) nodes. Second, it matches only the business name and service name given in the WSDL document to collect service information. In order to overcome these difficulties, author have proposed an efficient and effective UDDI architecture called E-UDDI, which extends the UDDI design by incorporating a QoS in additional bag in the business entity data structure. Moreover, to enable service customer for easily finding more appropriate service information, an effective service matching mechanism is adopted in the E-UDDI so that the user can take the decisions. Service discovery and publishing is improved considerably in the proposed system by means of an effective UDDI registry with flexible and more suitable service searching facility.

1 Introduction

A major turn in the industry for loosely linked service-oriented architecture and interoperable solutions over heterogeneous platforms and systems is the web service. From industries and standard bodies, it has received outstanding attention and adoption [1–10]. For dependable service invocation and event notification between two endpoints, the two-way web service interaction ought to have its Service Local Registry that reveals the WSDL interfaces of both the server and the client [11].

The two significant registries employed by the majority of people today are UDDI (Universal Description Discovery and Integration) and ebXML. For facilitating businesses to quickly, easily, and dynamically discover web services and interact with each other, an industrial initiative known as UDDI [12] is employed which, creates an Internet-wide network of registries of web services. [13] UDDI permits businesses to register their presence on the web. A set of Application Programming Interfaces (APIs) is being offered by UDDI, which can be employed to publish or explore information stored within the directory [14]. Most significantly, the information about the technical interfaces of a business's services is available in UDDI. To determine technical data, such that those services can be cited and employed one can interrelate with UDDI at both design time and run time through a set of SOAP-based XML API calls [15–18].

© Springer International Publishing Switzerland 2016
N. Bjørner et al. (Eds.): ICDCIT 2016, LNCS 9581, pp. 92–96, 2016.
DOI: 10.1007/978-3-319-28034-9_11

In this paper, we have made some extension to the standard UDDI, called as E-UDDI which is designed by adding QoS for user driven query. Here QoS contains information of each web services in detail and it is stored in an additional bag to the business entity data structure [19].

2 Review of Related Research

Literature presents a lot of researches related to the use of UDDI registry, which plays an important role in helping requesters to find suitable web services. In recent times, the extension of UDDI registry has received significant interest among the researchers [20–26].

3 Proposed System Architecture for User Driven Web Service Registry and Discovery

In general, the web service provider and the user find some difficulties in UDDI usage due to its incapability in providing certain functionalities. Some of the limitations when we find and publish the web services in UDDI are described as follows. (1) UDDI in its current form is limited to three pages such as, yellow, green and white page. (2) The web service document gives only the abstract definition of the web services. (3) Only within business name, service name, service category and tModel restricted searching facilities are offered by the UDDI. (4) Based on user specified conditions web services are directly matched by the UDDI.

In order to overcome these difficulties, we have developed an E-UDDI registry that provides the following advantages compared to the standard UDDI-registry. (1) It contains QoS to describe the specific features and properties. (2) The detailed description of the web services is defined in additional bag. (3) The searching facility given by the proposed work is extended to additional bag. The proposed system architecture for user driven web service registry and discovery is shown in Fig. 1.

3.1 E-UDDI Data Model

Along with certain specific QoS related with business, businesses and web services are described in an XML schema by the E-UDDI data model. The choice of XML is because it offers platform-neutral view of data and permits natural way of describing hierarchical relationships. In E-UDDI data model, the core information regarding businesses and web services are organized as four different data structures. Each data structure within an E-UDDI registry is allocated a Universally Unique ID (or "key", also called UUID). The entire information given in the E-UDDI data model is theoretically signified into four elements such as, white page, yellow page, green page and additional page. The additional page contains the detailed description of the web services specified with QoS attributes.

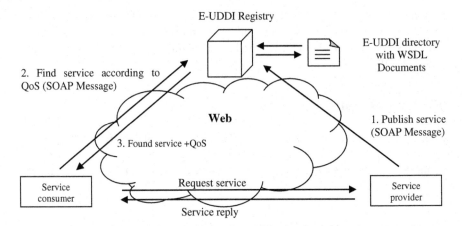

Fig. 1. Proposed system architecture for web service registry and discovery

3.2   Service Publishing and Discovery

This section describes the process of publishing web services with QoS in the E-UDDI registry and discovery of web services from the E-UDDI registry based on the user specified QoS attributes.

3.2.1   Service Publishing Phase

During the service publishing phase, an E-UDDI is used to update the specified QoS of the services. To update the Additional bag into the E-UDDI registry, we have used the *save _QoS API* which, is newly designed in the proposed work by exploiting the SOAP protocol. At first, SOAP message with empty additional bag is sent to the service provider and they submit the QoS in the SOAP message. Then, these specific QoS are stored as WSDL document in the E-UDDI registry. The updated QoS in the registry are named as additional bag. In order to enable the user to easily get the fully satisfied services from the common repository additional bag is used.

3.2.2   Service Discovery Phase

The service discovery phase uses QoS based retrieval of web services as an improvement over the standard API. Accordingly, the user can locate their QoS query to discover a set of services that satisfies the given QoS list. For matching the given QoS query with the QoS specified in the E-UDDI registry, the following two mechanisms are used. ***E-UDDI Matching Mechanism:*** Here, we have used two types of matching mechanism such as (1) Complete_QoS_detail (2) Fraction_ QoS_detail. Through the use of this, the QoS query given by the service customer is matched with the Additional bag of every WSDL document in the E-UDDI registry.

4 Conclusion

The proposed system architecture is an effective implementation of web service registry and an effective retrieval of web services based on the user's interest. The proposed system published all the web services in their public registry by obtaining all the service information from the service provider. The service information contained in the public registry was written in a WSDL document and it additionally, included the specific QoS of each web services. The published web services with its QoS were utilized to match the query QoS given by the user. If the given query QoS was exactly matched with the WSDL documents, the matched results are given to the user with its access information. Otherwise, the partially matched web services are given to the user, so that the user can select suitable web services after his/her own interest. The experimental results ensured that the proposed system provides fine-grained web services to the user by matching their input QoS.

References

1. Feng, L., Chou, W., Li, L., Li, J.: WSIP – web service SIP endpoint for converged multimedia/ multimodal communication over IP. In: Proceedings of the IEEE International Conference on Web Services (ICWS 2004), San Diego, California, USA, 6–9 June, pp. 690–697 (2004)
2. Haines, M.: Web service as information systems innovation: a theoretical framework for web service technology adoption. In: Proceedings of the IEEE International Conference on Web Services (ICWS 2004), San Diego, California, USA, 6–9 June, pp. 11–16 (2004)
3. Muhammad, M., Bin, T., Toshiro, K.: Introducing dynamic distributed coordination in web services for next generation service platform. In: Proceedings of the IEEE International Conference on Web Services (ICWS 2004), San Diego, California, USA, 6–9 June, pp. 296–305 (2004)
4. Vidyasankar, K., Vossen, G.: A multi-level model for web service composition. In: Proceedings of the IEEE International Conference on Web Services (ICWS 2004), San Diego, California, USA, 6–9 June, pp. 462–469 (2004)
5. Jinghai, R., Peep, K.: Logic-based web services compositions: from service description to process model. In: Proceedings of the IEEE International Conference on Web Services (ICWS 2004), San Diego, California, USA, 6–9 June, pp. 446–453 (2004)
6. Caromel, C., di Costanzo, A., Gannon, D., Slominski, A.: Asynchronous peer-to-peerweb services and firewalls. In: Proceedings of the 19th IEEE International Conference on Parallel and Distributed Symposium, Denver, CA, USA, 4–8 April, p. 1 83a (2005)
7. Standard ECMA-348: Web Services Description Language (WSDL) for CSTA Phase III, 2nd edn., June 2004
8. ECMA TR-90: Session Management, Event Notification, and Computing Function Services - an amendment to ECMA-348, ECMA International, December 2005
9. Eyhab, A., Qusay, H.M.: Investigating web services on the world wide web. In: Proceeding of the 17th International Conference on World Wide Web, Beijing, China, pp. 795–804 (2008)
10. Feng, L., Gesan, W., Li, L., Wu, C.: Web service for distributed communication systems. In: Proceedings of the IEEE International Conference on Service Operations and Logistics, and Informatics (SOLI 2006), Shanghai, China, pp. 1030–1035 (2006)

11. Feng, L., Gesan, W., Wu, C., Lookman, F., Li, L.: TARGET: two-way web service router gateway. In: IEEE International Conference on Web Services (ICWS 2006), pp. 629–636 (2006)
12. Oasis Consortium: UDDI the UDDI Technical White Paper (2000). http://www.uddi.org
13. Naveen, S., Massimo, P., Sycara, K.: Semantic web service discovery in the OWL-S IDE. In: Proceedings of the 39th Annual Hawaii International Conference on System Sciences, vol. 6, p. 109b (2006)
14. Jeckle, M., Zengler, B.: Active UDDI - an extension to UDDI for dynamic and fault-tolerant service invocation. In: Chaudhri, A.B., Jeckle, M., Rahm, E., Unland, R. (eds.) NODe-WS 2002. LNCS, vol. 2593, pp. 91–99. Springer, Heidelberg (2003)
15. Karsten, J.: Web Service Description and Discovery Using UDDI, Part I. Microsoft Corporation, 3 October 2001
16. Hartwig, G.: Introduction to Web Services. Borland, March 2002
17. Sheng, Q., Benatallah, B., Stephan, R., Oi-Yan Mak, E., Zhu, Y.Q.: Discovering e-services using UDDI in SELF-SERV. In: Proceedings of the International Conference on E-Business, Beijing, China, May 2002
18. David, C., Tyler, J.: Java web services, 1st edn., pp. 1– 276. O'Reilly, Sebastopol (2002). ISBN: 0-596-00269-6
19. Parimala, N., Anu, S.: Web service with criteria: extending WSDL. In: 2011 Sixth International Conference on Digital Information Management (ICDIM). IEEE (2011)
20. Du, Z., Huai, J.-P., Liu, Y.: Ad-UDDI: an active and distributed service registry. In: Bussler, C.J., Shan, M.-C. (eds.) TES 2005. LNCS, vol. 3811, pp. 58–71. Springer, Heidelberg (2006)
21. Edgardo, A., Marco, B., Carlo, G., Giorgio, G., Flavio, L.: Extending the UDDI API for service instance ranking. In: Proceedings of the International Symposium on Web Services, Las Vegas, Nevada, USA, June 2005
22. Powles, A., Krishnaswamy, S.: Extending UDDI with recommendations: an association analysis approach. In: Proceedings of 19th International Conference on Advanced Information Networking and Applications, vol. 2, pp. 715–720 (2005)
23. Matjaz, B.J., Ana, S., Bostjan, B., Ivan, R.: WSDL and UDDI extensions for version support in web services. J. Syst. Softw. **82**(8), 1326–1343 (2009)
24. Zhang, M., Cheng, Z., Zhao, Y., Huang, J.Z., Li, Y., Zang, B: ADDI: an agent-based extension to UDDI for supply chain management. In: Proceedings of the Ninth International Conference on Computer Supported Cooperative Work in Design, Shanghai, China, vol. 1, pp. 405– 410 (2005)
25. Huimin, H., Haiyan, D., Dongxia, H., Yuemei, H.: Research on the models to customize private UDDI registry query results. In: Proceedings of 3rd International Conference on Innovative Computing Information and Control, ICICIC, Dalian, Liaoning, 22 August, p. 205 (2008)
26. Xiang, L., Lin, L., Lei, X.: I-UDDI4 M: improved UDDI4 M protocol, vol. 259, pp. 859–866. Springer, Boston (2008). 978-0-387-77252-3

Long Wire Length of Midimew-Connected Mesh Network

M.M. Hafizur Rahman[1]($\boxtimes$), Rizal Mohd Nor[1], Md. Rabiul Awal[1],
Tengku Mohd Bin Tengku Sembok[2], and Yasuyuki Miura[3]

[1] DCS, KICT, IIUM, 50728 Kuala Lumpur, Malaysia
{hafizur,rizalmohdnor}@iium.edu.my
[2] Cyber Security Center, UPNM, 57000 Kuala Lumpur, Malaysia
tmtsembok@gmail.com
[3] Graduate School of Technology, SIT, Fujisawa, Kanagawa, Japan
miu@info.shonan-it.ac.jp

Abstract. Minimal DIstance MEsh with Wrap-around links (Midimew) connected Mesh Network (MMN) is a hierarchical interconnection network consists of several Basic Modules (BM), where the BM is a 2D-mesh network and the higher level network is a midimew network. In this paper, we present the architecture of MMN and evaluate the number of long wires, length of a long wire, and the total length for the long wire of MMN, TESH, and torus networks. It is shown that the proposed MMN possesses simple structure and moderate wire length. The long wire length of MMN is slightly higher than TESH network and far lower than that of 2D torus network. Overall performance suggests that, MMN is a good choice for future generation massively parallel computers.

Keywords: Massively parallel computers · Interconnection network · MMN · Long wire length

1 Introduction

The demand for computation power is increasing rapidly and found as constant over the last half century. Massively parallel computer (MPC) is introduced to meet this increasing demand. Nevertheless, the scaling of MPC is increasing as well. In nearby future, MPC will contain 10 to 100 millions of nodes [1] in a single system with computing capability at the exaflops level. In MPC, interconnection network dominates the system performance [2]. In relation, hierarchical interconnection network (HIN) is a plausible alternative way to interconnect the future generation MPC systems [3]. However, the performance of already proposed HIN does not yield an ultimate choice of a network for MPC. Among a lot of HINs, several k-ary n-cube based HIN proposed [4,5] for good performance.

Small transistor size and its greater density make the MPC with millions of nodes using VLSI and NoC technology. Hence, the functionality becomes more complex of an MPC system with the shrinking geometry. As a matter of fact,

© Springer International Publishing Switzerland 2016
N. Bjørner et al. (Eds.): ICDCIT 2016, LNCS 9581, pp. 97–102, 2016.
DOI: 10.1007/978-3-319-28034-9_12

interconnection network becomes the steering point, in the context of power dissipation and cost. In an MPC system, more than 50 % of total power dissipated by the interconnection network and the cost of MPC is related to the communication links of the network. Hence, the network is wire limited on a VLSI surface. Wire length determines the communication delay of the network [6]. Among the total wire length long wire is also a determining factor. It occupied significantly the allocated wire area for a network on a VLSI surface. Total wire length of network indicates the average locality of links of the network. Therefore long wire length is an influential factor for the interconnection network to be implemented in a VLSI plane.

MMN [7] was proposed to improve performance of fixed degree network while keeping short diameter which is still desirable [8]. BM of MMN is 2-D mesh and higher level network are midimew network. Hence, MMN offers simple and hierarchical structure and this translate to the ease of VLSI implementation. The main focus of this paper is to explore the long wire length of a MMN for VLSI implementation. We compare the number of long wire and length of long wire for the several degree 4 networks.

The remainder of the paper is organized as follows. In Sect. 2, we present the basic architecture of the MMN. Long wire length evaluation is discussed in Sect. 3. Finally, in Sect. 4 we conclude this paper.

2   Architecture of the MMN

Midimew connected Mesh Network (MMN) is a HIN, where multiple basic modules (BM) are hierarchically interconnected to form a higher level network of MMN. BM is the basic building blocks of MMN and it is a 2D-mesh network of size $(2^m \times 2^m)$. BM consists of 2^{2m} processing elements (PE). PEs are arranged in 2^m rows and 2^m columns. Considering $m = 2$, a BM of size (4×4) is portrayed in Fig. 1. Each BM has $2^{(m+2)}$ free ports at the contours for higher level interconnection. All Intra-BM links are done by free ports of the interior nodes. All free ports of the exterior nodes, either one or two, are used for inter-BM links to form higher level networks. In this paper, BM refers to a Level-1 network.

Successive higher level networks are built by recursively interconnecting 2^{2m} immediate lower level sub-networks in a $(2^m \times 2^m)$ midimew network. As portrayed in Fig. 2, considering (m = 2) a Level-2 MMN can be formed by interconnecting $2^{(2 \times 2)} = 16$ BMs. Similarly, a Level-3 network can be formed by interconnecting 16 Level-2 sub-networks, and so on. Each BM is connected to its logically adjacent BMs. It is useful to note that for each higher level interconnection, a BM uses $4 \times (2^q) = 2^{q+2}$ of its free links, $2^{(2q)}$ free links for diagonal interconnections and $2^{(2q)}$ free links for horizontal interconnections. Here, $q \in \{0, 1, ..., m\}$,, is the inter-level connectivity. $q = 0$ leads to minimal inter-level connectivity, while $q = m$ leads to maximum inter-level connectivity.

A MMN(m, L, q) is constructed using $(2^m \times 2^m)$ BMs, has L levels of hierarchy with inter-level connectivity q. In principle, m could be any positive integer. In this paper, we focus on a class of MMN(2,L,q) networks. The highest level

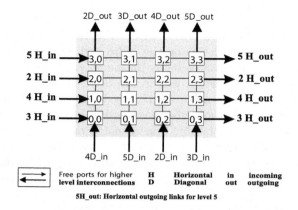

Fig. 1. Basic Module of MMN

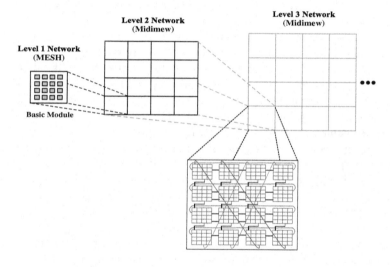

Fig. 2. Higher Level Networks of MMN

network which can be built from a $(2^m \times 2^m)$ BM is $L_{max} = 2^{m-q} + 1$ with $q = 0$ and $m = 2$, $L_{max} = 5$, Level-5 is the highest possible level. The total number of nodes in a network having $(2^m \times 2^m))$ BMs is $N = 2^{2mL}$.

3   Long Wire Length Evaluation

In our previous study, we have evaluated the total wire length of a MMN along with the other networks in a 2D-planar implementation [9]. The wire length is evaluated using 45 nm technology. And according to 45 nm technology, the tile height is 5.2 mm and tile width is 3.6 mm [10]. Each node of an interconnection network is in one tile of a VLSI implementation. And wire length depends on the tile size. We have considered horizontal and vertical direction to evaluate the total wire length. Here the wire length in horizontal and vertical direction depends on tile width and height, respectively. Wire length between two particular nodes is the number of tiles needs to pass to interconnect the nodes. Therefore, wire length between two nodes in horizontal direction is the product of number of tiles needs to be passed and tile width. Similarly for vertical direction, wire length is the product of number of tiles needs to be passed and tile height. Consequently, total wire required to connect all the nodes of a network is the number of total tiles needs to be passed and can be expressed as, $Wire\ Length = Tile\ distance_X + Tile\ distance_Y$ and $Tile\ distance = \#\ of\ tiles \times \#\ of\ groups$. Here $\#\ of\ groups$ indicate the total number of similar communication links.

Considering 45 nm CMOS 5.2 mm × 3.6 mm tile [10], the wire length between two neighboring nodes in horizontal direction is 3.6 mm and for vertical direction is 5.2 mm. Total wire length is evaluated using the wire length required for BM and the inter-BM link length for higher level networks. The wire length of a BM is 105.6 mm which yields 1689.6 mm for 16 BMs. As portrayed in Fig. 2, 4 diagonal links and 4 horizontal wrap-around links are the long wire of an MMN. For the TESH network 4 vertical and 4 horizontal wrap-around links are the long wire. For a 16 × 16 torus network, 16 vertical wrap-around links and 16 horizontal wrap-around links are the long wire. And the mesh network don't have any long link because it is not using the wrap-around links. Therefore, MMN, TESH, and torus networks have, 8, 8, and 32 long wires, respectively.

The length of long wire is a crucial parameter to design of an interconnection network. The performance of a network is strongly influenced by the long links because the delay caused by these interconnections is a limiting factor. The operating speed of a network is limited by the physical length of its links. Thus, the long length of a wire can be used to describe and compare the maximum physical speeds that the various networks can attain.

Each wrap-around links has a length of 54 mm and 4 wrap-around horizontal links length is 4 × 54 mm = 216 mm. According to the layout of diagonal links on a 2D-plane, the longest wires are two diagonal links. The distance of the longest wire is 121.2 mm. The length of other two diagonal links is 109.6 mm. Thus, the total length for the long wire in a MMN is (4 × 54 mm) + (2 × 121.2 mm) + (2 × 109.6 mm) = 677.6 mm = 67.76 cm. Similarly the length of 8 long wires in a TESH network is 42.24 cm. Also the length of 16 horizontal wrap-around links and 16 vertical wrap-around links of a 16 × 16 torus network is 211.2 mm.

Networks with much wire eventually results a high installation cost and a large VLSI area which responsible for poor performance. On the contrast, diameter is the maximum number of links that must be traversed to send a packet to any node of an interconnection network among all distinct pairs of nodes along the shortest path. Diameter indicates the worst case scenario of a network and has direct influence on the overall static network performance. Hence, the product of total wire length and diameter is a good criteria to get the static operating cost of the network. We can express the static operating cost as $C_{static} = L \times D$.

Here, C_{static} represents the static operating cost, L for total wire length and D stands for diameter. The real cost of a system depends on the VLSI realization. However, the static operating cost is a good criterion to indicate the relationship between cost and performance of a network.

The wiring complexity, total wire length, diameter, static operating cost, number of long wire, length of these long wire, longest wire length of 2D-mesh, 2D-torus, TESH, MMN networks have been evaluated and tabulated in Table 1. For fair comparison we consider degree 4 networks only.

Table 1. Comparison of Total Wire Length of Various Networks

Network	Wiring Complexity	Total Wire Length (cm)	Diameter	Static Operating Cost	# of Long Wire	Length of Long Wire (cm)	Longest Wire Length (cm)
2D-Mesh	480	211.75	30	6352.50	x	x	x
2D-Torus	512	422.95	16	6767.20	32	211.20	7.80
TESH(2,2,0)	416	253.99	21	5333.79	8	42.24	6.24
MMN(2,2,0)	416	263.43	17	4478.31	8	67.76	12.12

Due to the absence of wrap-around links in a 2D mesh network, it results small wire length and large diameter. From Table 1, it is clearly seen that 2D-mesh network can be constructed with minimum wire length among the networks, 211.75 cm in total. On the other hand, 2D-torus network contains 32 long wrap-around links and among them the longest wire is vertical wrap-around link and its length is 7.80 cm. Due to presence of numerous long links, the wire require for a 2D torus is 422.95 cm. This long wire results high static operating cost which is 6767.2 regardless of low diameter. TESH (2,2,0) is a hierarchical and optimized architecture with the combination of 2D mesh and 2D torus network. Due to the hierarchy in nature, the longest wire length and the number of long wire is less which results less wiring complexity and requires small wire length than that of torus network. Eventually, TESH has less static operating cost than mesh and 2-D torus network and higher than MMN and it is 5333.79.

Like TESH, MMN (2,2,0) is also a hierarchical network with the combination of mesh and midimew networks. The number of long wire is the same as that of TESH network. However, due to diagonal midimew connection and 2D-planar implementation in VLSI the longest wire length is a bit higher than that of TESH network. Eventually the total wire length is also a bit high. On the contrast, this diagonal connection substantially reduces the diameter of the MMN. Therefore, this small diameter yields small static operating cost for the MMN than that of 2D-mesh, 2D-torus, and TESH network and that is 4478.31.

4 Conclusion

The architecture and wire length, number of long wire, and the longest wire length of the MMN have been discussed in detail. In addition the wire length evaluation of 2D mesh, 2D torus, and TESH are also explored and compared with MMN as well. It is shown that the MMN possess a simple architecture, composed of 2D mesh and midimew network. From the wire length evaluation, it is clear that, the MMN presents moderate wire length in total with fixed degree nodes. The number of long wire of MMN is same as TESH network, the longest wire length is a bit high, the total wire length of MMN is slightly higher than that of 2D mesh and TESH network. However total wire length of MMN is far lower in comparison with 2D torus. This paper focused on the architectural structure and wire length evaluation. Issues for future work include wire length evaluation of MMN in a 3D VLSI realization.

Acknowledgments. This work is supported by FRGS13-065-0306, Ministry of Education, Malaysia. The authors would like to thank the anonymous reviewers for their insightful comments and suggestions to improve the clarity and quality of the paper.

References

1. Beckman, P.: Looking toward exascale computing. In: 9th PDCAT, p. 3 (2008)
2. Yang, Y., Funahashi, A., Jouraku, A., Nishi, H., Amano, H., Sueyoshi, T.: Recursive diagonal torus: an interconnection network for massively parallel computers. IEEE Trans. Parallel Distrib. Syst. **12**, 701–715 (2001)
3. Abd-El-Barr, M., Al-Somani, T.F.: Topological properties of hierarchical interconnection networks: a review and comparison. J. Elec. Comp. Engg. **1** (2011)
4. Lai, P.L., Hsu, H.C., Tsai, C.H., Stewart, I.A.: A class of hierarchical graphs as topologies for interconnection networks. J. Theoret. Comput. Sci. **411**, 2912–2924 (2010)
5. Jain, V.K., Ghirmai, T., Horiguchi, S.: TESH: a new hierarchical interconnection network for massively parallel computing. IEICE Trans. IS **80**, 837–846 (1997)
6. Dally, W.J., Towles, B.: Route packets, not wires: on-chip interconnection networks. In: Proceedings of Design Automation Conference, pp. 684–689 (2001)
7. Awal, M.R., Rahman, M.M.H., Akhand, M.A.H.: A new hierarchical interconnection network for future generation parallel computer. In: Proceedings of 16th International Conference on Computers and Information Technology, pp. 314–319 (2013)
8. Camarero, C., Martinez, C., Beivide, R.: L-networks: a topological model for regular two-dimensional interconnection networks. IEEE Trans. Comput. **62**, 1362–1375 (2012)
9. Awal, M.R., Rahman, M.M.H., Nor, R.M., Sembok, T.M.B.T., Miura, Y., Inoguchi, Y.: Wire length of midimew-connected mesh network. In: Hsu, C.-H., Shi, X., Salapura, V. (eds.) NPC 2014. LNCS, vol. 8707, pp. 132–143. Springer, Heidelberg (2014)
10. Howard, J., Dighe, S., Vangal, S.R., Ruhl, G., Borkar, N., Jain, S., Erraguntla, V., Konow, M., Riepen, M., Gries, M., Droege, G., Larsen, T.L., Steibl, S., Borkar, S., De, V.K., Wijngaart, R.V.D.: A 48-core IA-32 processor in 45 nm CMOS using on-die message-passing and DVFS for performance and power scaling. IEEE J. Solid-State Circ. **46**(1), 173–183 (2011)
11. Awal, M.R., Rahman, M.M.H.: Network-on-chip implementation of midimew-connected mesh network. In: Proceedings of 14th PDCAT, pp. 265–271 (2013)

K-means and Wordnet Based Feature Selection Combined with Extreme Learning Machines for Text Classification

Rajendra Kumar Roul$^{(\boxtimes)}$ and Sanjay Kumar Sahay

BITS-Pilani, K.K. Birla Goa Campus, Goa, India
{rkroul,ssahay}@goa.bits-pilani.ac.in

Abstract. The incredible increase of online documents in digital form on the Web, has renewed the interest in text classification. The aim of text classification is to classify text documents into a set of pre-defined categories. But the poor quality of features selection, extremely high dimensional feature space and complexity of natural languages become the roadblock for this classification process. To address these issues, here we propose a k-means clustering based feature selection for text classification. Bi-Normal Separation (BNS) combine with Wordnet and cosine-similarity helps to form a quality and reduce feature vector to train the Extreme Learning Machine (ELM) and Multi-layer Extreme Learning Machine (ML-ELM) classifiers. For experimental purpose, 20-Newsgroups and DMOZ datasets have been used. The empirical results on these two benchmark datasets demonstrate the applicability, efficiency and effectiveness of our approach using ELM and ML-ELM as the classifiers over state-of-the-art classifiers.

Keywords: Bi-Normal Separation · Extreme Learning Machine · Feature selection · K-means · Multi-layer ELM · Text classification

1 Introduction

Text classification is one of the most important technique of text mining and become more popular with the increase in popularity of the internet. However, the booming of internet increases the size of the problem and hence it is necessary to improve the accuracy of the classification further. Most of the methods of text classification use 'bag of words' model where each unique term of a document is a feature. But the dynamic growth of the internet highly increases the number of documents on the Web which in turn increases the number of features in the range of millions. Many algorithms of Information Retrieval (IR) either can not be run or take long running time on a large number of features. Hence, it is essential to use feature selection for removing redundant features from the corpus. The main purpose of the feature selection is to determine which features are most suitable to the present classification technique. No new features are created in feature selection but some important features are

© Springer International Publishing Switzerland 2016
N. Bjørner et al. (Eds.): ICDCIT 2016, LNCS 9581, pp. 103–112, 2016.
DOI: 10.1007/978-3-319-28034-9_13

selected from the existing features. Many studies have been done on good feature selection techniques for text classification [1,2]. Algorithms of Feature selection can be broadly classified into filter, wrapper and embedded methods [3]. Filter method uses a proxy score instead of a predictive score to judge a subset. On the other hand, wrapper method gives a predictive score to each subset when the model is trained with respect to those features. In embedded method, the feature selection is done as a part of the model construction process. For example, LASSO (Least Absolute Shrinkage and Selection Operator), which involves penalizing the absolute size of the regression coefficients is a regression method. Feature selection techniques can be broadly classified into two categories - unsupervised and supervised. The unsupervised methods like Document Frequency, Term Strength, Term-Contribution, TF-IDF etc. do not require class labels of documents to choose the best features while the supervised methods like Accuracy, Bi-Normal Separation (BNS), Odds Ratio, Probability Ratio, Chi-Squared Metric, Information Gain (IG), MI-Judge etc. do require class labels for calculating the best features. A lot of research work has been done in the field of text classification using various state-of-the-art classifiers [4–7]. But very few researchers have used Extreme Learning Machines (ELM and ML-ELM) as the classifiers for text classification.

In this paper, the best features have been selected using the traditional k-means clustering technique where we divided a class (cluster assumed here) into a number of sub-classes (or sub-clusters) so that it can further bring more similar documents into the same group which in turn strengthen the relationship between the features (or keywords) of that sub-cluster. From each sub-cluster, we select the top features using Wordnet and cosine-similarity after forming the synonym lists of each feature selected based on their BNS score (a best performing measures in the probit classifier [8]). Finally, all top features of each sub-cluster are combined to form a reduced feature vector of the corresponding cluster for training the ELM and ML-ELM classifiers. The experimental results on two large datasets (20-Newsgroups and DMOZ) highlight the significance of ELM and ML-ELM over other established classifiers in the field of text classification.

The paper is outlined as follows: Sect. 2 describe the background details of our approach. In Sect. 3, we describe our proposed approach adopted to classify the text documents. The experimental work carried out is detailed in Sect. 4 and finally in Sect. 5, we concluded with some future enhancement of our proposed work.

2   Background

2.1   Extreme Learning Machine

Extreme Learning Machine (ELM), a classification technique proposed by Huang [9] is a combination of Single Layer Feed-forward Neural networks (SLFNs) and Support Vector Machine [10]. Neural networks and SVM are two state-of-the-art machine learning classifiers. But despite of their superiority, they have many limitations such as for neural network, some of the main challenges are rate of learning compare to their expected rate, unable to handle non-linear separable data, proneness to over fitting and sensitive to noisy data etc. and in the same way for SVM, algorithmic complexity, unstandardized probabilities of class membership, difficult to interpret the parameters for a solved model etc. are some of the prime challenges which still need to be addressed. ELM on the other hand has the potential to become a better classifier than other traditional classifiers due to many important reasons such as no adjustment of input weights and hidden layer biases are required, gives very good performance with less human intervention, easy to implement and learning speed is very fast etc. Figure 1 shows the system diagram of ELM.

Brief on ELM: For N arbitrary distinct samples (x_i, y_i), where $x_i = [x_{i1}, x_{i2}, ...,$ $x_{in}]^T \in R^n$ and $y_i = [y_{i1}, y_{i2}, ..., y_{im}]^T \in R^m$, such that $(x_i, y_i) \in R^n \times R^m$ where $(i = 1, 2, ..., N)$, along with L hidden nodes, and an activation function $g(x)$. The output function of ELM for a given input $\mathbf{x}$ is:

$$g_L(x_j) = \sum_{i=1}^{L} \beta_i g(w_i \cdot x_j + b_i) = y_j, j = 1, ..., N \tag{1}$$

where, $(w_i, b_i), i = 1, ..., L$ is randomly generated hidden node parameters such that $w_i = [w_{i1}, w_{i2}...w_{in}]^T$ is the weight vector connecting all n input nodes to the ith hidden node. b_i is the bias of ith hidden node. $\boldsymbol{\beta} = [\beta_1, ..., \beta_L]^T$ is the weight vector between the ith hidden node and the output nodes. $g(\mathbf{x})$ is the output vector which maps the input space of n-dimension to feature space of L-dimension, H (called ELM feature space, also known as hidden layer output matrix). Compact format of Eq. (1) can be written as follows:

$$H\beta = Y \tag{2}$$

where,

$$
\mathbf{H} = \begin{bmatrix} g(w_1 \cdot x_1 + b_1) & \cdots & g(w_L \cdot x_1 + b_L) \\ g(w_1 \cdot x_2 + b_1) & \cdots & g(w_L \cdot x_2 + b_L) \\ \cdot & \cdots & \cdot \\ \cdot & \cdots & \cdot \\ \cdot & \cdots & \cdot \\ g(w_1 \cdot x_N + b_1) & \cdots & g(w_L \cdot x_N + b_L) \end{bmatrix}_{N \times L} \quad \beta = \begin{bmatrix} \beta_{11} & \cdots & \beta_{1m} \\ \beta_{21} & \cdots & \beta_{2m} \\ \cdot & & \\ \cdot & & \\ \beta_{L1} & \cdots & \beta_{Lm} \end{bmatrix}_{L \times m} \quad Y = \begin{bmatrix} y_{11} & \cdots & y_{1m} \\ y_{21} & \cdots & y_{2m} \\ \cdot & & \\ \cdot & & \\ y_{N1} & \cdots & y_{Nm} \end{bmatrix}_{N \times m}
$$

$$\tag{3}$$

2.2 Multi-layer ELM

Multi-layer ELM (ML-ELM) is a machine learning technique of artificial neural network which uses deep learning (a multi-layer perceptron) [11] and ELM extensively. Deep networks outperform the traditional multi-layer neural network, SVMs and SLFNs, but have slow learning speed. Kasun et al. [12] first proposed the multi-layer form of ELM known as ML-ELM in which unsupervised learning is performed from layer to layer and it does not require any fine tuning. Hence, there is no need to spend a long time on the network training. It has a better

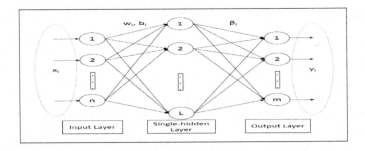

Fig. 1. ELM as a model

or comparable performance in comparisons with other deep networks. Figure 2 shows how ML-ELM combines both ELM-AE and ELM together. ELM-AE, just like regular ELMs is a good universal approximator, and its main aim is to represent the input features in a meaningful way by transforming the input data to a N dimensional feature space of hidden nodes. Thus, the resulting representation is either a compressed, equal or sparse representation depending on whether the input features are mapped to a lower, equal or higher dimensional feature space than their own. In an ELM network, for N training examples (x_j, y_j) and L hidden nodes, we have:

$$g_L(x_j) = \sum_{i=1}^{L} \beta_i g_i(x_j, w_i, b_i) = y_j, \ j = 1, ..., N \tag{4}$$

where (w_i, b_i), $i = 1, ..., L$ are the randomly generated hidden node parameters and H is the hidden layer output matrix. The output weights β which map the hidden nodes feature space to the output nodes can be computed depending on the number of training samples greater than, equal to or less than the hidden layer nodes. ELM-AE works in a manner similar to regular ELM except for a few modifications in order to perform unsupervised learning. ML-ELM makes use of ELM-AE to train the parameters in each layer. In other words, the hidden layer weights of ML-ELM are initialized by ELM-AE from layer to layer using unsupervised learning, and ML-ELM hidden layer activation functions can be either linear or non-linear piecewise. All output weights are determined analytically. The output of the ith hidden layer of ML-ELM can be obtained from the output of $(i-1)^{th}$ hidden layer and the output weight of β^i of the ith hidden layer. The output weight of β^i of the ith hidden layer is obtained layer wise from the ELM-AE, and its transpose. ML-ELM with 'L' hidden nodes can be represented as:

$$H^n = g((\beta^n)^T H^{n-1}) \tag{5}$$

2.3   Bi-Normal Separation (BNS)

According to Forman [2], Bi-Normal Separation (BNS) can be defined as $\phi^{-1}(tpr)$ - $\phi^{-1}(fpr)$ where ϕ is the standard normal distribution, and ϕ^{-1} is its

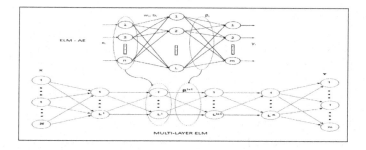

Fig. 2. Multi-layer ELM and ELM-AE

corresponding inverse, *tpr* is true positive rate and *fpr* is false positive rate respectively.

$$BNS(x, c_k) = \left| \phi^{-1}\left(\frac{n_{kw}}{n_k}\right) - \phi^{-1}\left(\frac{n_{\overline{k}w}}{n_{\overline{k}}}\right) \right| \qquad (6)$$

n_k is the number of documents in class c_k, $n_{\overline{k}}$ is the number of documents that are not in class c_k, n_{kw} is the number of documents in class c_k with word w and $n_{\overline{k}w}$ is the number of documents not in class c_k with word w.

3   Proposed Approach

The reduce training feature vector preparation for each cluster by selecting the top features is described as follows:

Step 1 Consider a given corpus consisting of number of classes (i.e. clusters C) of documents. Construct the term-document matrix for each such cluster C after pre-processing all the documents and select noun as the keywords of the entire corpus using minipar[1]

Step 2 For each cluster C, calculate the TF-IDF vector[2] and BNS score of each keyword of all the documents belonging to that cluster.

Step 3 Run the traditional k-means clustering algorithm on the term-vectors (i.e. keywords) of the cluster C and it returns k sub-clusters ($C' = \{c_1, c_2, ..., c_k\}$).

Step 4 For each $C' \in C$, calculate the cosine similarities[2] of all keywords with the centroid of C' and then select the top keywords from each C' in the following ways:

  (i) Select a keyword X having highest BNS score from the keyword-list of C' and using Wordnet prepare an initial synonym-list for X.

  (ii) Next, we need to check those keywords which are present both in the keyword-list of C' and in the synonym-list of X. If any such keywords are found then create a new synonym-list (*new-synonym-list*) of X and add

[1] http://ai.stanford.edu/~rion/parsing/minipar_viz.html.
[2] https://radimrehurek.com/gensim/tutorial.html.

all those keywords one by one to the new-synonym-list of X after discarding them from the keyword-list of C'. In this way the *new-synonym-list* of X is created. Now discard the initial synonym-list of X.

(iii) Repeat Step 4(i) and 4(ii) till the keyword-list of C' gets exhausted. Finally, we will have a *new-synonym-list* for those keywords which are selected based on their BNS scores from the keyword-list of C'. This gives us a lists of *new-synonym-list* of C'.

(iv) Select the top $m\%$ keywords (determined by experiment[3]) from each *new-synonym-list* of C' which have highest cosine-similarity (tightly bound to the centroid of C') values. We then combine all those top keywords of C' from each *new-synonym-list* and discard the remaining keywords to obtain the reduced feature vector of C'.

(v) Repeat the above steps (4(i)-4(iv)) for every $C' \in C$ and at the end, combine all the reduced feature vectors into a list to obtain the final reduce feature vector of C.

Step 5 Repeat Step 2 to 4 for each cluster C to obtain the final reduce feature vectors of all the clusters in the corpus. The final reduced feature vector of each cluster is then used to train ELM and ML-ELM and other traditional classifiers for text classification. Using the output prediction generated by a classifier and the known class label of the test data, calculate the precision, recall, F-measure and accuracy to quantify the performance of ELM, ML-ELM and other conventional classifiers.

The details of selection of top features from a sub-cluster are discussed in Algorithm 1.

4 Experimental Results

The proposed method has tested on the 20-Newsgroups[4] and DMOZ open directory project[5] datasets. 20-Newsgroups is a collection of nearly 20,000 documents of newsgroup and divided into 20 different newsgroups. It has Web pages categorized into 7 categories namely "Alt", "Computer", "Miscellaneous", "Recreation", "Science", "Social" and "Talk". The dataset has 18,846 documents out of which 7,528 are put into testing set and remaining in training set. Similarly for DMOZ in which Web pages are divided into 14 categories namely "Arts", "Computers", "Business", "Home", "Health", "Games", "News", "Reference", "Recreation", "Regional", "Shopping", "Science", "Sports", "Society". We considered approximately 60,000 Web pages and utilized nearly 30,000 Web pages each for our training and testing set. We first ran our feature selection algorithm on these datasets separately. For the k-means clustering, k was set as 10 (determined by the experiment for which the result is best). For implementing the

---

[3] Iteratively running the script over a range of values of m and finally select that value of m for which the result is best.
[4] http://qwone.com/~jason/20Newsgroups/.
[5] http://www.dmoz.org.

Algorithm 1. Selecting top features of a sub-cluster

Input: Sub-Cluster ($C' = \{c_1, c_2, ..., c_k\}$) generated by traditional k-means algorithm with cosine-similarity values of each keyword
Output: Reduce feature vector (FV) of C'
Keyword_List(KL) $\leftarrow \phi$
$Synonym\_List_w(SL_x) \leftarrow \phi$
$New\_Synonym\_List_x(NSL_x) \leftarrow \phi$
$List\_of\_List(LL) \leftarrow \phi$ //contains the synonyms list of each keyword selected based on their BNS score
$KL \leftarrow$ keywords from all documents $D \in C'$
for all keyword $X \in KL$ (selected based on their BNS score) **do**
  $SL_x \leftarrow$ all the synonyms of X found in Wordnet
  for all keyword $U \in KL$ **do**
    $flag \leftarrow 0$
    if U present in SL_w **then**
      add it to the NSL_x of X and remove from KL
      if $flag = 0$ **then**
        $flag = 1$
      end if
    end if
    if $flag = 1$ **then**
      $KL \leftarrow KL - \{X\}$
    end if
  end for
  $LL \leftarrow LL \cup NSL_x$ //appended the synonym required list of X to LL
  $NSL_x \leftarrow \phi$
end for
for all $NSL_x \in LL$ **do**
  select the top m % keywords K(determined by experiment[3]) having highest cosine-similarity values from NSL_x
  $FV \leftarrow FV \cup K$ //append all the top features into a list
end for
return FV

---

entire approach, python language has been used. A machine with Intel Core 2 Duo Processor, 2.1 GHz, with 64 GB RAM and running Ubuntu 14.04 has been used to execute the algorithms.

Figures 3 and 4 show the average precision, recall, F-Measure and accuracy of different classifiers on the 20-Newsgroups and DMOZ dataset respectively. The number of internal nodes = '2000' set for both ELM and ML-ELM (with number of hidden layers ='3') on 20-Newsgroups dataset which gives us the best results. Similarly, for DMOZ dataset, we set the number of internal nodes = '2500' for both ELM and ML-ELM (with number of hidden layers = '5') to achieve the best results. For demonstration purpose, we have just shown the category wise performance of ELM and ML-ELM for 20-Newsgroups (feature vector length of 1852) in Tables 1 and 2 and for DMOZ dataset (feature vector length of 2260) in

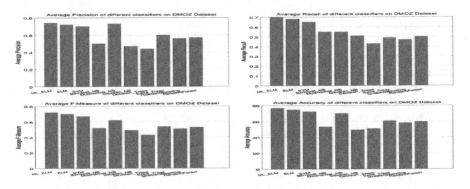

Fig. 3. Average precision, recall, F-measure and accuracy of various classifiers on 20Newsgroups Dataset

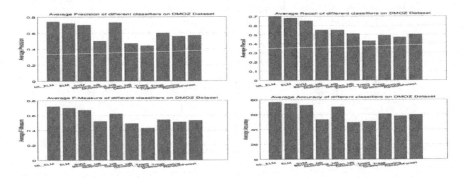

Fig. 4. Average precision, recall, F-measure and accuracy of various classifiers on DMOZ Dataset

Table 1. ELM (20-Newsgroups)

Category	Total testing documents	Precision	Recall	F-measure
Alt	320	0.6201	0.6261	0.6221
Computers	1952	0.8137	0.8444	0.8343
Miscellaneous	390	0.7431	0.7083	0.7243
Recreation	1590	0.7980	0.8189	0.8072
Science	1580	0.7430	0.7059	0.7256
Social	399	0.7610	0.5459	0.6364
Talk	1297	0.7001	0.7499	0.7258
Average	1075	0.7398	0.7142	0.7251

Table 2. ML-ELM (20-Newsgroups)

Category	Total testing documents	Precision	Recall	F-measure
Alt	320	0.6242	0.6224	0.6234
Computers	1952	0.8186	0.8429	0.8344
Miscellaneous	390	0.7769	0.7030	0.7244
Recreation	1590	0.9298	0.8140	0.8680
Science	1580	0.8010	0.7015	0.7456
Social	399	0.6299	0.7635	0.6997
Talk	1297	0.7058	0.7608	0.7268
Average	1075	0.7542	0.7440	0.7460

Tables 3 and 4 respectively. It can be observed from the diagrams that ML-ELM performs the best out of all the traditional classifiers. ML-ELM has an impressive average F-measure and average accuracy of 0.7460 and 79 % on 20-Newsgroups dataset and 0.7195 and 76.7 % on the DMOZ dataset, which signifies that our promising feature selection method works well for both the datasets.

Table 3. ELM (DMOZ)

Category	Total testing documents	Precision	Recall	F-measure
Arts	1396	0.7388	0.6815	0.7090
Business	3384	0.7556	0.7014	0.7275
Computers	1494	0.7434	0.6912	0.7164
Games	5757	0.6914	0.6845	0.6879
Health	1491	0.6958	0.7019	0.6988
Homes	1405	0.7314	0.6855	0.7077
News	1504	0.7411	0.6518	0.6936
Recreation	1410	0.6969	0.7015	0.6992
Reference	1301	0.7015	0.6716	0.6862
Regional	1307	0.7114	0.6515	0.6801
Science	1390	0.7275	0.6610	0.6927
Shopping	6209	0.7281	0.6525	0.6882
Society	1505	0.7445	0.6871	0.7146
Sports	1515	0.7215	0.6659	0.6926
Average	2219	0.7235	0.6778	0.6996

Table 4. ML-ELM (DMOZ)

Category	Total testing documents	Precision	Recall	F-measure
Arts	1396	0.7321	0.6819	0.7061
Business	3384	0.7645	0.6923	0.7266
Computers	1494	0.7115	0.7238	0.7176
Games	5757	0.7662	0.7149	0.7397
Health	1491	0.7550	0.6822	0.7168
Homes	1405	0.7139	0.7237	0.7188
News	1504	0.7425	0.6912	0.7159
Recreation	1410	0.7917	0.6823	0.7329
Reference	1301	0.7239	0.6779	0.7001
Regional	1307	0.7732	0.6645	0.7147
Science	1390	0.7882	0.7012	0.7422
Shopping	6209	0.7121	0.7249	0.7184
Society	1505	0.7312	0.6843	0.7070
Sports	1515	0.7442	0.6898	0.7160
Average	2219	0.7464	0.6954	0.7195

5   Conclusion

This paper proposed a new technique for feature selection using clustering. By using k-means techniques, a number of sub-clusters are generated for a cluster. Checking synonyms using Wordnet and finally selecting important keywords using cosine-similarity helps us to obtained the reduces feature vector. For text classification, ELM and ML-ELM classifiers have been used. We tested our approach on 20-Newsgroups and DMOZ datasets and the results witness the suitability and importance of our approach using ELM and ML-ELM as the classifiers in the field of text classification. This work can be further extended by combining ELM and ML-ELM hidden layer feature space with SVM to improve the results. Also, implementing the proposed approach in a distributed systems using Hadoop can help in load balancing and faster processing.

References

1. Yang, Y., Pedersen, J.O.: A comparative study on feature selection in text categorization. In: ICML, vol. 97, pp. 412–420 (1997)
2. Forman, G.: An extensive empirical study of feature selection metrics for text classification. J. Mach. Learn. Res. **3**, 1289–1305 (2003)
3. Guyon, I., Elisseeff, A.: An introduction to variable and feature selection. J. Mach. Learn. Res. **3**, 1157–1182 (2003)
4. Aggarwal, C.C., Zhai, C.: A survey of text classification algorithms. Mining Text Data, pp. 163–222. Springer, New York (2012)
5. Qiu, X., Huang, X., Liu, Z., Zhou, J.: Hierarchical text classification with latent concepts. In: Proceedings of the 49th Annual Meeting of the Association for Computational Linguistics: Human Language Technologies: short papers, vol. 2. Association for Computational Linguistics, pp. 598–602 (2011)

6. Qiu, X., Zhou, J., Huang, X.: An effective feature selection method for text categorization. In: Huang, J.Z., Cao, L., Srivastava, J. (eds.) PAKDD 2011, Part I. LNCS, vol. 6634, pp. 50–61. Springer, Heidelberg (2011)
7. Sebastiani, F.: Machine learning in automated text categorization. ACM Comput. Surv. (CSUR) **34**(1), 1–47 (2002)
8. Eyheramendy, S., Madigan, D.: A novel feature selection score for text categorization. In: Proceedings of the Workshop on Feature Selection for Data Mining, in conjunction with the 2005 SIAM International Conference on Data Mining, pp. 1–8 (2005)
9. Huang, G.-B., Zhu, Q.-Y., Siew, C.-K.: Extreme learning machine: theory and applications. Neurocomputing **70**(1), 489–501 (2006)
10. Vapnik, V., Golowich, S.E., Smola, A.: Support vector method for function approximation, regression estimation, and signal processing. In: Advances in Neural Information Processing Systems, vol. 9. Citeseer (1996)
11. Hinton, G.E., Salakhutdinov, R.R.: Reducing the dimensionality of data with neural networks. Science **313**(5786), 504–507 (2006)
12. Kasun, H.G.V., Zhou, H.: Representational learning with elms for big data scholarly article. IEEE Intell. Syst. **28**(6), 31–34 (2013)

Language Identification and Disambiguation in Indian Mixed-Script

Bhumika Gupta[1(✉)], Gaurav Bhatt[2], and Ankush Mittal[3]

[1] College of Engineering Roorkee, Roorkee, Uttarakhand, India
bhumikagupta0206@gmail.com
[2] Indian Institute of Technology, Roorkee, Uttarakhand, India
gauravbhatt.coer@gmail.com
[3] Graphic Era University, Dehradun, Uttarakhand, India
director5research@gmail.com

Abstract. The algorithm that has been proposed in this paper tries to segregate words from various languages (namely Hindi, English, Bengali and Gujarati) and provide relevant replacements for the misspelled or unknown words in a given query. Thus, generating a relevant query in which the original language of each word is known. First, the words are matched directly with the dictionaries of each language transliterated into English. And then, for those that do not match, a set of probable words from all the dictionaries taking words that are closest to the given spelling is shortlisted using the Levenshtein algorithm. After this, to achieve a higher level of generalization, we use a list of probabilities of doublets and triplets of words occurring together that are computed from a training database. The probabilities computed further determine the relevance of those words in the given text allowing us to pick the most relevant match.

Keywords: Mixed-script · Transliteration · Similarity matching · Supervised machine learning · Information retreival

1 Introduction

Mixed-script or Macaronism is basically a fusion of two or more languages by phonetic representation of words from these different languages into one script. A huge majority of the population of the world is either bilingual or multilingual. These people use code-mixing (CM) and code-switching (CS) on a regular basis. The main purpose of this amalgamation is to allow people to express and communicate beyond the constraints of one language [1, 2]. Even though the definitions of code-mixing and code-switching are very vague and sometimes overlapping, most people refer to CM as using words from another language while speaking is some other and CS is defined as switching between speeches from two or more languages in one particular conversation. Both the forms of Macaronisms are very common on news, advertising and microblogs currently. For instance, advertisement taglines like, *"yehi hai right choice"* and *"hungry kya?"*. They

© Springer International Publishing Switzerland 2016
N. Bjørner et al. (Eds.): ICDCIT 2016, LNCS 9581, pp. 113–121, 2016.
DOI: 10.1007/978-3-319-28034-9_14

aid as an enhancement to the lucidity of what one is trying to convey and also as a medium to reach a wider audience. This can imply that multilingual queries can help users to ask questions more expressively and also to be able to access a wider source of retrieval.

Previous work in this area mostly focuses on Cross Language Information retrieval (CLIR) which, by definition, is the task of retrieving information in a language, L1, when the query is posed in a language, L2, but may also refer to posing a query in one language when the retrieval can be from documents in multiple languages. A more demanding scenario would be if the query contained more than one script transliterated into one language and the source of retrieval is also in various languages. This was first cited by Gupta et al. [3] as Mixed-Script Information Retrieval (MSIR) and was later followed by introduction of tasks in the field of transliterated search by the Forum for Information Retrieval Evaluation. Bhat et al. in their submission for the FIRE 2014 shared task on transliterated search [4] used an SVM classifier for query word labeling and a letter based language model to determine the probabilities of words for query expansion.

The problem in case of MSIR is that there is no common script to represent all these languages and hence, various forms of transliterations are used. Usually most Indian languages are phonetically represented in English or the Roman script for easier readability. This leads to variations in spellings and a lot of times words are misspelled and might turn out to be unknown to the predefined database.

2   Our Contribution

In an attempt to solve the earlier mentioned issues of misspelled or unknown words in a multilingual environment we tried some combinations of the concepts of LCS, Edit Distance and Naive Bayes applied on the N-Gram Markov model.

Firstly, to find a replacement of the word that turns out to be unknown, in a given query, we used the technique of finding the longest common subsequence of that word with all the English words and the words from other languages transliterated into English. Upon doing this we picked one of the words randomly from those that yielded the longest common subsequence with the unknown word.

This approach did not result in a very relevant match for the word in most cases as more than one word gave the maximum value for the LCS.

As LCS gave very irrelevant matches in a lot of cases, to generate matches that were closer to the entered word, we employed the Levenshtein algorithm. Using the edit distance we were able to generate a list of reasonably more relevant words but the ambiguity still lied in the fact that the minimum edit distance value could also be same for two or more words.

Thus, a combination of Edit Distance and Naive Bayes was used. The method can be broken down into the following set of phases, as shown in Fig. 1:

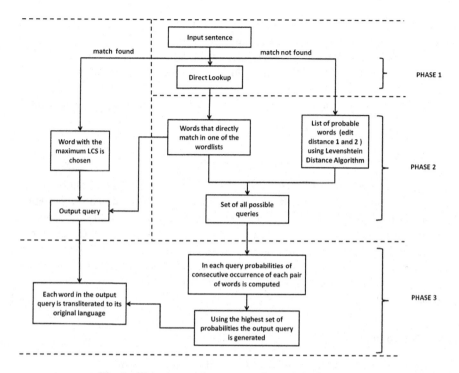

Fig. 1. Flowchart to demonstrate the proposed method

Phase 1: Where we first lookup all the words, from a given query, directly in the dictionaries for all four languages.

Phase 2: For the words that do not match in any of the dictionaries, we first shortlisted the closest matches on the basis of smallest edit distance with the words in the dictionaries.

Phase 3: Then we computed probabilities of these shortlisted words of consecutive occurrence with their neighbors in the original query. The probabilities were computed from a training database of about 5000 queries. This database contains single language English queries from a database provided for the FIRE 2014 FAQ Retrieval task and also, multilingual Hindi-English, Bengali-Hindi-English and Gujarati-Hindi-English queries which were manually translated into mixed transliterated scripts. Now the word picked with the highest probability of occurrence with its neighbors is considerably more relevant.

3   Technique Used

The technique can be used to discern the original language of each word of an input query. The query is written in English transliterations of a combination of one or more languages. The languages we worked with are English, Hindi, Bengali and Gujarati but the technique can be modified to work for any number of languages. The algorithm works for spelling variations and misspelled words with an error of one or two characters but can be modified to check for bigger errors. The limitation of the methodology appears in the case where the word entered occurs in more than one dictionary, for instance, the English word "to" might be present in the Hindi dictionary as well where it represents the English transliteration of the word "तो". In this case the ambiguity might not be resolved.

3.1 Language Identification

The process of identification of the original language starts with a basic lookup approach where each word is looked up in the three lists containing transliterated pairs of Hindi-English, Bengali-English and Gujarati-English words and a fourth list containing English words. For this we create a list of four hash tables and store the transliterated pairs of words in them so that the words from the input queries can be directly matched in these dictionaries. The words that go unmatched are directed to another function which works to determine the most appropriate replacement for it from one of the four word lists for the purpose of disambiguation.

3.2 Disambiguation

For the words that went unidentified in the first lookup based scan:

(a) *LCS:* Longest common subsequence refers to the longest common sequential set of characters between two strings where these characters do not necessarily occur consecutively.
The algorithm is a technique of dynamic programming that uses memorization by maintaining a table for the LCS at each step.
The implementation can be represented by:

$$LCS\left(x_i, y_j\right) = \begin{cases} 0 & \text{if } i = 0 \text{ or } j = 0 \\ LCS\left(x_{i-1}, y_{j-1}\right) & \text{if } x = y \\ Larger\left(LCS\left(x_{i-1}, y_j\right), LCS\left(x_i, y_{j-1}\right)\right) & \text{if } x! = y \end{cases} \tag{1}$$

Where x and y represent the two words whose LCS is being computed and $LCS\left(x_i, y_j\right)$ is the LCS up to the *(i, j)th* position in the LCS table.
An LCS is computed for the ambiguous word and each word from all the four wordlists. The maximum value of LCS is stored and the word corresponding to that value is used as a replacement.
For instance, considering the example illustrated in Fig. 2, it is inferred that LCS might not always give exactly one maximum value.

Input Query:	She	is	cluless	
Phase I(lookup):	/E	/E	/Ukn	
LCS:			**clue**	*LCS = 4*
			clueless	*LCS = 7*

*"clueless" should be picked
because of higher value
of LCS
But, words like*

c**olo**u**rless**	*LCS = 7*
cluele**ss**ness	*LCS = 7*
clo**udless**	*LCS = 7*

also give the same LCS value.

Fig. 2. Illustration for the LCS method

This makes it difficult to choose the most relevant replacement rendering the method highly inaccurate in most cases.

(b) *Using Edit Distance:* As LCS did not result in promising outputs for resolving the ambiguity of the misspelled words, a method involving the Levenshtein algorithm using Edit Distance from the NLTK Library was adopted.
Edit distance is a measure of difference in characters between two strings. It uses character based editing operations like deletion, addition and substitution to measure this difference between the two given strings.
Mathematically represented as,

$$lev\,(i,j) = min \begin{cases} lev\,(i-1,j) + 1 \\ lev\,(i,j-1) + 1 \\ lev\,(i-1,j-1) + 1_{(x_i \neq y_j)} \end{cases} \qquad (2)$$

Where *lev(i, j)* represents the minimum Levenshtein distance between two word *x[1...i]* and *y[1...j]*.
Edit distance is calculated for each word from all the dictionaries with the misspelled word and the word with minimum edit distance is chosen as the replacement.
As shown in Fig. 3, the same edit distance can occur for more than one word. Thus, although Edit distance generates a set of more relevant matches for the ambiguous words compared to the LCS algorithm, it still does not provide us with satisfactorily accurate results.

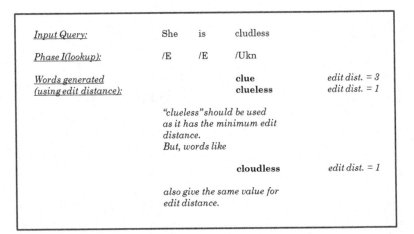

Fig. 3. Illustration for Edit distance method

(c) *Using a combination of Edit distance and Naive Bayes on modified N-gram Markov Model:* To refine the results obtained from the Levenshtein algorithm we train a database containing mixed-script queries using a version of the N-gram Markov model. From this database we compute probabilities of consecutive occurrence of pairs of words and store these probabilities in a hash table. Now, to pick the most relevant result from the list of words generated by the Levenshtein algorithm, we compare the probabilities of occurrence of these words with their neighbors in the input query using the already created hash table. The highest probabilities are given preference to generate the corrected query.

The relation for calculation of probabilities can be represented as:

$$P(x \cap y) = \left[\frac{f(x \text{ and } y) + 1}{f(\text{all words}) + |V| + 1} \right] \tag{3}$$

Where P is the probability of occurrence of two words, x and y, together,
$f(x, y)$ represents the frequency of consecutive occurrence of x and y in the training dataset,
$f(\text{all words})$ is the count of words in the database and V ie vocabulary is the count of unique words.

Now, we consider an example, as shown in Fig. 4, of a medical query that is a blend of English, Hindi and Gujarati scripts transliterated into English language.

The output query is chosen based on the highest probabilities of each pair of words. The resultant query in this case is *"Cosmetic surgery ke baad swelling kam karne ke liye shu karvu chhe"*.

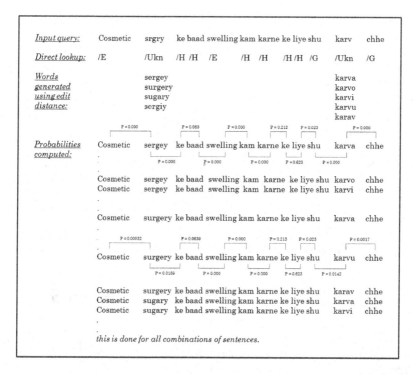

Fig. 4. Illustration for the proposed method which uses Edit Distance and Naïve Bayes theorem implemented on the modified N-Gram Markov model

Each word in the query is then transliterated back to its original language using dictionaries that are created from the dataset containing pairs of transliterated Hindi, Bengali and Gujarati words.

Thus, final result is *"Cosmetic surgery* के बाद *swelling* कम करने के लिए *शुं કરવું છે"*.

4   Experiment and Results

For the application of the proposed methodologies the dataset was taken from FIRE 2015 task on Mixed-Script Information Retrieval. A set of commonly used English words, along with lists of common Hindi, Bengali and Gujarati words along with their English translations was provided under the task.

Now, for the Naïve Bayes applied on the N-Gram model using supervised machine learning a training dataset was created. This contained a set of FAQs that were taken from FIRE 2014 task for FAQ Retrieval. Some of these queries were manually translated into mixed-script. About 1000 queries each of Hindi-English, Bengali-Hindi-English and Gujarati-Hindi-English mixed-script were constructed. The resulting database that was used as the training dataset was a collection of over 5000 mixed-script and single-script queries in domains like medicine and banking.

The model designed on this training dataset using the proposed methodology was tested on a set of 300 random queries. Table 1 demonstrates the output of some of these queries. The method worked flawlessly for most of these queries yielding an accuracy of about 97.6 %. The queries were mostly in the same domain as the training dataset. As a limitation of the relatively small database than the one's usually used to train machine learning algorithms, some words might be unknown and hence even the relevant words might generate a very low probability of occurrence. A wider training database might eradicate this issue.

Table 1. Sample queries with respective output for the proposed method

Input Query	Output Query
Wht are the **smptms** of smallpox	What are the symptoms of smallpox
Back pain ki **sbse** aam wajah **ky** hai	Back pain की सबसे आम वजह क्या है
Asperger syndrome kevi **rte affct kre** chhe	Asperger syndrome કેવી રીતે affect કરે છે
Aami **aamr** debit **crd** keman reactivate **kra skta** hai	আমি আমরা debit card কিভাবে reactivate করা সकता है

5   Conclusion and Future Work

In this paper we addressed the problems of language identification in case of Indian mixed-script queries for the misspelled and ambiguous words. Approaches like the LCS algorithm and Levenshtein distance were tested which, though resolved the problem to some extent, had a lot of limitations and did not work for a wide range of cases. The method stated was, hence, a combination of Levenshtein algorithm and supervised machine learning. The use of Naïve Bayes theorem using the N-Gram model considerably reduced the scope of error and gave a reasonably higher accuracy for maintaining a check on misspelled words.

The method can be improved on using techniques like deep learning and can be trained to work better for the out-of-vocabulary words. Another improvement would be the verification of correct original language for words that are found in more than one dictionary after transliteration into English language. This can be done by tagging words with their original language in the training database.

References

1. Vyas, Y., Gella, S., Sharma, J., Bali, K., Choudhury, M.: POS tagging of English-Hindi code-mixed social media content. In: Proceedings of the EMNLP 2014, pp. 974–979 (2014)
2. Chittaranjan, G., Vyas, Y.: Word-level language identification using CRF: code switching shared task report of MSR india system. In: Proceedings of the EMNLP (2014)
3. Gupta, P., Bali, K., Banchs, R.E., Choudhury, M., Rosso, P.: Query expansion for mixed-script information retrieval. In: Proceedings of the 37th International ACM SIGIR Conference on Research and Development in Information Retrieval (2014)
4. Bhat, I.A., Mujadia, V., Tammewar, A., Bhat, R.A., Shrivastava, M.: IIIT-H system submission for FIRE 2014 shared task on transliterated search. In: Proceedings of the Forum for Information Retrieval Evaluation (2014)
5. King, B., Abney, S.: Labelling the languages of words in mixed-language documents using weakly supervised methods. In: Proceedings of NAACL-HLT (2013)
6. Gupta, P., Rosso, P., Banchs, R.E.: Encoding transliteration variation through dimensionality reduction: FIRE shared task on transliterated search. In: Proceedings of the 5th Forum for Information Retrieval Evaluation (2013)
7. Raghavi, K.C., Chinnakotla, M.K., Shrivastava, M.: Answer ka type kya he? Learning to classify questions in code-mixed language. In: Proceedings of the 24th International Conference on World Wide Web Companion, pp. 853–858. International World Wide Web Conferences Steering Committee (2015)
8. Roy, R.S., Choudhury, M., Majumder, P., Agarwal, K.: Overview and datasets of FIRE 2013 track on transliterated search. In: Proceedings of the 5th Forum for Information Retrieval Evaluation (2013)
9. Marton, Y., Callison-Burch, C., Resnik, P.: Improved statistical machine translation using monolingually-derived paraphrases. In: Proceedings of the 2009 Conference on Empirical Methods in Natural Language Processing, vol. 1, pp. 381–390. Association for Computational Linguistics (2009)
10. Callison-Burch, C., Koehn, P., Osborne, M.: Improved statistical machine translation using paraphrases. In: Proceedings of the Main Conference on Human Language Technology Conference of the North American Chapter of the Association of Computational Linguistics, pp. 17–24. Association for Computational Linguistics (2006)
11. Dolan, B., Quirk, C., Brockett, C.: Unsupervised construction of large paraphrase corpora: exploiting massively parallel news sources. In: Proceedings of the 20th International Conference on Computational Linguistics, p. 350. Association for Computational Linguistics (2004)
12. Gupta, K., Choudhury, M., Bali, K.: Mining Hindi-English transliteration pairs from online Hindi lyrics. In: LREC, pp. 2459–2465 (2012)

A Dynamic Priority Based Scheduling Scheme for Multimedia Streaming Over MANETs to Improve QoS

Syed Jalal Ahmad[1], V.S.K. Reddy[2], A. Damodaram[3],
and P. Radha Krishna[4(✉)]

[1] J B Institute of Engineering and Technology, Hyderabad, India
jalal0000@yahoo.com
[2] Malla Reddy College of Engineering and Technology, Hyderabad, India
vskreddy2003@gmail.com
[3] Jawaharlal Nehru Technological University, Hyderabad, India
damodarama@rediffmail.com
[4] Infosys Labs, Infosys Limited, Hyderabad, India
radhakrishna_p@infosys.com

Abstract. In MANETs, delay and loss of packets need to be reduced in order to provide a good quality of multimedia data transmission over MANETs. To achieve this, we propose a *Priority Based Mapping Method*, which provides priority in the order of I (intra coded), P (predictive coded) and B (bidirectional predictive coded) frame packets. In addition, our approach handles the expiry time of the packets as well as damaged acknowledgement of the packets/frames. We validate our approach through simulations.

Keywords: Virtual buffer · Multimedia · MANET · Video streaming · QoS

1 Introduction

The most important features of Quality of Service (QoS) for multimedia and real time traffic in Mobile Adhoc Networks (MANETs) are delay and loss of packets. For successful communication between a pair of end users, delay should be low and kept within the tolerable limits.

The 802.11e standard [3] guarantees the QoS requirements for multimedia applications by giving differential services at MAC level and improves the performance of physical level in the critical traffic condition. This standard defines *access categories* based on transmission priorities at channel level. However, their approach consider only single multimedia flow. Lee and Chung [2] proposed Scalable Video Coding (SVC) to overcome the drawbacks of 802.11e by providing priorities to the multimedia frame packets. However, these priorities are pre-defined in the field which causes reduction in Packet Delivery Ratio (PDR). This is because, SVC does not pay attention towards the packets whose acknowledgements are damaged or the packets that are not received in a finite order, which results in degradation of QoS. Also Shin et al. [5] proposed a cross line video transmission scheme having three types of video frames:

© Springer International Publishing Switzerland 2016
N. Bjørner et al. (Eds.): ICDCIT 2016, LNCS 9581, pp. 122–126, 2016.
DOI: 10.1007/978-3-319-28034-9_15

Intra coded (**I**), *Predictive coded* (**P**) and *Bidirectional predictive coded* (**B**). The priority of these frames are pre-defined resulting into reduction of QoS as well as increase in the loss of packets. Raji and Kumar [4] presented an approach to provide QoS for multimedia applications. However, their approach do not provide any guarantee if packets are not positively acknowledged at the receiver side.

In this paper, we present a *Priority Based Mapping Method* (**PBMM**), which gives first priority to *I* frame packets, second priority to P frame packets and finally *B* frame packets. Our approach also takes care of expiry time of the packets (i.e., time of *I*, *P* and *B* frame packets). Before the expiry time of any packet, the scheduler send these packets to a buffer (called *Q* buffer in our approach) by using a *switching property* of packets, where these packets are directly go to the next anchoring node. Further, the proposed approach handles the negative acknowledgement of the packets/frames. We used *selective repeat technique* to consider the negative acknowledgement of the packets that are either not received in a proper order or the packets which are damaged due to noise. Thus, the priority of the packets in our approach changes dynamically. The benefits of our approach is two-fold: (i) reduced delay by maintaining the time count of the packets and (ii) reduced loss of packets by controlling the order of packets.

2   PBMM Scheme

Our approach dynamically assigns the priority to the multimedia data packets based on the threshold time of the packet, that is, the *laxity time period* of the packet. Figure 1 shows the proposed buffer architecture for multimedia data packets. In the proposed PBMM scheme, we divide the

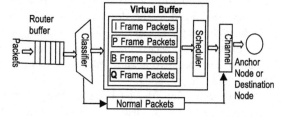

Fig. 1. Architecture of PBMM for multimedia packets

virtual buffer into four sub buffers namely *I, P, B* and *Q* frame buffers. The first three buffers are used for compression of video information. The additional *Q* frame buffer is used to store and forward the packets towards the next anchoring node or destination whose acknowledgements are not yet received positively within the specified time limit due to either congestion or noise during transmission.

Figure 2 depicts the scheduler mechanism for the packets where first priority is given to *I* frame packets, followed by *P* and finally *B* frame packets. This is because loss of I frame packet will have more effect on multimedia applications [6]. On the other hand, if *B* frame packet is lost, it just affects itself. In this work, we introduce a service to forward the packets called *Packet Forwarding Service* (PFS) by keeping an additional field

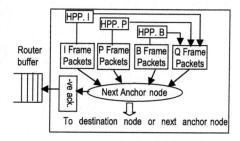

Fig. 2. Scheduler mechanism

in the header. In this scheme, an additional field of 6 bytes is considered as part of the packet header to store the laxity time of the packet and the hop count [2]. Here, *laxity time* is the difference between deadline and current local time. Packets whose time expires after the laxity time limit are directly given to the Q buffer by using a switching technique where they can move towards the destination and can overcome the delay as well as the loss of packets. We call these packets as *High Priority Packets* (HPPs). The HPPs are those packets whose access time is greater than the threshold limit. Such type of packets waste the bandwidth unnecessarily. In the present approach, we assume that a separate threshold is defined for each type of packet.

The Q buffer takes care of the packets, whose acknowledgements are not received positively within the specified time limit, by using a feedback mechanism (see Fig. 2). The incoming packets are first stored in the router buffer as per the scheduler. If the Q buffer is empty, it sends the I frame packets and at the same time checks the *Threshold Limit* of I frame packets T_{LI}. If the threshold limit is less than the laxity time, then it continuously transmits the packets towards destination through the I frame buffer. Suppose any *Packet Time* (P_t) is equal to its laxity time (for instance, laxity time period for voice packet is 150 ms and for video it is 400 ms [2]), then the packet is directly given to the Q buffer, where it will be accessed directly towards the next anchoring node or destination. Similarly, if the threshold of P and B packets, say T_{LP} & T_{LB} respectively, is equal to the laxity limit, such packets will also directly access the Q buffer and can reach to the destination. The buffer Q is further divided into three sub-buffers called Q_I, Q_P and Q_B which access priority wise damaged acknowledgement packets. First it access the negative acknowledged packets of I frame through Q_I sub buffer, next negative acknowledged packets of P frame through Q_P and finally B frame through Q_B.

Our approach differs from the Lee and Chung [2] approach in three ways: (a) we use the virtual buffer at the intermediate node (which is the router in MANETs) to prioritize the packets, (b) we only consider the acknowledgements of those packets which either received out of order or damaged due to noise or any other effect in the network and (c) additional buffer Q is used along with I, P and B frame buffers.

3   Results and Discussion

We used NS-2 Simulator to demonstrate our approach and compared the results with two existing approaches namely SVC [2] and Raji [4]. Figure 3 shows the variation of PDR with simulation time of the source- destination pair. It can be observed that if the source- destination pair is far away (i.e., multiple hops) from each other, as the simulation time increases, the PDR also increases in all the three approaches (i.e., SVC, Raji and our approach). However, our approach

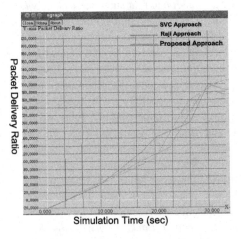

Fig. 3. PDR vs simulation time

produces better results. Initially the PDR of SVC and Raji approaches is better when compared to our approach as it maintains a routing table which leads to an initial overhead. However, after elapse of certain time period, our approach has much higher PDR as we are saving more *I*, *P* and *B* frame packets that are lost in the cases of SVC and Raji approaches.

Figure 4 shows the variation of delay with simulation time for the three approaches. Here, the delay in our approach is less in comparison with the SVC and Raji approaches. This is because, as the number of hops increases, SVC and Raji approaches take more time to sense and access the channel that inturn increases the delay. Also, the results show that if intermediate nodes are busy with other source-destination pairs for communication, still our approach maintains the PDR higher than the existing approaches. We used *location aware and energy efficient routing protocol* [1] to maintain the routing table in the network. Table 1 shows the simulation environment and parameters considered.

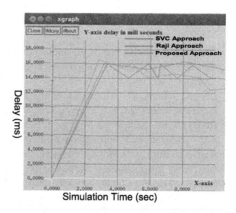

Fig. 4. Delay vs simulation time

Table 1. Simulation values

Network parameters	Values
Simulation time	50 s
No. of nodes	2 to 50
Packet size	512 bytes
Pause time	30 s
MAC type	PBMM
Radio propagation model	Two-ray ground
Queue type	Drop-tail
Antenna	Omni antenna
Routing	LAEERP
Simulation speed	2, 5, 8, 10, 12 m/s
Channel capacity	2 Mbps
Traffic	Video
Network area	1000 m × 1000 m

4   Conclusion

In this paper, we presented a PBMM scheme to improve QoS for multimedia applications in MANETs by exploiting the characteristics of the video frame and the priority of the packets. Unlike the SVC and Raji approaches, our approach guarantee the transmission of all type of packets (i.e. I, P, & B frame packets) without any increase in the delay. Our approach also reorganizes the order of packets according to the time schedule of the packet. The presented approach is very effective for multimedia applications in multi-hop networks.

References

1. Ahmad, S.J., Reddy, V.S.K., Damodaram, A., Krishna, P.R.: Location aware and energy efficient routing protocol for long distance MANETs. Int. J. Netw. Virtual Organ. **13**(4), 327–350
   (2013)
2. Lee, S., Chung, K.: The study of dynamic video frame mapping scheme for multimedia
   streaming over IEEE 802.11e WLAN. Int. J. Multimedia Ubiquit. Eng. **8**(1), 163–174 (2013)
3. Reddy, T.B., John, P.J., Murthy, C.S.R.: Providing MAC QoS for multimedia traffic in
   802.11e based multi hop ad hoc wireless networks. Comput. Netw. **51**(1), 153–176 (2007)
4. Raji, V., Kumar, N.M.: An effective stateless QoS routing for multimedia applications in
   MANETs. Int. J. Wireless Mob. Comput. **7**(5), 456–464 (2014)
5. Shin, P., Lee, S., Chung, K.: A cross-layer based video transmission scheme using efficient
   bandwidth estimation in IEEE 802.11e EDCA. J. KIISE Inf. Netw. **35**(3), 173–182 (2008)
6. Takeuchi, S., Sezaki, K., Yasuda, Y.: Dynamic adaptation of contention window sizes in
   IEEE 802.11e Wireless LAN. In: International Conference on Information, Communications
   and Signal Processing, Bangkok, Thailand (2009)

Improved Bug Localization Technique Using Hybrid Information Retrieval Model

Alpa Gore[1(✉)], Siddharth Dutt Choubey[2], and Kopal Gangrade[2]

[1] Department of Computer Science and Engineering, Shri Ram Institute of Technology,
Jabalpur, Madhya Pradesh, India
`Gore.Alpa@gmail.com`
[2] Department of Information Technology, Shri Ram Institute of Technology,
Jabalpur, Madhya Pradesh, India
`{Siddharth.Choubey,Kopal.Gangrade}@gmail.com`

Abstract. The need of bug localization tools and increased popularity of text based IR models to locate the source code files containing bugs is growing continuously. Time and cost required for fixing bugs can be considerably minimized by improving the techniques of reducing the search space from few thousand source code files to a few files. The main contribution of this paper is to propose a Hybrid model based on two existing IR models (VSM and N-gram) for bug localization. In the proposed hybrid model performance is further improved by using word based bigrams. We have also introduced a weighing factor beta β to calculate the weighted sum of unigram and bigram and analyzed its accuracy for values ranging from (0–1). Using TopN, MRR and MAP measures, we have conducted experiments which show that the proposed hybrid model outperforms some existing state-of-art bug localization techniques.

1 Introduction

Bug fixing is an important activity and improving its performance in terms of time and efforts required, has become a major area of concern. This is the reason that bug fixing techniques have gained special attention for researchers. The steps involved in traditional bug fixing are as follows: 1. Bug reports are received and verified. 2. The developer team locates the buggy source code files to be fixed. 3. The source code files are fixed. The second step is a time consuming activity if done manually. The bug fixing efforts and time can be minimized by using tools to locate the buggy source code files. This process of using tools to locate the buggy source code files is termed as *bug localization*. Previous work done on bug localization using information retrieval techniques are: 1. Lukins et al. in 2010 [3] worked on applying LDA (Latent Dirichlet Allocation) model for bug localization. 2. Rao and Kak [4] in 2011 did a comparative analysis of various IR techniques like Unigram, Latent Semantic Analysis (LSA), VSM, LDA and Cluster. 3. Zhou et al. [5] proposed BugLocator which used sophisticated TF.IDF formulation, length of file factor and similarity among bugs previously fixed. 4. Saha et al. [7] proposed BLUiR and suggested and tested an approach based on concept of using code structural information for information retrieval. 5. Lal and Sureka [6] proposed and

N. Bjørner et al. (Eds.): ICDCIT 2016, LNCS 9581, pp. 127–131, 2016.
DOI: 10.1007/978-3-319-28034-9_16

tested hypothesis of applying the concepts of character based n-gram to achieve bug localization.

2 Architecture of Hybrid Model

In Vector Space Model (VSM) vector value is calculated based on token frequency *tf* and inverse document frequency *idf* of each token [2]. One of the disadvantages of VSM is that it does not include term dependencies into the model, for instance for modeling phrases or adjacent terms. Using N-gram model Song and Croft [1] proposed the use of statistical language model approximated by N-gram models in information retrieval. Unigram model assumes that each word occurs independently. The bigram model takes the local context into consideration. The proposed hybrid model captures the relevance of adjacent terms by using bigrams model and calculating bigram based vectors.

2.1 Overview of Proposed Approach

We propose a hybrid model that uses word based N-gram model [1] in conjunction with VSM model [4]. The proposed hybrid model along with single terms (unigrams) also performs indexing for bigrams. A weighing factor **beta** (β) ($0 \leq \beta \leq 1$) is used to combine scores from both unigram and bigram terms and then final ranking of documents is done. The data set used for experiment is SWT(v3.1), AspectJ and Eclipse(v3.1) (Table 3) which is a subset of the data set used by BugLocator and the comparative study of the result is done. TopN, MRR (Mean Reciprocal Rank) and MAP (Mean Average Precison) is used as evaluation matrix. Figure 1 shows the architecture of the proposed hybrid model. Improvement in the performance of bug localization is based on utilizing semantic similarity by applying statistical language model like N-gram Model. TF.IDF model is used for indexing and calculating scores. We have used rVSM proposed by Zhou et al. [5] for length normalization, TF.IDF and final score calculations.

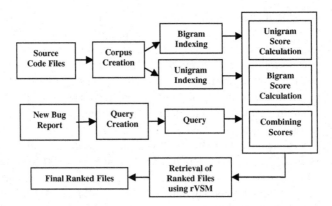

Fig. 1. Overall architecture of the new hybrid approach using unigram and Bigram scores

Every bug report is a search query and is matched against each source code to calculate scores. In the proposed hybrid approach we calculate uScore (from Unigram Vector)

and bScore (from Bigram Vector) using rVSM [5]. After calculating uScore and bScore for each file we combine the two scores by calculating weighed sum of the two using the following:

$$\text{fScore} = \text{uScore} \times (1 - \beta) + \text{bScore} \times \beta \qquad (1)$$

where β is a weighing factor and $(0 \leq \beta \leq 1)$. The fScore is the final score and is weighted sum of uScore and bScore. The source code files are ranked using fScore and the Final-Rank is returned to the user.

3 Experimental Result

We have evaluated the value of MRR (Mean Reciprocal Rank) measure for various values of β (in range 0 to 1) which is shown in Table 1 to establish optimum value of β for each dataset. The comparative analysis of performance of our proposed hybrid approach with respect to Classical VSM and rVSM [5] on Top1, Top5, Top10, MRR and MAP measures is shown in Tables 2 and 3, Fig. 2.

Table 1. Value of MRR for SWT, AspectJ and Eclipse datasets for β range (0 to 1)

$\beta \rightarrow$	0.0	0.1	0.2	0.3	0.4	0.5	0.6	0.7	0.8	0.9	1.0
SWT	0.532	0.533	0.530	0.531	0.550	**0.553**	0.540	0.544	0.506	0.489	0.346
AspectJ	0.347	0.351	0.352	**0.353**	0.347	0.343	0.336	0.318	0.294	0.262	0.212
Eclipse	0.300	0.322	0.336	**0.381**	0.343	0.336	0.324	0.306	0.284	0.265	0.241

Table 2. Comparative analysis of MRR for rVSM and Hybrid model for benchmark dataset

Model	SWT	AspectJ	Eclipse
rVSM	0.47	0.33	0.35
Hybrid	0.553 ($\beta = 0.5$)	0.353 ($\beta = 0.3$)	0.381 ($\beta = 0.3$)

Table 3. Details of Benhmark Datasets

Project	#Bugs	#Files
SWT (v3.1)	98	484
AspectJ	286	6485
Eclipse (v3.1)	3075	12863

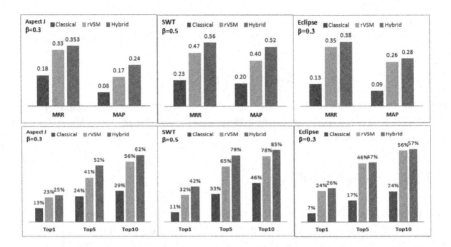

Fig. 2. Comparative analysis of Top1, Top5 and Top10, MAP and MRR for Classical, rVSM and Hybrid Model for data set SWT, AspectJ and Eclipse

4   Conclusion and Future Work

The experiment results from Table 1 show that optimum performance is achieved at $\beta = 0.5$, $\beta = 0.3$ and $\beta = 0.3$ for benchmark datasets SWT, AspectJ and Eclipse respectively. Also the proposed hybrid model shows consistent performance improvements on all the three TopN, MRR and MAP measures when compared with Classical and rVSM techniques. The future work will be focused on testing hybrid model on preprocessed large data sets.

References

1. Song, F., Croft, B.: A general language model for information retrieval. In: Proceedings of the 1999 ACM SIGIR Conference on Research and Development in Information Retrieval (1999)
2. Manning, C.D., Raghavan, P., Schütze, H.: Introduction to Information Retrieval. Cambridge University Press, Cambridge (2008)
3. Lukins, S., Kraft, N., Etzkorn, L.: Bug localization using latent Dirichlet allocation. Inf. Softw. Technol. **52**(9), 972–990 (2010)
4. Rao, S., Kak, A.: Retrieval from software libraries for bug localization: a comparative study of generic and composite text models. In: Proceeding of the 8th Working Conference on Mining Software Repositories (MSR 2011), pp.43–52. ACM, Waikiki, Honolulu, Hawaii (May 2011)
5. Zhou, J., Zhang, H., Lo, D.: Where should the bugs be fixed? - more accurate information retrieval-based bug localization based on bug reports. In: Proceedings of the 2012 International Conference on Software Engineering, ICSE 2012, pp. 14–24. IEEE Press, Piscataway, NJ, USA (2012)

6. Lal, S., Sureka, A.: A static technique for fault localization using character n-gram based information retrieval model. In: Proceedings of ISEC 2012, Kanpur, UP, India (22–25 February 2012)
7. Saha, R.K., Lease, M., Khurshid, S., Perry, D.E.: Improving bug localization using structured information retrieval. In: Proceedings of ASE, pp. 345–355, Heidelberg, New York (2013)

HGASA: An Efficient Hybrid Technique for Optimizing Data Access in Dynamic Data Grid

R. Kingsy Grace[1]([✉]) and R. Manimegalai[2]

[1] Sri Ramakrishna Engineering College, Coimbatore, India
kingsygrace.r@srec.ac.in
[2] Park College of Technology, Coimbatore, India
mmegalai@yahoo.com

Abstract. Grid computing uses computers that are distributed across various geographical locations in order to provide enormous computing power and massive storage. Scientific applications produce large quantity of sharable data which requires efficient handling and management. Replica selection is one of the data management techniques in grid computing and is used for selecting data from large volumes of distributed data. Replica selection is an interesting data access problem in data grid. Genetic Algorithms (GA) and Simulated Annealing (SA) are two popularly used evolutionary algorithms which are different in nature. In this paper, a hybrid approach which combines Genetic Algorithm with Simulated Annealing, namely, HGASA, is proposed to solve replica selection problem in data grid. The proposed algorithm, HGASA, considers security, availability of file, load balance and response time to improve the performance of the grid. GridSim simulator is used for evaluating the performance of the proposed algorithm. The results show that the proposed algorithm, HGASA, outperforms Genetic Algorithms (GA) by 9 % and Simulated Annealing (SA) by 21 % and Ant Colony Optimization (ACO) by 50 %.

Keywords: Replica selection · Data grid · Computational grid · Genetic algorithm · Simulated annealing

1 Introduction

The two major categories of grid computing [1] are: (i) Computational grid and (ii) Data grid. Computational grid is mainly used for compute intensive applications and data grid is an infrastructure for storing and sharing large volumes of data, for data intensive applications Data replication in data grid reduces the access latency in distributed systems by keeping multiple copies of the data file in geographically distributed sites [2]. In a data grid system, there are hundreds of clients across the globe submitting job requests. Usually, a grid job accesses multiple files for its job execution. In data-intensive applications, when a job accesses large file, the unavailability of that file can cause the whole job to hang up. Any node or network failure causes file unavailability. As a result, there has been an increasing research interest focusing on how to maximize the file availability. Data replication reduces the access latency in distributed systems by

© Springer International Publishing Switzerland 2016
N. Bjørner et al. (Eds.): ICDCIT 2016, LNCS 9581, pp. 132–136, 2016.
DOI: 10.1007/978-3-319-28034-9_17

keeping multiple copies of the data file in geographically distributed sites [2]. Each grid site has its own capabilities and characteristics; therefore, selecting one particular site which has the required data among many such sites, is an important and significant decision [3]. The replica selection problem has been investigated by many researchers and only response time is considered as a criterion for the selection process. In this work, the replica selection problem is addressed as an important decision to guarantee efficiency and to ensure the satisfaction of the grid users by providing replicas with reduced latency and improved security. The main contribution of this work is to produce an alternative solution to the replica selection problem based on response time, availability, security and load balancing. This work extends the replica selection using genetic algorithm [4] by employing hybrid approach. The proposed replica selection algorithm is based on both genetic algorithm and simulated annealing and is called as Hybrid of Genetic Algorithm and Simulated Annealing (HGASA). HGASA is implemented using GridSim 5.1 simulation toolkit [5]. Performance of the proposed HGASA approach is compared with Genetic Algorithm (GA), Ant Colony Optimization (ACO) algorithm, Simulated Annealing (SA) in terms of TASL (Response Time, Availability, Security and Load Balancing) value [4].

2 Related Work

Replica selection is one of the important tasks of data management in data intensive application. It decides which replica location is the best place to access the data for users. If several replicas are available for a file, the optimization algorithm determines which replica should be selected to execute the job. Lin et al. have proposed a Network Coordinate (NC) based nearest replica selection service called Rigel in [6]. Tim and Ambramson have proposed GriddLeS Data Replication Service (GRS) which provides limited support for automatic replica selection in [3]. Naseera and Murthy have proposed predictive replica selection using neural networks [7] based on [8]. Ishii and Mello have proposed a solution for Data Access Problem (DAP) in [9]. It is a prediction based optimization approach. Sun et al. have proposed an Ant Colony Optimization (ACO) algorithm for replica selection in [10]. It reduces data access latency, decreases bandwidth consumption and distributes the load evenly. Jadaan et al. have proposed a rank based elitist clustering genetic algorithm for replica selection in data grid [4].

3 HGASA: Hybrid of Genetic Algorithm and Simulated Annealing for Replica Selection

Genetic Algorithm (GA) was introduced by J. Holland in 1975 [11] and had been used for solving searching, learning and optimization problems. GA is a global search technique which is based on the mechanism of biological evolution inspired by Darwin's theory of evolution [12]. GA consists of two types of operations, namely, mutation and crossover. These operations are repeatedly applied to a population of chromosomes for obtaining a possible solution for the given search space. Simulated Annealing (SA) is a heuristic optimization algorithm [13] and is analogous to annealing in metals and solids.

SA was first introduced by Metropolis et al. in [14]. The idea in Metropolis et al. is used by Kirkpatrick et al. in [13] to search for an optimal solution in optimization problems. Combining GA which is a global search technique with SA which is a local search technique gives the benefit of both, at the same time avoids problems such as premature convergence and local optimum [15]. In the proposed replica selection architecture, if a user requests for a replica, the replica selection algorithm gets all information regarding the replica from the Replica Location Service (RLS) [16]. The best replica location site is selected based on four parameters: response time, availability, security and load balancing. The network related information such as bandwidth is gathered with the help of Network Weather Service (NWS). A hybrid evolutionary algorithm, HGASA, which employs both Genetic Algorithm (GA) and Simulated Annealing (SA), is proposed in this work. TASL values are used to compare the performance of the proposed algorithm with the existing algorithms. During GA implementation, a Model Replica (MR) [4] is set with maximum (100 %) of response Time T, Availability A, Security S and Load balancing L. i.e. MR (T, A, S, L) = (100, 100, 100, 100). The distance between MR and the available replica is computed using the Eq. (1). T_1, A_1, S_1 and L_1 are the TASL values of MR and T_0, A_0, S_0 and L_0 are the TASL values of available replica.

$$TASL = \sqrt{((T_1 - T_0) + (S_1 - S_0)^2 + (A_1 - A_0)^2 + (L_1 - L_0))} \qquad (1)$$

The replicas that are closer to MR are grouped to form a cluster. The replica with the shortest distance from the MR is selected as the best replica. The cluster metric, M, is calculated as in [4]. The implementation parameters for the proposed algorithm, HGASA are initial population is 50, mutation probability is 0.9, crossover probability is 0.1, initial temperature is 10000 and cooling rate is 0.9. The implementation of HGASA algorithm for replica selection problem is shown in Algorithm 1.

4   Experimental Results

The ACO, GA, SA and HGASA algorithms are implemented using Intel CORE i5 processor and simulated in GridSim toolkit [5] for selecting best replica location. The number of sites in the grid network will be defined by the user and with varying performance in time, availability, security and load balancing. The number of grid sites is twenty in the simulation of existing and proposed algorithms. The performance of the ACO, GA, SA and HGASA are calculated for two different scenarios such as 10 user requests and 25 user requests. The efficiency is calculated using the Formula in [4]. GA is 44 % more efficient than ACO algorithm for selecting replica in data grid. HGASA shows 21 %, 9 % and 50 % more improvement in efficiency when compared to SA, GA and ACO respectively. When two or more sites have the best possible performance in terms of response time, security, availability and load balancing which are equal in proportional value but vary in the order, then randomly one among them is selected for creating the replica. All the factors are equally considered and one factor is not preferred over the other during replication. The response time, security, availability and load balancing for all the twenty sites are generated randomly from 75 to 95.

Algorithm HGASA ()
{
1. Input all necessary Parameters
2. Generate Initial Population
3. Generate Initial Temperature to all the individuals
4. Calculate the fitness of all the chromosomes
5. Select a random node as parent node
6. Perform crossover with some other node satisfying fitness function
7. Check the fitness probability of the child chromosome [17]
8. Apply mutation operation
9. Calculate the fitness function of the new population [4]
10. Set T[i]=T[i]*Cooling Rate
11. If the child's fitness is better than the parent, the child replaces the parent
12. Repeat steps 5-11 until termination condition is met
}

Algorithm 1: HGASA

5 Conclusion

HGASA based Replica Selection in Data Grid improves the efficiency of selecting the best replica site for user requests during job execution. The efficiency is improved by increasing the number of parameters such as response time, availability of the file, security and load balancing. The efficiency of the HGASA algorithm is compared with GA, SA and ACO. ACO algorithm does not deal with availability, security and load balancing, and therefore not efficient when compared to genetic algorithm, simulated annealing and HGASA. The efficiency of genetic algorithm and simulated annealing is 44 % and 36 % greater than ACO algorithm. The proposed algorithm, HGASA, performs better than all the three algorithms, namely, GA, SA and ACO by 9 %, 21 % and 50 % respectively. The efficiency can be improved further by considering other parameters such as bandwidth, scheduling strategies, access pattern that are important for job execution.

Acknowledgements. The authors would like to thank the Management & Principal of Sri Ramakrishna Engineering College, and the Head of the Department of Computer Science and Engineering, for their support in completing this work.

References

1. Foster, I., Kesselman, C.: The Grid: Blueprint for a New Computing Infrastructure. Morgan Kaufmann, San Francisco (1999)
2. Khanli, L.M., Isazadeh, A., Shishavan, T.N.: PHFS: a dynamic replication method, to decrease access latency in the multi-tier data grid. Future Gener. Comput. Syst. **27**(3), 233–244 (2011)

3. Tim, H., Abramson, D.: The griddles data replication service. In: Proceedings of the 1st International Conference on E-Science and Grid Computing, pp. 271–278 (2005)
4. Jadaan, O.A., Abdulal, W., Hameed, M.A.: Enhancing data selection using genetic algorithm. In: Proceedings of IEEE International Conference on Computational Intelligence and Communication Networks, pp. 434–439 (2010)
5. Buyya, R., Murshed, M.: GridSim: A toolkit for the modeling and simulation of distributed resource management and scheduling for grid computing. J. Concurrency Comput. Pract. Experience **14**, 1175–1220 (2002)
6. Lin, Y., Chen, Y., Wang, G., Deng, B.: Rigel: a scalable and lightweight replica selection service for replicated distributed file system. In: 10th IEEE/ACM International Conference on Cluster, Cloud and Grid Computing, CCGC, pp. 581–582 (2010)
7. Naseera, S., Murthy, K.V.M.: Performance evaluation of predictive replica selection using neural network approaches. In: Proceedings of International Conference on Intelligent Agent and Multi-Agent Systems, IAMA 2009, p. 1 (2009)
8. Rahman, R.M., Baker, K., Alhajj, E.: A predictive technique for replica selection in grid environment. In: Seventh IEEE International Symposium on Cluster Computing and the Grid, pp. 163–170 (2007)
9. Ishii, R.P., De Mello, R.F.: An online data access prediction and optimization approach for distributed systems. IEEE Trans. Parallel Distrib. Syst. **23**(6), 1017–1029 (2012)
10. Sun, M., Sun, J., Lu, E., Yu, C.: Ant algorithm for file replica selection in data grid. In: Proceedings of First International Conference on Semantics, Knowledge and Grid, p. 64 (2005)
11. Holland, J.: Adaptation in Natural Artificial Systems. University of Michigan Press, Ann Arbor (1992)
12. Olivas, E.S., Guerrero, J.D., Martinez-Sober, M., Magdalena-Benedito, J.R., Serrano Lopez, A.J.: Handbook of Research on Machine Learning Applications and Trends: Algorithms, Methods, and Techniques. IGI Global, Hershey (2010). doi:10.4018/978-1-60566-766-9
13. Kirkpatrick, S., Gelatt, C., Vecchi, M.: Optimization by simulated annealing. Science **220**, 671–680 (1983)
14. Metropolis, N., Rosenbluth, A.W., Rosenbluth, M.N., Teller, A.H., Teller, E.: Equation of state calculation by fast computing machines. J. Chem. Phys. **21**(1087), 1087–1091 (1953)
15. Yoshikawa, M., Yamauchi, H., Terai, H.: Hybrid architecture of genetic algorithm and simulated annealing. Eng. Lett. **16**(3), EL_16_3_11 (2012)
16. Chervenak, A., Schuler, R., Ripeanu, M., Amer, M.A., Bharathi, S., Foster, I., Kesselman, C.: The globus replica location service: design and experience. IEEE Trans. Parallel Distrib. Syst. **20**(9), 1260–1272 (2009)
17. Gandomkar, M., Vakilian, M., Ehsan, M.: A combination of genetic algorithm and simulated annealing for optimal DG allocation in distribution networks. In: Proceedings of Canadian Conference on Electrical and Computer Engineering, pp. 645–648 (2005)

Energy Efficient SNR Based Clustering in Underwater Sensor Network with Data Encryption

Sahu Bandita[1] [✉] and Khilar Pabitra Mohan[2]

[1] Padmanava College of Engineering, Rourkela, India
bandita.sahu@gmail.com
[2] National Institute of Technology, Rourkela, India

Abstract. In Under Water Sensor Network (UWSN), design of clustering protocol is challenging due to the energy constrained sensor nodes. Therefore, energy saving is considered to be an important issue. In this paper, a new clustering protocol is proposed which is named as energy efficient SNR based clustering in UWSN with Data Encryption (EESCDE). Using this, one percent improvement in the residual energy as compared to the algorithm ESRPSDC is achieved.

Keywords: Signal-to-noise ratio · Cluster head · Data encryption · Residual energy

1 Introduction

In UWSN, number of sensing devices are used and called as sensor nodes [1–3]. These nodes are responsible for gathering, processing and transmitting the data to the specified sensor node. A large number of applications are enabled by UWSN such as monitoring the environmental condition for scientific application, navigation assistance, oil monitoring, disaster prevention and many more. Underwater Sensor Networks (UWSN) [4] use acoustics signal as its communication media [2] as propagation delay of the acoustic signal is 1500 m/s that is higher than that of the radio signal.

The proposed protocol is used for UWSN for short term application to monitor the underwater environment and improve the residual energy.

2 Related Work

Several clustering [7] techniques have already been developed. Table 1 describes various protocols and their applications.

In UWSN model, a UWSN [4] is modeled as a graph G= (V, E) where, set of vertices V= $V_1, V_2, V_3, ...V_n$ and set of edges E= $E_1, E_2, E_3, ...E_M$. If a data d comes under the sensing range r of a sensor node S_i, the data d can be

© Springer International Publishing Switzerland 2016
N. Bjørner et al. (Eds.): ICDCIT 2016, LNCS 9581, pp. 137–141, 2016.
DOI: 10.1007/978-3-319-28034-9_18

Table 1. Protocol Comparison

Protocol	Base Concept	Energy Utilization	Designed for	Hop	Communication	Phases	Application	Environment
LEACH [6]	distributed clustering	mode-rate	homogeneous	single	CH	set up and steady phase	Continuous monitoring	TWSN
HEED [7]	periodic CH selection	less	heterogeneous	single	CH	initialization, setup, and steady	environmental monitoring	TWSN
PEGASIS [8]	chain based,transmission through neighbor nodes	less	homogeneous	multi	leader	chain formation and broadcasting	disaster management	TWSN
PEACH [9]	overhearing	mode-rate	homogeneous	multi	CH	Cluster formation and data transmission	automation, robot control	TWSN
ESRP [4]	SNR based CH selection	less	homogeneous	multi	CH	Initialization, CH selection,data transmission	environmental monitoring	TWSN
PROPOSED	SNR based CH selection	very less	homogeneous	multi	CH	initialization, CH selection,data encryption, and data transmission	disaster management, submarine detection	TWSN UWSN

sensed. Similarly a node S_i can communicate with another sensor node S_j, if and only if, the $distance(S_i, S_j) <= c(communication range)$.

Energy and Data model includes different types of consumed energy.

The parameter b1 is the total packet size of a cluster, which can be obtained as, $b1 = b * number\ of\ sensor\ nodes\ in\ that\ cluster$.

3 Proposed Algorithm

It consists of four phases such as: Initialization phase, CH selection phase, Data encryption phase, and Data transmission phase. In initialization phase, nodes are deployed, assigned with some identification, and parameters are initialized.

```
Algorithm: Data Encryption
1: for i = 1 → n do
2:     Sensor nodes sense data
3:     if (node[i].energy >0) then
4:         if ((node[i].energy >energyThreshold) && (
           node[i].clusterindex==-1) ) then
5:             Assumed to be a CH,Performs CH functions
6:             node[i].energy − node[i].energy - node[i].cEnergy
7:         else Assumed to be a NCH,Performs NCH function
8:             node[i].energy = node[i].energy - node[i].cEnergy
9:         i=i+1
10:    Node dies
```

```
Algorithm: Cluster Head Selection
1: Set clusterindex = 0
2: for i = 1 → n do
3:     Compute Euclidian distance from the BS
4:     node[i].SNR = SL-TL-P_noise
5:     i=i+1
6: for j = 1 → n do
7:     Select and remove the Highest SNR value
8:     Store it in remove list.
9:     for numclust = 0 → k do
10:        if ((node[j].energy > energyThreshold) &&
          (node[i].clusterindex==0)) then
11:            node[i].clusterindex=-1
12:            numclust += 1
13:        i=i+1
```

In the second phase, the variables numclust and clusterindex are initialized to zero. Depending on the computed euclidean distance of nodes with respect to BS, SNR value [4] is obtained. The SNR value is computed as the difference between the received power signal and noise power in DB.

Data encryption phase performs encryption by applying the Hill Cipher [10]. So as to encrypt a block of data at a time,it is useful. The cryptanalysis of this type of cipher is difficult because the key size is an m × m matrix. Each entry in the matrix can have values between 1 to 1499 (the chosen prime number). As the size of the key domain became $1499^{m \times m}$, the brute-force attack is extremely difficult. The cryptanalysis of the known-plain text is also not so easy. As the key matrix is not transmitted, man in middle attack is not possible. If the residual energy of the CH becomes less than the threshold value, then that node cannot act as a CH for further transmission.

In data transmission phase, transmission process starts after the cluster [5] is created and the TDMA scheduled is derived. To avoid the replay attack, a nonce is provided by the CH. If the hashed value of on both side CH and NCH is matched,data transmission process is initiated.

4   Simulation and Results

In this section, we have evaluated the proposed model using network simulator NS3. In a 100 m × 100 m planar square region, 50 sensor nodes are deployed randomly (Table 2).

Table 2. Simulation Parameters

Parameter	Value	Parameter	Value
Packet size	2 Kb	Topology	Random
Sensor nodes type	Passive omnidirectional	Number of cluster	5
Threshold energy	1.5 j	Initial energy	2.4 j
Initial battery power	3.3 volt	Depth	4 m
Transmission power	2 w	Frequency	2.4 GHz
Data rate	6 Kbps	Communication range	20 m

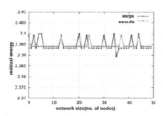

Fig. 1. Comparison of network size vs residual energy

Figure 1 shows the energy utilization on increasing the network size. Figure 2 describes that on increasing message complexity the no transmission also increases, and the residual energy decreases. It is observed in Fig. 3 that this protocol is well suited for UWSN as compared to TWSN. Figure 4 shows the comparison of TL of the protocols esrps and eescde. In Fig. 5 the position of the CHs are compared in UWSN and Terrestrial WSN.

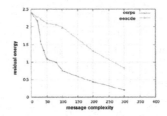

Fig. 2. Comparison of message complexity vs residual energy

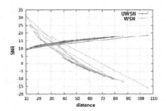

Fig. 3. Comparison of SNR vs distance

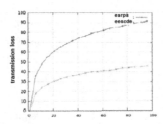

Fig. 4. Comparison of transmission loss vs distance

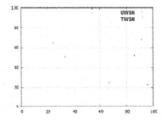

Fig. 5. Comparison of CH position in a 100 × 100 grid of UWSN and TWSN

5   Conclusion

This cluster model is an energy-based model, which has been developed and simulated using the Network simulator NS3. Using this protocol, 1 percent improvement in residual energy has been achieved.

References

1. Abbasi, A.A., Younis, M.: A Survey on Clustering Algorithms for Wireless Sensor Networks Computer Communications. Elsevier, New York (2007)
2. Akyildiz, I., Pompili, D., Melodia, T.: Challenges for efficient communication in underwater acoustic sensor networks. ACM Sigbed Rev. **1**, 3–8 (2004)
3. Akyildiz, I.F., Pompili, D., Melodia, T.: Underwater acoustic sensor networks: research challenges. Ad hoc Netw. **3**, 257–279 (2005)
4. Ganesh, S., Amutha, R.: Efficient and secure routing protocol for wireless sensor networks through snr based dynamic clustering mechanisms. J. Commun. Netw. **15**, 422–429 (2013). Ad hoc and sensor networks, wireless networks, 2007 - Springer
5. Li, L., Dong, S., Wenl, X.: An energy efficient clustering routing algorithm for wireless sensor networks. J. China Univ. Posts Telecommun. **13**, 71–75 (2006)
6. Handy, M.J., Marc, H., Dirk, T.: Low energy adaptive clustering hierarchy with deterministic cluster-head selection. In: 4th International Workshop on Mobile and Wireless Communications Network. IEEE (2002)
7. Chen, G., Li, C., Ye, M., Jie, W.: An unequal cluster-based routing protocol in wireless sensor networks. Wireless Netw. **15**(2), 193–207 (2009)
8. Lindsey, S., Cauligi, S.R.: PEGASIS: power-efficient gathering in sensor information systems. In: Aerospace Conference Proceedings, vol. 3. IEEE (2002)
9. Yi, S., et al.: PEACH: power-efficient and adaptive clustering hierarchy protocol for wireless sensor networks. Computer Commun. **30**(14), 2842–2852 (2007)
10. Toorani, M., Abolfazl, F.: A secure variant of the hill cipher. In: IEEE Symposium on Computers and Communications, ISCC 2009. IEEE (2009)

Collaborative Access Control Mechanism for Online Social Networks

Nemi Chandra Rathore[✉], Prashant Shaw, and Somanath Tripathy

Department of Computer Science and Engineering,
Indian Institute of Technology, Patna, India
{nemi,prashant.cs11,som}@iitp.ac.in

Abstract. Online Social Networks (OSNs) offer an attractive mean for digital social interactions and information sharing among the users. At the same time, it raises a number of security and privacy issues. Especially, there is no efficient mechanism to enforce privacy over data associated with multiple users. This paper proposes a privacy preserving mechanism to allow the users to control access of their shared resources in a collaborative manner. We have developed a Facebook application "msecure" and made a 'survey based user study' of the app with a user base of ($n = 50$). The results of the study reveals popularity of it among users. The study indicates that users are still concerned about the privacy of their shared contents and they believe that a tool like "msecure" could be useful for managing their shared images and other shared contents.

Keywords: Privacy · Multi-party resources · Trust · Stakeholders

1 Introduction

Emergence of Online Social Network (OSN) is a major technological phenomenon seen in recent years that has united millions of people across the globe. OSNs are web based platforms that offer various types of information sharing services to their users. These services are designed to enable peoples to share their personal and public information with their family, friends, colleagues and even strangers [10]. Some of the giant OSNs are Facebook, Twitter, Google+. Facebook, itself claims 1.49 billion monthly active users [6].

Almost all social networks allow their users to have a personal profile containing personal attributes. Through OSNs users interact with each other for variety of purposes. During interactions, users share large volume of information in form of posts, comments, pictures, videos and many more. Many times, these contents reveal sensitive and personal information about the users or their friends. It results in potential risk to their privacy. Moreover, the users are often either unable to figure out or unaware about the audience that can access their resources. The situation becomes worse when the resource is shared among multiple users (i.e. multi-party resources) who may have different access preferences. For addressing these critical issues, existing OSNs allow the user to set the target audience for the data items exclusively owned by him. For the data items

© Springer International Publishing Switzerland 2016
N. Bjørner et al. (Eds.): ICDCIT 2016, LNCS 9581, pp. 142–147, 2016.
DOI: 10.1007/978-3-319-28034-9_19

belonging to more than one user, OSNs offer privacy protection mechanisms that are either too loose or too restrictive. So, there is a need for an effective and flexible multi-party access control mechanism where all the stakeholders can specify their own access preferences collaboratively.

A number of relationship-based access control models have been proposed to protect privacy of OSN users in [2–4,7,9]. These models exploit relationships between users and resources, to control the access of user data. Unfortunately, none of these solutions address the problem of controlling the access of multi-party resources. Recently, different solutions for multi-party access control have been proposed [1,8,10]. The limitations of these solutions include the inflexibility and user-unfriendliness. Also, these models ignore the trust level between controllers of the content and its requester which is the important parameter taken into consideration in real life, while sharing sensitive content with others.

In this paper, we propose a *collaborative access control model* (CACM) to control the access of multi-party contents that considers the level of trust each stakeholder of the resource have on the requesting user. We also have developed a prototype application for Facebook to show its effectiveness.

The organization of the paper is as follows. Section 2, describes the proposed collaborative access control mechanism (CACM). Section 3 provides details about implementation and evaluation of the mechanism in the form of an app named as *msecure*. The survey study and results are discussed in Subsect. 3.1 to understand the popularity this tools. Section 4 concludes the work.

2   System Model and the Proposed Mechanism

2.1   System Model

OSN is a relationship network with a set of user groups and data items. Let $\mathcal{L}$ be the finite set of labels representing the relationships supported by OSN. $\mathcal{D}$ is the set of all the *data items/resources/contents*[1] uploaded to OSN by the users. The relationship network of OSN can be represented as a directed labeled graph, $G = (V, E)$, where a node $v \in V$ denotes a user and each directed edge $e \in E$ represents the relationship between two users. Formally, an edge $(v_i, v_j) \in E$ labeled with $l \in \mathcal{L}$ is represented by a 4-tuple, (v_i, v_j, l, t), where $0 \leq t \leq 100$ represents trust of v_i for v_j. Every OSN user $v \in V$ have a set of data items $\mathcal{D}_v$. These resources can be classified in two classes namingly *exclusive* resources and *multi-party* resources. A data item $d \in \mathcal{D}_v$ owned by more than one user is called multi-party resource, otherwise, it is referred as exclusive or single-party resource.

2.2   Collaborative Access Control Mechanism (CACM)

The major objective of our proposed technique CACM is to preserve privacy suitably, for the contents of multiple stakeholders. Collaborative policy specification is the primary component of CACM that uses user trust discussed in this section. Following terms are used to describe CACM.

---

[1] In this paper, we use the terms resource, content and data item as synonyms.

- **Owner:** Let $d \in \mathcal{D}_v$ be a data item in the space of a user $v \in V$ in the social network. The user v is called the owner of data item d.
- **Stakeholder:** Let $d \in \mathcal{D}_v$ be a data item in the space of the user $v \in V$, in the social network. Let $S_d \subset V$ be the set of users associated with d. A user $v' \in V$ is called a stakeholder of d, if $v' \in S_d$.
- **Trust Level:** Trust Level is the amount of trust (or degree of intimacy) a user v has on his direct friends on a scale of 0–100. The trust of users v_1 on v_2 is represented as $T_{v_1}^{v_2}$. Every OSN user assigns a trust level to his direct connections in his network. Our mechanism uses trust level between the controllers and the requester to make any access decision.

Computing Trust Level. For deciding the trust level of his/her direct friends a user has to divide its friends into different groups like Family, Close, Normal, Public. Each group has a range (denoted by pair min-max) of trust values and a default trust value T_G (which is the minimum value of the range). User can change the values of trust within the specified range for each friend individually. For instance the ranges (minimum – maximum) for the different groups which could be defined as: (i) *Family:* 100–76 (ii) *Close Friends:* 75–51 (iii) *Normal Friends:* 50–26 (iv) *Public:* 25–0.

Collaborative Policy Specification. Let a user $v \in V$ uploads a resource d in his user space. Let S_d be the set of all the stakeholders of d. After the upload of d, CACM invites all the stakeholders of d to define the collaborative access policy for it. The policy specification is done as follows:

- Each stakeholder $v' \in S_d$ specifies the *minimum trust level* $t_{min}^{v'}$ need to be possessed by the requester to access d.
- The *average trust threshold* (T_{avg}^d) and *minimum trust threshold* (T_{min}^d) for d are calculated as follows.

$$T_{avg}^d = \lfloor \frac{\sum_{v' \in V}(t_{min}^{v'})}{|S_d|} \rfloor; \quad T_{min}^d = min\{t_{min}^{v'} : v' \in S_d\} \tag{1}$$

Access of d to the requesting user $z \in V$ is given only if, the following equation is satisfied:

$$\frac{1}{|S_d|}\left(\sum_{i=1}^{m} T_i^z\right) \geq T_{avg}^d; \quad T_i^z \geq T_{min}^d, \forall i \tag{2}$$

If z is not a direct friend of any user from the set S_d, but have a mutual friend k with stakeholder $v \in S_d$, then the trust for z can be computed as follows:

$$\frac{T_k^z + T_v^k}{2} \to T_v^z; v \in S_d \tag{3}$$

This is to note that k is the mutual friend of v and z such that T_v^k is maximum. If z neither have a direct friend nor a mutual friend with any user from the set S_d, then trust level of z is set to 0.

3   Implementation and Evaluation

We have developed a Facebook Canvas app "msecure", which has been provided with the permissions for accessing user information like public profile, photos, publish actions, email and friends of the users who are using the application. The application development uses Apache Tomcat version 2.2.24., MYSQL version 5.1.61-rel13.2-log, PHP version 5.2.17.

At present, this application is limited to the access control of photos only but can be extended to other type of multi-party resources later. Figure 1(a) explains, the design of the application. When a Facebook user accesses the application, and gives it, the required permissions, the Facebook server sends request to the application server on which the application is hosted. When the process is completed the application server accesses the Facebook Graph API [5] and retrieves the required data. With the data collected, it implements the mechanism on its back end. After the application of CACM logic, results are posted back on Facebook through the Graph API. Figure 1(b) shows the homepage of "msecure". The homepage features several options as described below:

– **msecure Profile:** This option shows the profile information of the currently logged in user like profile id, name, email-id of the user.
– **Trust Values:** This option allows the users to group their friends and set trust values for them.
– **Contents:** This option forms the main part of the application. Using this option the user can apply the access policies easily. It displays a gallery containing the images of the logged in users. The user can select one of these images and proceed further for setting the custom privacy of the photograph. After selecting a photograph the user is displayed a page that contains the photograph with options like *View photograph details*, *Current Owner's Information*, *Participating stakeholders*, *Set Privacy for Photograph* and *Delete previous privacy settings*.
– **Instructions:** The instruction section elaborates the steps the user has to undergo for applying the mechanism onto a photograph.
– **Feedback:** Feedback section is for the user to apply feedback to the developers of the application.

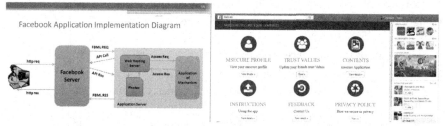

(a) Application Implementation Design   (b) Homepage of *msecure*

Fig. 1. *msecure* Design and Interface

- **Privacy Policy:** Privacy policy shows and explains how the application secures data of the logged in user.

3.1 Survey and Results

CACM is inspired by the fact that most of us share our private and sensitive information with others according to the amount of trust we have on them. It allows all the stakeholders of a data item to specify the trust level which would be required to access the data item at the time of collaborative policy specification. Then, it calculates average threshold and minimum threshold trust level that are stored in form of the access policy of the resource.

We conducted a survey study among Facebook users that include students, research scholars and faculties from IIT, Patna, to examine whether users would like to perceive tools such as *msecure* as being useful. Further, to know whether they intend to adopt such tools to empower their collaborative privacy control with their social groups.

Among the 50 users participated in the study, 43 were males and 7 were females. Number of people who reported using the Facebook application at least once in a week were 39. Users were given a short demo about the working of the application and then after a usage of the application for 4 days, a feedback was taken from them on a set of questions. Table 1, shows the results of survey.

Many users vowed to use the application on the regular basis. Most of the users feel that the interface of the application is very user friendly. Moreover, more than 90 % of users felt that using the application helped them to secure the privacy of the contents effectively. The results of the survey indicates the popularity of our model among users. Following are the features and advantages of CACM:

Table 1. Results of the survey

Questions (Rate on the scale of 5 to 1)	5	4	3	2	1
How often would you like to use the application?	32	8	7	3	-
Do you intend to install this application on your Facebook profile in the near future?	3	10	8	2	-
Do you predict that you will use this application in near future?	33	9	4	4	-
Using the application helped me protect my shared photographs better	41	8	1	-	-
User interface of this interface was user friendly	46	3	1	-	-
Instructions given in the application makes it easy to use	42	8	-	-	-
Interaction with the application does not require much of mental effort	41	-	9	-	-
There is high potential risk involved in sharing personal information on Facebook	48	2	-	-	-
I would like to see more such applications on Facebook	39	1	9		-

- It allows controllers of the resource to share it only with users whom they trust.
- The mechanism has been popular among the tested user base.
- About 80 % data processing is done in real time by the application.
- The application does not use any centralized data manager for implementation of the mechanism.
- The application has a light and sleek user interface making it easy for novice users to understand the application.

4   Conclusion and Future Work

In this paper, we have proposed a simple trust-based collaborative access control mechanism tailored to multiple stakeholders. We also have developed a Facebook app to realize the correctness and effectiveness the scheme. We conducted a survey study which confirms that our application is effective and appreciated by all the users. At present, our application allows only the trust level between stakeholders and requester to control the access of a multi-party resource. In future, we are planing to extend CACM to include more attributes to define access policies for the resources. Moreover, we also would like to add a semi-automatic mechanism to help the users to assign trust value to their contacts.

References

1. Carminati, B., Ferrari, E.: Collaborative access control in on-line social networks. In: 2011 7th International Conference on Collaborative Computing: Networking, Applications and Worksharing (CollaborateCom), pp. 231–240 (October 2011)
2. Carminati, B., Ferrari, E., Perego, A.: Rule-based access control for social networks. In: Meersman, R., Tari, Z., Herrero, P. (eds.) OTM 2006 Workshops. LNCS, vol. 4278, pp. 1734–1744. Springer, Heidelberg (2006)
3. Cheng, Y., Park, J., Sandhu, R.: Relationship-based access control for online social networks: Beyond user-to-user relationships. In: 2012 International Conference on Social Computing (SocialCom), Privacy, Security, Risk and Trust (PASSAT), pp. 646–655 (September 2012)
4. Cheng, Y., Park, J., Sandhu, R.: Attribute-aware relationship-based access control for online social networks. In: Atluri, V., Pernul, G. (eds.) DBSec 2014. LNCS, vol. 8566, pp. 292–306. Springer, Heidelberg (2014)
5. Facebook. Facebook graph api, v2.4 (2015)
6. Facebook. Facebook news room (June 2015)
7. Fong, P.: Relationship-based access control: protection model and policy language. In: Proceedings of the First ACM Conference on Data and Application Security and Privacy, pp. 191–202. ACM, New York, USA (2011)
8. Hu, H., Ahn, G.J., Jorgensen, J.: Multiparty access control for online social networks: model and mechanisms. IEEE Trans. Knowl. Data Eng. 25(7), 1614–1627 (2013)
9. Pang, J., Zhang, Y.: A new access control scheme for facebook-style social networks. CoRR, abs/1304.2504 (2013)
10. Squicciarini, A., Xu, H., Zhang, X.L.: Cope: enabling collaborative privacy management in online social networks. J. Am. Soc. Inf. Sci. Technol. 62, 521–534 (2011)

i-TSS: An Image Encryption Algorithm Based on Transposition, Shuffling and Substitution Using Randomly Generated Bitmap Image

Kanagaraj Narayanasamy[✉] and Padmapriya Arumugam

Department of Computer Science and Engineering, Alagappa University,
Karaikudi 630 003, Tamilnadu, India
kanagaraj.n.in@ieee.org, mailtopadhu@yahoo.co.in

Abstract. In the digitalized era, an enormous amount of digital images are being shared over the different networks and also available in different storage mediums. Internet users enjoy this convenient way of sharing images and at the meantime, they need to face the consequences like chosen plain-text, statistical, differential attacks, and brute-force attack. These attacks and noises create the need of enhancing the image information security. An image encryption algorithm needs to be robust. An image encryption algorithm (*i*-TSS) based on transposition, shuffling, and substitution is presented in this paper, that provides better security to the image. This algorithm is implemented using Java. By assessing the results of image quality metrics, this algorithm proves to be secured and robust against the external attacks.

1 Introduction

Cryptography is one of the best ways to communicate secretly even over the insecure channels [1]. Image encryption means converting the original image to disguised form, just like text encryption. AES, RSA and IDEA [3–5] were widely used text encryption algorithms. These text encryption algorithms can be modified to handle the image data, but the textual data differ from the image data. For instance, if the RGB color model based image's size is 512×512 then there would be 786432 numbers of data to be handled. This much of data can be handled by the algorithms which are developed particularly for the image or Multimedia data [2].

Usually, an image encryption system is made up of several components (Fig. 1). As illustrated in the figure, the image is encrypted using an algorithm and a respective key to produce the encrypted/disguised image. Similarly, the encrypted image is decrypted using the key to get the plain image.

According to the usage of the key, the algorithm technique differs. In Symmetric technique, encryption key and decryption key are same; and in Asymmetric technique, encryption key and decryption key differ. It is possible for an adversary to obtain the original image without the respective key by means of cryptanalysis. The proposed algorithm comes under the Symmetric key cryptographic technique.

© Springer International Publishing Switzerland 2016
N. Bjørner et al. (Eds.): ICDCIT 2016, LNCS 9581, pp. 148–156, 2016.
DOI: 10.1007/978-3-319-28034-9_20

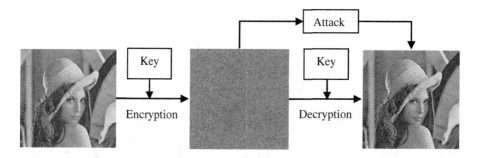

Fig. 1. Process of image encryption and decryption

The security of the image is the primary concern in this paper. The traditional image encryption algorithms such as AES, DES, RSA and the family of ECC based algorithms may not be the best one to choose for image encryption, specifically for speed and applicability in real-time applications. In recent years, several image encryption algorithms [6–12] have proposed. Zang and Liu [6] proposed an image encryption methodology based on permutation – diffusion based image encryption system. The position of the image pixels are shuffled to obtain high plain image sensitivity. The key and plain image decides the key stream in the diffusion step. Lin and Wang [7] proposed an image encryption based on chaos with the Piece Wise Linear (PWL) memristor in Chua's circuit. Diaconu et al. [8], Dascalescu and Boriga [9], and Dalhoum et al. [10] have proposed various image encryption algorithms based on Image scrambling technique. Askar et al. [11] and Zhang et al. [12] have proposed image encryption algorithms based on the chaotic economic map and DNA encoding respectively. Both these algorithms use a chaotic map, but in the [12] logistic chaotic map is used in the shuffling phase, and further DNA coding, and Chebyshev's chaotic map is used in algorithm in different phases. The proposed algorithm is seriously tested using different images and compared with other research works [7, 11, 12] to prove that the proposed algorithm is more effective in resisting attacks.

The rest of the paper is organized as follows. In the second section, the proposed algorithm is explained; in the next section, the experimental study is done; in the fourth section, the results and discussion are done to justify the efficiency of the algorithm; and the last section deals about the conclusion of the proposed algorithm.

2   Proposed Algorithm

The proposed image encryption algorithm *i*-TSS, basically works based on the Transposition, Shuffling, and Substitution processes. Transposition is the process of interchanging pixel's position. During Shuffling, the pixels are scrambled in order to confuse the adversaries. Substitution process is done with the help of a Randomly Generated bitmap image (RGbmp). RGbmp is created with the randomly generated values according to the size of the input image. Those values are assigned to Red, Green, and Blue components to form RGbmp. The transposed and shuffled image is XOR-ed with the RGbmp to obtain the better encrypted image as shown in Fig. 2.

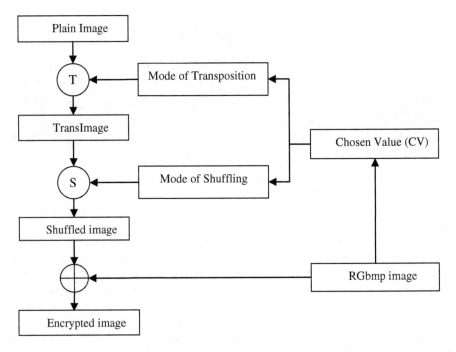

Fig. 2. Overall workflow of Proposed Algorithm (i-TSS)

2.1 Transposition Process

This is the first process in the algorithm. The transposition process starts from an initial position, most probably from the center of the image or nearby position from the center of the image. The initial position changes according to a 'Chosen Value (CV)'. This CV is chosen from the RGbmp with some simplified constraints. The pixels are taken in a spiral manner from the center of the image and repositioned from top to bottom. The CV also decides the number of transposition rounds. This transposition process will totally scramble the plain image.

2.2 Shuffling and Substitution Processes

In the second phase, shuffling the pixel's position is done. The transpositioned-image (TransImage) enters into this stage as input. The TransImage is shuffled either in even or odd order. The order of shuffling is determined based on the chosen value (CV). In the last phase, the Shuffled-image is XOR-ed with Randomly Generated bitmap image (RGbmp). The XOR operator has been used in this phase because it has distinctive properties when compared with other operators [13]. The Red, Green, and Blue values of the shuffled image are XOR-ed with Red, Green, and Blue values of the RGbmp. The resultant images possess better encryption.

3   Experimental Study

Experiments are done on the proposed algorithm (*i*-TSS) to find out the performance, and results are taken into account to assess the robustness and secrecy of the proposed algorithm. The images [14] with various resolutions are considered for the experimental study. The encryption and decryption process of the algorithm is explained in this section.

3.1   Encryption and Decryption Processes

Once the RGbmp is created, a value (CV) is chosen based on some conditions. It will be used to determine the mode of transposition and mode of shuffling. In the transposition process, the plain image is repositioned. The below Table 1 shows the usage of rounds in the process of transposition.

Table 1. Peak Signal-to-Noise Ratio (PSNR) values for a transposition image with various rounds

	Transposition (Round = 1)	Transposition (Round = 45)	Transposition (Round = 150)
PSNR (RGB)	28.5636	28.3612	28.3318

PSNR (RGB band) values for the various transposition images are grouped in the above table. The PSNR (RGB) values clearly reveal the essentiality of the rounds in transposition process. The next phase is shuffling the RGB values. The RGB values are loaded into a one dimensional array and get shuffled in either odd or even order. This single step of the shuffling process makes adversaries to be in the confused state. In the last phase, the randomly generated bitmap image is used to encrypt the shuffled image. The Red, Green and Blue values of the RGbmp are XOR-ed with the respective Red, Green and Blue values of the shuffled image to obtain the encrypted image. The RGbmp is sent as a matrix key file to the receiver end.

In the decryption phase, the RGbmp is recreated using the received matrix key file from the sender. The CV is retrieved from the RGbmp by the same condition used as in the process of encryption. The processes in the encryption work are reversed to get the original image. In the first phase, the RGbmp is used to decrypt the encrypted image using XOR operator. By using the CV, the mode of shuffling and transposition can be found and those findings are used to do the reverse processes of shuffling and transposition.

3.2   Execution Time

The average encryption and decryption speed is determined using Lena image with different sizes varying from 64×64 to 1024×1024 pixels are 982 ms and 1003 ms respectively on personal computer equipped with an Intel processor (Core i3) with clock speed of 1.7 GHz, 2 GB of RAM and 520 GB of Hard disk capacity.

4   Results and Discussion

The techniques like PSNR [15, 16] and Mean Squared Error (MSE) [17] are the two commonly adopted image quality measures, in which PSNR is actually based on the value of MSE. These two measures are easy to use and have a convenient procedure to implement in mathematical aspect. Mostly all metrics compare the original image with the distorted image and provide the result about the difference or similarity. Later, these metrics are found to be insufficient to assess the quality. New metrics like Structural Similarity Index Measure (SSIM) [18], NPCR (Number of Pixels Change Ratio) [19], Unified Averaged Changed Intensity (UACI) [19] have introduced. PSNR, MSE, NPCR, and UACI metrics have taken into account to assess the encryption work.

4.1   Histogram

Color Histogram is a graphical representation of the colors distribution in an image. If the histogram exhibits the uniform distribution of colors, then the adversaries cannot get any information through statistical attacks [20]. Table 2 illustrates the histograms (RGB) plotted for various original images and histograms (Only Red band) plotted for respective encrypted images. The histograms and the mean values (Table 3) clearly show the uniformity in distribution of colors. This reveals that the encrypted images of *i*-TSS algorithm can easily withstand the statistical attacks.

Table 2. Histogram results for original and respective encrypted images

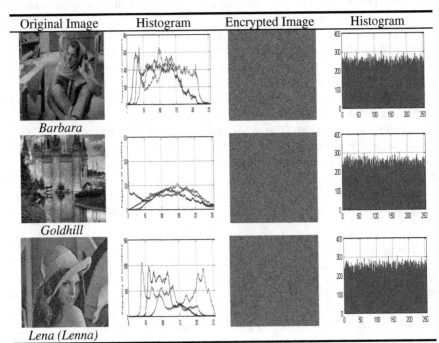

Original Image	Histogram	Encrypted Image	Histogram
Barbara			
Goldhill			
Lena (Lenna)			

Table 3. Mean values for original and respective encrypted image

Image name	Mean value (original image)	Mean value (encrypted image)
Barbara	Red: 134.42	Red: 127.59
	Green: 102.04	Green: 127.39
	Blue: 93.41	Blue: 127.24
Goldhill	Red: 137.84	Red: 127.11
	Green: 138.82	Green: 127.36
	Blue: 109.45	Blue: 127.48
Lena	Red: 177.24	Red: 128.32
	Green: 127.92	Green: 127.92
	Blue: 99.17	Blue: 127.13

4.2 PSNR and MSE

PSNR is used to compute the ratio between the maximum possible value of a signal and the power of distorting noise that changes the representation quality [16]. PSNR is expressed in decibel (dB) unit. PSNR is based on the MSE value. MSE is used to calculate the amount of deviation between the original and its disguised image. If the comparing images are identical then the MSE value will be zero and PSNR would be infinity. If the PSNR value is less; then, the quality of the image encryption is better. PSNR and MSE values are calculated between different original image and its encrypted image; and it is tabled in Table 4.

Table 4. PSNR and MSE values between the original and respective encrypted image

Image name	PSNR	MSE
Barbara	20.5113	4.461
Goldhill	19.7036	5.161
Lenna	20.1267	4.822

4.3 NPCR and UACI

In differential attack, an attacker tries to find the plain image by changing a specific pixel in image and traces the differences in the respective output image. A general consideration for all encryption algorithms is that the encrypted image must be different from its original image. This deviation can be measured by means of two criteria: NPCR and UACI. The NPCR is used to measure the rate of change in an encrypted image when a bit is changed in the plain image. The UACI is used to calculate the unified average changing intensity between two encrypted images with a deviation in only one bit in respective plain images. In Table 5, NPCR and UACI values are tabled for different images. In Table 6, NPCR and UACI values of the proposed algorithm are compared with other research results and found to provide better results.

Table 5. Values of NPCR and UACI tests of encrypted images

Image name	NPCR (%)	UACI (%)
Lena	99.62	33.46
Goldhill	99.59	33.46
Barbara	99.60	33.46

Table 6. Comparative results of NPCR and UACI

Measure	[12]	[8]	[9]	[10]	Ours
NPCR (%)	99.7017	99.489	99.431	90.126	99.62
UACI (%)	28.7051	29.006	25.032	NaN	33.46

4.4   Entropy Measure

Entropy is a statistical measure that deals with the randomness of a bundle of data. Theoretically, if the entropy measure of the encrypted images nearly equal to 8 (sh); then the image encryption algorithm is highly robust against entropy attack. From Table 7, it is possible to know justify the leakage of information of the proposed algorithm against entropy attack to be negligible. Further, in Table 8 entropy measure of the i-TSS compared with other research results, this shows the betterment in handling entropy attack.

Table 7. Entropy values of the original images and respective encrypted image

Images	Entropy	
	Original image	Encrypted image
Lena	7.6553	7.9989
Goldhill	7.8644	7.9990
Barbara	7.6283	7.9990

Table 8. Comparative results of Entropy measure

Algorithm	Entropy (sh)
[7]	7.9890
[11]	7.9961
[12]	7.9854
Ours	7.9990

5 Conclusion

In this paper a new transposition, shuffling and substitution based cryptosystem has been introduced for image encryption. Improving the randomness in transposition process is the main advantage of the system. The results of a security analysis for three different images show the resistance to chosen plain-text, differential and statistical attacks on the encrypted images. In addition to these, a large key space makes the brute force attack to be impractical; the entropy measure of the proposed algorithm is close to the principle value 8 and the average execution time is 993 ms. Hence, it is suitable for the practical usage in real-time. In future, this work can be combined with chaotic functions to enhance the security of the encryption process.

References

1. Schneier, B.: Applied Cryptography, 2nd edn. Wiley, New York (1996). ISBN 0-471-11709-9
2. Soleymani, A., Ali, Z., Nordin, M.: A survey on principal aspects of secure image transmission. In: Proceedings of World Academy of Science, Engineering and Technology, pp. 247–254 (2012)
3. Stalling, W.: Cryptography and Network Security: Principles and Practice, 6th edn. Prentice Hall, Upper Saddle River (2013). ISBN 978-0133354690
4. Mollin, R.A.: An Introduction to Cryptography. CRC Press, Boca Raton (2006)
5. Vanstone, S.A., Menezes, A.J., Oorschot, P.C.: Handbook of Applied Cryptography. CRC Press, Boca Raton (1996)
6. Zhang, G., Liu, Q.: A novel image encryption method based on total shuffling scheme. Opt. Commun. **284**, 2775–2780 (2011)
7. Lin, Z., Wang, H.: Efficient image encryption using a chaos-based PWL memristor. IETE Tech. Rev. **27**, 318–325 (2010)
8. Diaconu, A.V., Costea, A., Costea, M.A.: Color image scrambling technique based on transposition of pixels between RGB channels using Knight's moving rules and digital chaotic map. In: Mathematical Problems in Engineering (2014)
9. Dascalescu, A.C., Boriga, R.E.: A novel fast chaos-based algorithm for generating random permutations with high shift factor suitable for image scrambling. Nonlinear Dyn. **74**, 307–318 (2013)
10. Dalhoum, A.L.A., Mahafzah, B.A., Awwad, A.A., Aldamari, I., Ortega, A., Alfonseca, M.: Digital image scrambling using 2D cellular automata. IEEE Trans. Multimedia **19**, 28–36 (2012)

11. Askar, S.S., Karawia, A.A., Alshamrani, A.: Image encryption algorithm based on chaotic economic model. In: Mathematical Problems in Engineering (2015)

12. Zhang, J., Fang, D., Ren, H.: Image encryption algorithm based on DNA encoding and chaotic maps. In: Mathematical Problems in Engineering (2015)

13. http://www.cs.umd.edu/class/sum2003/cmsc311/Notes/BitOp/xor.html. Accessed 10 October 2015

14. http://sipi.usc.edu/database/. Accessed 10 October 2015

15. http://in.mathworks.com/help/images/image-quality-metrics.html and http://in.mathworks.com/help/images/image-quality.html. Accessed 10 October 2015

16. Peak Signal-to-Noise Ratio as an Image Quality Metric: White paper published by National Instruments China (2013)

17. Wang, Z., Bovik, A.C.: Mean squared error: Love it or leave it?—A new look at signal fidelity measures. IEEE Signal Process. Mag. **26**(1), 98–117 (2009)

18. Wang, Z., Bovik, A.C., Sheikh, H.R., Simoncelli, E.P.: Image quality assessment: From error visibility to structural similarity. IEEE Trans. Image Process. **13**, 600–612 (2004)

19. Wu, Y., Noonan, J.P., Agaian, S.: NPCR and UACI randomness tests for image encryption. Cyber J. Multidiscip. J. Sci. Technol. J. Sel. Areas Telecommun. (JSAT), April Edition, 31–38 (2011)

20. Shannon, C.: Communication theory of secrecy systems. Bell Syst. Techn. J. **28**, 656–7151 (1949)

A Type System for Counting Logs
of Multi-threaded Nested Transactional
Programs

Anh-Hoang Truong[1]([✉]), Dang Van Hung[1], Duc-Hanh Dang[1],
and Xuan-Tung Vu[2]

[1] VNU University of Engineering and Technology, Hanoi, Vietnam
hoangta@vnu.edu.vn
[2] Japan Advanced Institute of Science and Technology, Nomi, Japan

Abstract. We present a type system to estimate an upper bound for the resource consumption of nested and multi-threaded transactional programs. The resource is abstracted as transaction logs. In comparison to our previous work on type and effect systems for Transactional Featherweight Java, this work exploits the natural composition of thread creation to give types to sub-terms. As a result, our new type system is simpler and more effective than our previous one. More important, it is more precise than our previous type system. We also show a type inference algorithm that we have implemented in a prototype tool.

Keywords: Resource bound · Software transactional memory · Type systems

1 Introduction

Software Transactional Memory [9] has been introduced as an alternative to the locked-based synchronization for the shared memory concurrency. It has become a focus for intensive theoretical researches and practical applications for quite a long time. One of the recent transactional models that support advanced features of programming such as nested and multi-threaded transactions is described in [6]. In this model, a transaction is said to be nested if it is contained in another transaction; the former is called child transaction, and the latter is called parent transaction. The rule is that the child transaction must commit before their parent does. Furthermore, a transaction is multi-threaded when threads are created and run inside the transaction. These threads when created, run in parallel with the thread executing that transaction. For independent manipulation of shared variables, a child thread will make a copy of all variables of its parent thread.

This research is funded by Vietnam National Foundation for Science and Technology Development (NAFOSTED) under grant number 102.03-2014.23. The research is also partly supported by the research project QG.14.06, Vietnam National University, Hanoi.

© Springer International Publishing Switzerland 2016
N. Bjørner et al. (Eds.): ICDCIT 2016, LNCS 9581, pp. 157–168, 2016.
DOI: 10.1007/978-3-319-28034-9_21

When the parent thread commits a transaction, all the child threads created inside that transaction must join the commit of their parent. We call this kind of commits *joint commits*, and the time when these commits occur *joint commit point*. Joint commits act as the synchronizations of parallel threads.

In the implementations in practice, each transaction has its own local copy of memory called log to store shared variables for independent accesses during its execution. Each thread may execute a number of nested transactions, and thus may contain a corresponding number of logs. In addition, a child thread also stores a copy of its parent's logs so that it can be executed independently with its parents until a joint commit point. At the time when all child threads and their parent are synchronized via joint commits, their own logs and the copies they keep relating to the transaction are consulted to check for conflicts and potentially performing a roll-back. These logs are then discarded – the corresponding memory resources are freed. A major complication for the static analysis is that the number of logs cloned (resource allocation) when a new thread is created is implicit and the commit statements (resource deallocation) that need to synchronize with each other are also implicit, so the resources used by these programs are difficult to estimate.

The number of cloned logs may affect the efficiency of parallel threads and the maximal number of logs that coexist may affect the safety of the program when the memory is limited. Therefore, a precise estimation of the upper bound of number of coexisting logs in a multi-threaded, nested transactional memory program plays a crucial role.

In our previous works [7,10] we gave type and effect systems for estimating the upper bounds of number of logs that coexist at the same time. We are not satisfied with those estimations, and take a new approach to solve the problem. This work was initiated from our previous work [10] with the advantage that our new system can infer more precise bound, and it is simpler with some natural sacrifice on the compositionality. The main contributions of this work are: (1) A simpler type system with natural composition of terms; (2) Our correctness proofs are all briefly shown; (3) A type inference algorithm and a tool for inferring types for the core part of the language.

Related Work. Estimating resource usage has been studied in various settings.

Hofmann and Jost [4] compute the linear bounds on heap space for a first-order functional language. In terms of imperative and object-oriented languages, Wei-Ngan Chin et al. [3] verify memory usages for object-oriented programs. In [5], Hofmann and Jost use a type system to calculate the heap space bound as a function of input for an object oriented language. In [2] the authors statically compute upper bounds of resource consumption of a method using a non-linear function of method's parameters. In [1] the authors propose type systems for component languages with parallel composition but the threads run independently. [8] proposes a fast algorithm to statically find the upper bounds of heap memory for a class of JavaCard programs.

Our analysis not only takes care of multi-threading – many of the cited works are restricted to sequential or functional languages – but also of the complex and implicit synchronization (by joint commits) structure entailed by the transactional model.

The rest of the paper is structured as follows. In the next section we will explain informally the problem and the approach by a motivating example. Section 3 introduces the formal syntax and operational semantics of the calculus. Section 4 presents a new type system. The soundness of the analysis is sketched in Sect. 5 and then, a type inference algorithm is sketched in Sect. 6. Section 7 is the conclusion of the paper.

2   Motivating Example

We use the following example program (see Listing 1.1) which is taken from our previous work [7,10] as our running example to demonstrate the problem and our new approach.

Listing 1.1. A nested multi-threaded program.

```
1   onacid;//thread 0
2     onacid;
3       spawn(e1;commit;commit);//thread 1
4       onacid;
5         spawn(e2;commit;commit;commit);//thread 2
6       commit;
7       e3;
8     commit;
9     e4;
10  commit
```

In this program, the statements `onacid` and `commit` are to start and to close a transaction, respectively, and must be paired. The expressions `e1`, `e2`, `e3` and `e4` represent subprograms. The statement `spawn` is to open a thread with the code represented by the parameter of the statement. The command `spawn` creates a new thread running in parallel with its parent thread. The new thread duplicates the logs of the parent thread for storing a copy of variables of the parent thread. In our example, when spawning `e1` the main thread has opened two transactions; so thread 1 executes `e1` inside these two transactions and must do two commits to close them. This is why after `e1`, thread 1 needs to execute two `commit` commands.

In our previous work, we allowed more freedom in splitting the whole program term into arbitrary sub-terms and then we gave types to all these sub-terms. This approach leads to a bit complex type systems as we have to handle quite lot of possible combinations. In this work we restrict the way to combine terms. We type the inner most thread first and then combine with its sibling threads (parent) and so on.

3   The Language TFJ

Syntax. The syntax of TFJ is given in Fig. 1, and it is similar Featherweight Java (FJ) except for the first and the last line. The first line is for defining run time threads/processes and the last line is three commands for creating a thread, starting and committing a transaction. These three commands make the language multi-threaded and transactional. Other commands are of the FJ language: L is class definition, M is method declaration, the values of v can be reference, variable, or **null**, and the term e can be a value, a field access, an assignment, a method call, a object creation in the first line for e. The second syntax line for e is for sequencing and choice. $\bar{x}$ ($\bar{v}$) is vector of x (v). The detailed explanation of the syntax was given in [7]. In this paper, we restrict ourselves to a sub-language of TFJ in which we use only the simple form of the expression **let** for sequencing. Namely, $e_1; e_2$ can be expressed by **let** $x = e_1$ **in** e_2 where x does not occur in e_2 with the assumption that no lazy evaluation applied. We allow only this form of **let** from now on.

Dynamic Semantics. The semantics of TFJ is given by two sets of operational rules: the rules for the object semantics in Table 1, and the rules for the transactional and multi-threaded semantics in Table 2. The object semantics rules are standard and similar to Featherweight Java. We highlight here only the key points concerning creating and removing logs of the transactional and multi-threaded semantics rules. The readers are referred to [7] for a detailed explanation of the semantics. Generally, the (global) runtime environment is a collection of threads. Each thread contains a local environment which is a sequence of logs. For managing these threads and logs we give an id to each thread and log. The object semantics mainly works on the local environment and does not manipulate logs as well as threads. This part is similar to Featherweight Java. The transactional and multi-threaded semantics creates and destroys threads and logs. Now we formally define the local and global environments and explain in more details about the transactional and multi-threaded semantics rules.

Definition 1 (Local environment). *A local environment E is a finite sequence of labeled logs $l_1:log_1; \dots ; l_k:log_k$, where the ith element of the sequence consists of a transaction label l_i (a transaction name) and the log log_i corresponding to the transaction l_i.*

$$
\begin{aligned}
P &::= \mathbf{0} \,|\, p(e) \,|\, P \parallel P && \text{processes} \\
L &::= \mathbf{class}\ C\{\bar{f}, \bar{M}\} && \text{class definition} \\
M &::= m(\bar{x})\{e\} && \text{methods} \\
v &::= r \,|\, x \,|\, \mathbf{null} && \text{values} \\
e &::= v \,|\, v.f \,|\, v.f := v \,|\, v.m(\bar{v}) \,|\, \mathbf{new}\ C() && \text{expressions} \\
  &\quad |\, \mathbf{let}\ x = e\ \mathbf{in}\ e \,|\, \mathbf{if}\ v\ \mathbf{then}\ e\ \mathbf{else}\ e \\
  &\quad |\, \mathbf{spawn}(e) \,|\, \mathbf{onacid} \,|\, \mathbf{commit}
\end{aligned}
$$

Fig. 1. TFJ syntax.

Table 1. Object semantics.

$$E, \text{let } x = v \text{ in } e \to E', e[v/x] \quad \text{L-RED}$$
$$E, \text{let } x_2 = (\text{let } x_1 = e_1 \text{ in } e) \text{ in } e' \to E, \text{let } x_1 = e_1 \text{ in } (\text{let } x_2 = e \text{ in } e') \quad \text{L-LET}$$
$$E, \text{let } x = (\text{if true then } e_1 \text{ else } e_2) \text{ in } e \to E, \text{let } x = e_1 \text{ in } e \quad \text{L-COND}_1$$
$$E, \text{let } x = (\text{if false then } e_1 \text{ else } e_2) \text{ in } e \to E, \text{let } x = e_2 \text{ in } e \quad \text{L-COND}_2$$

$$\frac{read(E, r) = E', C(\bar{u}) \quad fields(C) = \bar{f}}{E, \text{let } x = r.f_i \text{ in } e \to E', \text{let } x = u_i \text{ in } e} \quad \text{L-LOOKUP}$$

$$\frac{read(E, r) = E', C(\bar{u}) \quad write(r \to C(\bar{u}) \downarrow_i^{u'}, E') = E''}{E, \text{let } x = r.f_i := u' \text{ in } e \to E'', \text{let } x = u' \text{ in } e} \quad \text{L-UPD}$$

$$\frac{read(E, r) = E', C(\bar{u}) \quad mbody(C, m) = (\bar{x}, e)}{E, \text{let } x = r.m(\bar{r}) \text{ in } e' \to E', \text{let } x = e[\bar{r}/\bar{x}, r/this] \text{ in } e'} \quad \text{L-CALL}$$

$$\frac{r \text{ fresh} \quad extend(r \mapsto C(\bar{\text{null}}), E) = E'}{E, \text{let } x = \text{new } C() \text{ in } e \to E', \text{let } x = r \text{ in } e} \quad \text{L-NEW}$$

For $E = l_1:log_1; \ldots; l_k:log_k$, we call k the size of E, and denote by $|E|$. The size $|E|$ is the nesting depth of transactions, namely l_1 is the outer-most transaction and l_k is the inner-most one. Note that the inner-most one exists for each thread. The empty environment is the empty sequence of labeled logs, and is denoted by ϵ.

Transactional and Multi-threaded Semantics. We will give the transition rules for the semantics in the form $\Gamma, P \Rightarrow \Gamma', P'$ or $\Gamma, P \Rightarrow error$, where Γ is a global environment and P is a set of processes of the form $p(e)$. A global environment contains local environments of threads and is defined as follows.

Definition 2 (Global environment). *A global environment Γ is a finite mapping from thread id to its local environment, $\Gamma = p_1:E_1, \ldots, p_k:E_k$, where p_i is a thread id and E_i is the local environment of the thread p_i.*

We denote by $|\Gamma|$ the size of Γ which is the total number of logs in Γ, i.e., $|\Gamma| = \sum_{i=1}^{k} |E_i|$. At the staring point, the global environment for the main thread p_1 of the program is $p_1 : \epsilon$. During the execution of the program, the global environment changes according to the semantic rules. Our goal is to effectively find an upper bound of $|\Gamma|$ as it represents the number of logs in all (concurrent) threads. Note that testing all possible paths is not feasible because of parallel threads and the choice expression.

The global steps make use of a number of functions accessing and changing the global environment: $reflect(p_i, E_i', \Gamma)$, $spawn(p, p', \Gamma)$, $start(l, p_i, \Gamma)$, $intranse(\Gamma, l)$, and $commit(\bar{p}, \bar{E}, \Gamma)$. These functions were defined in [7]. Their brief explanations are as follows. In rule G-PLAIN, the function $reflect$ only update the local changes to the global environment. In rule G-SPAWN, the function $spawn(p, p', \Gamma)$ creates a new thread p' with a cloned copy of transactions in p, so the number of logs in p is duplicated. In rule G-TRANS, the function $start(l, p_i, \Gamma)$ creates one more log with the fresh label l in thread p_i. In rule G-COMM, we denote $\coprod_1^k p_i(e_i)$ for $p_1(e_1) \parallel \ldots \parallel p_k(e_k)$. The rule requires k

Table 2. Transactional and threading semantics.

$$\frac{E, e \to E', e' \quad p : E \in \Gamma \quad reflect(p, E', \Gamma) = \Gamma'}{\Gamma, P \parallel p(e) \Rightarrow \Gamma', P \parallel p(e')} \text{ G-PLAIN}$$

$$\frac{p' \ fresh \quad spawn(p, p', \Gamma) = \Gamma'}{\Gamma, P \parallel p(\textbf{let } x = \textbf{spawn}(e_1) \textbf{ in } e_2) \Rightarrow \Gamma', P \parallel p(\textbf{let } x = \textbf{null in } e_2) \parallel p'(e_1)} \text{ G-SPAWN}$$

$$\frac{l \ fresh \quad start(l, p, \Gamma) = \Gamma'}{\Gamma, P \parallel p(\textbf{let } x = \textbf{onacid in } e) \Rightarrow \Gamma', P \parallel p(\textbf{let } x = \textbf{null in } e)} \text{ G-TRANS}$$

$$\frac{p : E \in \Gamma \quad E = ..; l : log; \quad intranse(\Gamma, l) = \bar{p} = p_1..p_k \quad commit(\bar{p}, \bar{E}, \Gamma) = \Gamma'}{\Gamma, P \parallel \coprod_1^k p_i(\textbf{let } x = \textbf{commit in } e_i) \Rightarrow \Gamma', P \parallel (\coprod_1^k p_i(\textbf{let } x = \textbf{null in } e_i))} \text{ G-COMM}$$

$$\frac{\Gamma = \Gamma''; p : E \quad |E| = 0}{\Gamma, P \parallel p(\textbf{let } x = \textbf{commit in } e) \Rightarrow error} \text{ G-ERROR}$$

threads to do joint commit, and each thread releases one log, so k logs are to be removed as expressed in the function *commit*. k threads are all threads that are synchronized by the joint commits. They contains one parent threads and $k - 1$ child threads that were directly spawned by the parent. The function *intranse* identifies the k threads with the same label l for the synchronization.

Note that a global environment may contain threads with their own local environments, and each local environment in turn contains transactions with their own logs. Therefore, a global environment may contain transactions with the same labels because some transactions are copied by a **spawn** operation.

4   Type System

Types. To represent the transactional behaviour of a term, we use a set of four symbols (called *tags* or *signs*) $\{+, -, \neg, \sharp\}$. The tags $+$ and $-$ abstractly represent the starting of a transaction and the committing of a transaction, respectively. The tag $\neg$ is used for the joint commit of transactions in parallel threads and the last one, $\sharp$, is used for accumulating the maximum number of logs created. To make it more convenient for computing on these sequences later, we associate a tag with a non-negative natural number $n \in \mathbb{N}^+ = \{0, 1, 2, ..\}$ to form *tagged numbers*. So our types use finite sequences over the set of tagged numbers $^T\mathbb{N} = \{ ^+n, \ ^-n, \ ^\sharp n, \ ^\neg n \mid n \in \mathbb{N}^+ \}$. We will try to give rules to associate a sequence of tagged numbers with a term (expression) of TFJ.

During computation, a tag with zero may be produced but it has no effect to the semantics of the sequence so we will automatically discard it when it appears. To simplify the presentation[1], we also automatically insert $^\sharp 0$ element whenever needed. In our type inference implementation we do not need to insert these elements. Intuitively, for a term to type, ^+n (^-n) means there are n consecutive **onacid** (**commit**) in the term, and $^\neg n$ means that there are n threads needed to

---

[1] We can avoid the insertion as shown in our implementation for the type inference algorithm in Sect. 6.

be synchronized with some **onacid** in a joint commit to complete the transaction in the term, and $^\sharp n$ says n is the maximal number of logs created by the term.

In the sequel, let s range over $^T\mathbb{N}$, $^T\bar{\mathbb{N}}$ be the set of all sequences of tagged numbers, and S range over $^T\bar{\mathbb{N}}$ and $m, n, l, ..$ range over $\mathbb{N}$. The empty sequence is denoted by ϵ as usual. For a sequence S we denote by $|S|$ the length of S, and write $S(i)$ for the ith element of S. For a tagged number s, we denote $\mathrm{tag}(s)$ the tag of s, and $|s|$ the natural number of s (i.e., $s = {}^{\mathrm{tag}(s)}|s|$). For a sequence $S \in {}^T\bar{\mathbb{N}}$, we write $\mathrm{tag}(S)$ for the sequence of the tags of the elements of S, i.e., $\mathrm{tag}(s_1 \dots s_k) = \mathrm{tag}(s_1) \dots \mathrm{tag}(s_k)$ and $\{S\}$ for the set of tags appeared in S. We also write $\mathrm{tag}(s) \in S$ instead of $\mathrm{tag}(s) \in \{S\}$ for the simplicity.

The set $^T\bar{\mathbb{N}}$ can be partitioned into equivalence classes such that all elements in the same class represent the same transactional behaviour, and for each class we use the most compact sequence as the representative for the class and we call it canonical element.

Definition 3 (Canonical sequence). *A sequence S is canonical if $\mathrm{tag}(S)$ does not contain '$++$', '$--$', '$\sharp\sharp$', '$+-$', '$+\sharp-$', '$+\neg$' or '$+\sharp\neg$' as subsequences, and furthermore, $|s| > 0$ for all element s of S.*

The intuition here is that we can always simplify/shorten a sequence S without changing the interpretation of the sequence w.r.t. the resource consumption to make it canonical: simply all the tagged zero can be removed without any effect to the behavior of the term, and double tags can be converted to single tags by the following seq function. The seq function below is to reduce a sequence in $^T\bar{\mathbb{N}}$ to a canonical one. Note the pattern $+-$ does not appear, but we can insert $^\sharp 0$ for $^\sharp l$ in the last definition of seq to handle this case. The last two patterns, '$+\neg$' and '$+\sharp\neg$', will be handled by the function jc later (Definition 8).

Definition 4 (Simplify). *Function seq is defined recursively as follows:*

$$\mathrm{seq}(S) = S \text{ when } S \text{ is canonical}$$
$$\mathrm{seq}(S\ {}^\sharp m\ {}^\sharp n\ S') = \mathrm{seq}(S\ {}^\sharp \mathrm{max}(m, n)\ S')$$
$$\mathrm{seq}(S\ {}^+ m\ {}^+ n\ S') = \mathrm{seq}(S\ {}^+(m + n)\ S')$$
$$\mathrm{seq}(S\ {}^- m\ {}^- n\ S') = \mathrm{seq}(S\ {}^-(m + n)\ S')$$
$$\mathrm{seq}(S\ {}^+ m\ {}^\sharp l\ {}^- n\ S') = \mathrm{seq}(S\ {}^+(m - 1)\ {}^\sharp(l + 1)\ {}^-(n - 1)\ S')$$

As mentioned above, threads are synchronized by joint commits. So these joint commits split a thread into so-called *segments* and only some segments can run in parallel. For instance, in the running example of the paper e1 can run in parallel with e2 and e3, but not with e4. With the type given to an expression e, segments can be identified by examining the type of the expression e inside **spawn**(e) for extra $-$ or $\neg$. For example, in **spawn**$(e_1); e_2$, if the canonical sequence of e_1 has $-$ or $\neg$, then the thread of e_1 must be synchronized with its parent which is the thread of e_2. Function merge in Definition 6 is used in these situations, but to define it we need some auxiliary functions.

For $S \in {}^T\bar{N}$ and for a tag $sig \in \{+, -, \neg, \sharp\}$, we introduce the function $first(S, sig)$ that returns the smallest index i such that $tag(S(i)) = sig$. If no such element exists, the function returns 0. A commit can be a local commit or, implicitly, a joint commit. At first, we presume all commits be a local commit. Then when we discover that there is no local transaction starting command (i.e., **onacid**) to match with a local commit, that commit should be a joint commit. The following function performs that job and converts a canonical sequence (with no $+$ element) to a so-called *joint sequence*.

Definition 5 (Join). *Let $S = s_1 \ldots s_k$ be a canonical sequence and assume $i = first(S, -)$. Then function* join(S) *recursively replaces $-$ in S by $\neg$ as follows:*

$$\text{join}(S) = S \qquad\qquad\qquad\qquad\qquad\qquad\quad \textit{if } i = 0$$
$$\text{join}(S) = s_1..s_{i-1} \ {}^\neg 1 \ \text{join}({}^\neg(|s_i| - 1) \ s_{i+1}..s_k) \qquad \textit{otherwise}$$

Since the function join is idempotent, joint sequences are well-defined and do not contain elements with $+$ or $-$ tags. We also simplify it to its canonical form so we can assume that joint sequence contains only $\sharp$ elements interleaved with $\neg$ elements. A joint sequence is used to type a term inside a **spawn** or a term in the main thread. Now we can define the merge function.

Definition 6 (Merge). *Let S_1 and S_2 be joint sequences such that the number of $\neg$ elements in S_1 and S_2 are the same (can be zero). The* merge *function is defined recursively as:*

$$\text{merge}({}^\sharp m_1, {}^\sharp m_2) = {}^\sharp(m_1 + m_2)$$
$$\text{merge}({}^\sharp m_1 \ {}^\neg n_1 \ S_1', {}^\sharp m_2 \ {}^\neg n_2 \ S_2') = {}^\sharp(m_1 + m_2) \ {}^\neg(n_1 + n_2) \ \text{merge}(S_1', S_2')$$

The definition is well-formed, because joint sequences S_1 and S_2 have only $\sharp$ and $\neg$ elements. In addition, the number of $\neg$ are the same in the assumption of the definition. So we can insert ${}^\sharp 0$ to make the two sequences match over the defined patterns.

For the conditionals **if** v **then** e_1 **else** e_2, we require that the external transactional behaviours of e_1 and e_2 are the same, i.e., when removing all the elements with the tag $\sharp$ from them, the remaining sequences are identical. Let S_1 and S_2 be such two sequences. Then, they can always be written as $S_i = {}^\sharp m_i \ {}^* n \ S_i'$, $i = 1, 2$, $* = \{+, -, \neg\}$, where S_1' and S_2' in turn have the same transactional behaviours. On this condition for S_1 and S_2, we define the choice operator as follows.

Definition 7 (Choice). *Let S_1 and S_2 be two sequences such that if removing all $\sharp$ elements from them the remaining two sequence are identical. The* alt *function is recursively defined as:*

$$\text{alt}({}^\sharp m_1, {}^\sharp m_2) = {}^\sharp \max(m_1, m_2)$$
$$\text{alt}({}^\sharp m_1 \ {}^* n \ S_1', {}^\sharp m_2 \ {}^* n \ S_2') = {}^\sharp \max(m_1, m_2) \ {}^* n \ \text{alt}(S_1', S_2')$$

Table 3. Typing rules.

$$\frac{}{-1 \vdash \textbf{onacid} : {}^+1} \text{ T-ONACID} \qquad \frac{}{1 \vdash \textbf{commit} : {}^-1} \text{ T-COMMIT}$$

$$\frac{n \vdash e : S}{n \vdash \textbf{spawn}(e) : (\text{join}(S))^\rho} \text{ T-SPAWN} \qquad \frac{n \vdash e : S}{n \vdash e : \text{join}(S)^\rho} \text{ T-PREP}$$

$$\frac{n_1 \vdash e_1 : S_1 \quad n_2 \vdash e_2 : S_2 \quad S = \text{seq}(S_1 S_2)}{n_1 + n_2 \vdash \textbf{let } x = e_1 \textbf{ in } e_2 : S} \text{ T-SEQ}$$

$$\frac{n_1 \vdash e_1 : S_1 \quad n_2 \vdash e_2 : S_2^\rho \quad S = \text{jc}(S_1, S_2)}{n_1 + n_2 \vdash \textbf{let } x = e_1 \textbf{ in } e_2 : S} \text{ T-JC}$$

$$\frac{n \vdash e_1 : S_1^\rho \quad n \vdash e_2 : S_2^\rho \quad S = \text{merge}(S_1, S_2)}{n \vdash \textbf{let } x = e_1 \textbf{ in } e_2 : S^\rho} \text{ T-MERGE}$$

$$\frac{n \vdash e_i : T_i \quad i = 1, 2 \quad kind(T_1) = kind(T_2) \quad T_i = S_i^{kind(T_i)}}{n \vdash \textbf{if } v \textbf{ then } e_1 \textbf{ else } e_2 : \text{alt}(S_1, S_2)^{kind(S_1)}} \text{ T-COND}$$

$$\frac{mbody(m) = e \quad n \vdash e : T}{n \vdash v.m(\bar{v}) : T} \text{ T-CALL} \qquad \frac{e \in \{v, v.f, v.f = v', newC()\} \quad n \in \mathbb{N}}{n \vdash e : \emptyset} \text{ T-SKIP}$$

Typing Rules. Now we are ready to introduce our formal typing rules. The language of types T is defined by the following syntax:

$$T = S \mid S^\rho$$

The second kind of types, S^ρ, is used for terms inside a spawn expression which need to be synchronized with their parent thread. The treatment of two cases is different, so we denote $kind(T)$ the kind of T, which can be empty (normal) or ρ depending on which case T is. The type environment encodes the transaction context for the expression being typed. The typing judgement is of the form $n \vdash e : T$ where $n \in \mathbb{N}$ is the type environment. When n is positive, it represents the number of opening transactions that e will close, by commits or joint commits in e.

The typing rules for our calculus are shown in Table 3. We assume that in these rules the functions seq, jc, merge, alt are applicable, i.e., their arguments satisfy the conditions of the functions. The rule T-SPAWN converts S to the joint sequence and marks the new type by ρ so that we can merge with its parent in T-MERGE. The rule T-PREP allows us to make a matching type for the e_2 in T-MERGE. In T-CALL we assume that the auxiliary function $mbody$ returns the body of method m. For sequencing (let), we have three rules: T-SEQ, T-MERGE and T-JC, where our previous work [10] has only two. Here we simplify the typing by allowing only a certain combinations of sequencing. This increases the preciseness of the type system as shown by the example at the end of this section. The remaining rules are straightforward except for the rule T-JC in which we need the new function jc. This function is explained below.

In rule T-JC, e_2 may have several segments, and let l be the number of join commit threads. The last + element in S_1, say ${}^+n$, will be matched with the first $\neg$ element in S_2, say $\neg l$. But after ${}^+n$, there can be a $\sharp$ element, say $\sharp n'$, and the local maximal number of logs for ${}^+n \ \sharp n'$ is $n + n'$ (but we will define step-by-step so in the following definition of jc we only add 1 to n' at a time).

Similarly, before $\neg l$ there can be a $^\#l'$, so the maximum of log at this point is at least $l+l'$. After removing one $+$ from S_1 and one $\neg$ from S_2 we can simplify the new sequences so that the patterns can appear in the next recursive call of jc. Thus, the function jc is defined as follows. Note that we do not define the function for all patterns and this is a reason for the loss of compositionality.

Definition 8 (Joint commit). *Function* jc *is defined recursively as follows:*

$$\text{jc}(S_1' \,^{+}n \,^{\#}n' , \,^{\#}l' \,^{\neg}l\, S_2') = \text{jc}(\text{seq}(S_1' \,^{+}(n-1) \,^{\#}(n'+1)\,), \text{seq}(\,^{\#}(l'+l)\, S_2')) \ \textit{if } l, n > 0$$

$$\text{jc}(\,^{\#}n' , \,^{\#}l' \,^{\neg}l\, S_2') = \text{seq}(\,^{\#}\text{max}(n',l') \,^{\neg}l\, S_2')$$

In the definition of jc, we implicitly assume that the first definition will be applied if there exists $^\#n$ with $n > 0$. As we can see in Sect. 6, the type inference algorithm naturally satisfies this condition.

As our type reflects the behaviour of a term, so the type of a well-typed program contains only a sequence of single $\sharp$ element expressing the upper bound of logs that can be created when we execute the program and the typing environment is 0.

Definition 9 (Well-typed). *A term* e *is* well-typed *if there exists a type derivation for* e *such that* $0 \vdash e : \,^{\#}n$ *for some* n.

A typing judgment has a property that its environment has just enough opening transactions for the (join) commits in e as expressed by T. Due to the lack of space, the proof of the theorem is skipped here. You can find it in a complete version of this paper.

Theorem 1 (Type judgment property). *If* $n \vdash e : T$ *and* $n \geq 0$ *then* $\text{sim}(\,^{+}n , T) = \,^{\#}m$ *and* $m \geq n$ *where* $\text{sim}(T_1, T_2) = \text{seq}(\text{jc}(S_1, S_2))$ *with* S_i *is* T_i *without* ρ.

5   Correctness

To show that our type system meets our purpose mentioned in the introduction of this paper, we need to show that a well-typed program does not create more logs than the amount expressed in its type. Let our well-typed program be e and its type is $^\#n$. We need to show that when executing e according to the semantics in Sect. 3, the number of logs in the global environment is always smaller than n.

Recall, a state of a program is a pair Γ, P where $\Gamma = p_1 : E_1; \ldots ; p_k : E_k$ and $P = \coprod_1^k p_i(e_i)$. We say Γ satisfies P, notation $\Gamma \models P$, if there exist $S_1, \ldots, S_k$ such that $|E_i| \vdash e_i : S_i$ for all $i = 1, \ldots, k$. For a component i, E_i represents the logs that have been created or copied in thread p_i, and S_i represents the number of logs that will be created when executing e_i. Therefore, the behavior of thread p_i in term of logs is expressed by $\text{sim}(\,^{+}|E_i| , S_i)$, where the sim function is defined in Theorem 1. We will show that $\text{sim}(\,^{+}|E_i| , S) = \,^{\#}n$ for some n. We denote this value n as $|E_i, S_i|$. Then *the total number of logs* of a program state – ones in

Γ and the potential ones that will be created when the remaining program is executed – denoted by $|\Gamma, P|$, is defined by: $|\Gamma, P| = \sum_{i=1}^{k} |E_i, S_i|$. Since $|\Gamma, P|$ represents the maximum number of logs *from* the current state and $|\Gamma|$ is the number of logs *in* the current state, we have the following properties.

Lemma 1. *If* $\Gamma \models P$ *then* $|\Gamma, P| \geq |\Gamma|$.

Lemma 2 (Subject reduction 1). *If* $E, e \rightarrow E', e'$, *and* $|E| \vdash e : S$ *then there exists* S' *such that* $|E'| \vdash e' : S'$ *and* $|E, S| \geq |E', S'|$.

Lemma 3 (Subject reduction 2). *If* $\Gamma \models P$ *and* $\Gamma, P \Rightarrow \Gamma', P'$ *then* $\Gamma' \models P'$ *and* $|\Gamma, P| \geq |\Gamma', P'|$.

Theorem 2 (Correctness). *Suppose* $0 \vdash e : {}^\sharp n$ *and* $p_1 : \epsilon, p_1(e) \Rightarrow^* \Gamma, P$. *Then* $|\Gamma| < n$.

6   Type Inference

In this section we give an algorithm to compute types for the core of our TFJ calculus. Our main type inference algorithm is presented in Listing 1.2 in the functional programming style, which uses the functions defined in the previous sections to compute types (sequence of tagged numbers). The main function `infer` takes an expression `term` and a head 'environment' `hd` in line 6. The expression is encoded as a list of branches and leaves. A branch corresponds to a new thread. A leaf is a tagged number.

We have implemented the algorithm in F Sharp and tested on several examples[2]. The code contains automated tests and all test cases are passed, i.e., actual results is equal to our expected ones.

Listing 1.2. Type inference algorithm.

```
1   type TagNum = Tag * int
2   type Tree = | Branch of Tree list | Leaf of TagNum
3
4   let rec infer (term: Tree list) (hd: TagNum list) =
5     match term with
6     | [] -> seq hd (*simplifies the result*)
7     | x::xs ->
8       match x with
9       | Leaf tagnum -> (*expand the head part*)
10          let new_head = seq (List.append hd [tagnum]) in
11          infer xs new_head
12       | Branch br -> (*a new thread*)
13          let child = join (infer br []) in (*infer child*)
14          let parent = join (infer xs []) in (*infer parent*)
15          let tl = seq (merge child parent) in (*merge them*)
16          jc hd tl (*join commit with the head*)
```

---

[2] https://github.com/truonganhhoang/tfj-infer.

7 Conclusion

We have presented a new type system that have some advantages over our previous type systems [7,10] for a language that mixes nested transactional memory and multi-threading. Our type system is much simpler and gives more precise estimation for the maximum number of logs (in the worst case) that can coexist during the execution of a program being typed. Though the new type system is a bit less compositional than the previous ones, we believe that the inference algorithm developed based on this work is more efficient. Like the type system in [10], the one presented in this paper does not restrict opening new transactions after a joint commit as the one presented in [7]. Our next step is to generalize our type system for the larger class of TFJ with more language features.

References

1. Bezem, M., Hovland, D., Truong, H.: A type system for counting instances of software components. Theor. Comput. Sci. **458**, 29–48 (2012)
2. Braberman, V., Garbervetsky, D., Yovine, S.: A static analysis for synthesizing parametric specifications of dynamic memory consumption. J. Object Technol. **5**(5), 31–58 (2006)
3. Chin, W.-N., Nguyen, H.H., Qin, S.C., Rinard, M.: Memory usage verification for OO programs. In: Hankin, C., Siveroni, I. (eds.) SAS 2005. LNCS, vol. 3672, pp. 70–86. Springer, Heidelberg (2005)
4. Hofmann, M., Jost, S.: Static prediction of heap space usage for first-order functional programs. In: Proceedings of POPL 2003. ACM, January 2003
5. Hofmann, M.O., Jost, S.: Type-based amortised heap-space analysis. In: Sestoft, P. (ed.) ESOP 2006. LNCS, vol. 3924, pp. 22–37. Springer, Heidelberg (2006)
6. Jagannathan, S., Vitek, J., Welc, A., Hosking, A.: A transactional object calculus. Sci. Comput. Program. **57**(2), 164–186 (2005)
7. Mai Thuong Tran, T., Steffen, M., Truong, H.: Compositional static analysis for implicit join synchronization in a transactional setting. In: Hierons, R.M., Merayo, M.G., Bravetti, M. (eds.) SEFM 2013. LNCS, vol. 8137, pp. 212–228. Springer, Heidelberg (2013)
8. Pham, T.-H., Truong, A.-H., Truong, N.-T., Chin, W.-N.: A fast algorithm to compute heap memory bounds of Java Card applets. In: Software Engineering and Formal Methods (2008)
9. Shavit, N., Touitou, D.: Software transactional memory. In: Symposium on Principles of Distributed Computing, pp. 204–213 (1995)
10. Vu, X.-T., Mai Thuong Tran, T., Truong, A.-H., Steffen, M.: A type system for finding upper resource bounds of multi-threaded programs with nested transactions. In: Symposium on Information and Communication Technology SoICT 2012, pp. 21–30 (2012)

Proactive Resource Provisioning Model for Cloud Federation

Geethapriya Ramakrishnan[1]([✉]), Prashant Anantharaman[2],
and Saswati Mukherjee[1]

[1] Department of Information Science and Technology, Anna University,
Chennai, India
geethapriya.krish@gmail.com, msaswati@auist.net
[2] Department of Computer Science, Dartmouth College, Hanover, NH, USA
prashant.anantharaman.gr@dartmouth.edu

Abstract. Cloud federation addresses the resource scalability issue by enabling infrastructure sharing among multiple clouds. We propose a proactive resource provisioning model for federation based on sliding window prediction technique. We compare the results of the proposed prediction mechanism with the commonly used time series prediction algorithm ARIMA. We developed a simulation environment for cloud federation to investigate the impact of workload prediction based resource provisioning in cloud federation. Finally we compare it with that of resource provisioning without prediction in a federated environment, evaluate the profit and resource utilization associated with both the cases.

Keywords: Cloud federation · Resource provisioning · Workload prediction · Insource · Outsource · Sliding window · ARIMA

1 Introduction

A Cloud is imagined as an inexhaustible pool of computing resources; in reality they are limited. To meet peak demands beyond the resource limits, cloud federation has been proposed as a solution in which the resources are dynamically provisioned. Multiple clouds share their infrastructure and co-ordinate among themselves through SLA to meet the demands. If there is a resource limitation in a cloud, resources are borrowed from other clouds (Outsource) and if there are more unused resources in a cloud, those resources are rented to other clouds there by increasing the resource utilization and maximizing profit (Insource) [1]. In this paper, we propose a proactive resource provisioning mechanism in cloud federation by implementing a sliding window prediction algorithm.

2 Literature Survey

The authors of [1,2] proposed the decision equations for federation. In [3,4], an economic model for federation has been proposed based on game theory. In [5], the

© Springer International Publishing Switzerland 2016
N. Bjørner et al. (Eds.): ICDCIT 2016, LNCS 9581, pp. 169–174, 2016.
DOI: 10.1007/978-3-319-28034-9_22

authors propose a threshold based load balancing algorithm for federation that mainly addresses SLA violation. Authors of [6] propose a pre-emption based contention free federation environment. All the above mentioned resource provisioning mechanisms are reactive i.e., the federation decisions are made only when the resource limitation occurs. In the next section we propose proactive resource provisioning mechanism and discuss the impact of it in terms of profit and resource utilization.

3   Proactive Resource Provisioning in Cloud Federation

An intelligent resource provisioning mechanism is needed such that it adapts to the incoming workload. In our proposed technique, federation decisions are made in advance even before the resource shortage occurs and also achieves efficient resource utilization. Based on the predicted resource requirements and the current resource utilization, insourcing and outsourcing decisions are made in advance. Our proposed mechanism has three components namely Resource Allocator, Load Balancer and Workload Predictor. We discuss each of them in detail in the forthcoming sub sections.

3.1   Resource Allocator

The VM requests to a IaaS cloud are from two sources in a federated environment: direct customers and insource request from other CSPs. Resource Allocator component gets the incoming VM requests and allocates resources for the VM on a best effort basis. Resources allocation is done based on the insource and outsource flags set/reset by the Load balancer and Workload Predictor components. The flowchart of how the VM requests are served is shown in Fig. 1.

3.2   Load Balancer

We define two threshold values on load in a cloud namely, T_1 and T_2. This component computes the resource utilization of the cloud periodically and compares it with the threshold values. Three decision rules of Load Balancer are as follows:

1. If the resource utilization is less than T_1, the insource flag is enabled which denotes that insource requests are served in order to improve the utilization.
2. If the resource utilization is between T_1 and T_2, only direct requests are served and no new insource requests are served to reserve more resources for future direct requests that yields more profit.
3. If the resource utilization crosses T_2, the insource requests that are being served are pre-empted and the outsource flag is set to denote that the new requests from direct customers have to be outsourced.

These scenarios are with respect to scaling up of resources by a cloud. Similarly, the flags are reset when the load falls below the threshold values during which scale down occurs. Figure 2 is the flowchart of the load balancing mechanism.

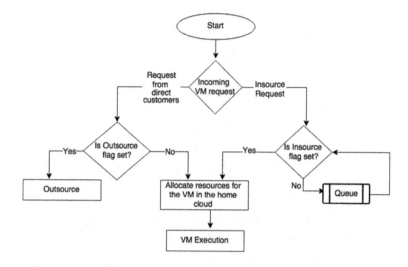

Fig. 1. Flowchart of resource allocation mechanism

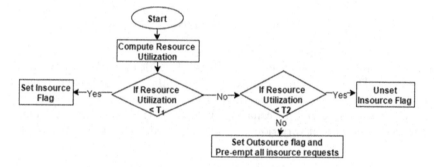

Fig. 2. Flowchart of load balancing mechanism

3.3   Workload Predictor

A time series based workload prediction algorithm runs at fixed time interval like load balancer and predicts the resource requirement of next interval based on which the resource utilization of next interval is estimated. Now a load balancing is performed by this component by comparing the estimated resource utilization with the threshold range based on which the insource and outsource flags are set/unset appropriately. The flowchart of the workload prediction mechanism is shown in Fig. 3. Though our prediction mechanism is intelligent enough to predict peak workloads and rejects new insource requests, few insource requests would have bypassed the prediction. Such insource requests are pre-empted when the resource utilization crosses T_2.

We propose a sliding window prediction algorithm that looks for a similar trend of events in the *training set* by matching the *current window* with the *training window* that keeps sliding until the entire training set is covered. The best matching

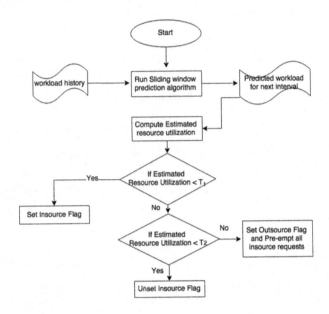

Fig. 3. Flowchart of workload prediction mechanism

training window is the one that has minimum Euclidean distance with the *current window*. The resource requirement in the *training set* that is next to the best matching training window is the predicted resource requirement. The Sliding window technique is useful in this scenario as it captures the variations in training set that matches the current variation and very well predicts the peak workloads.

4   Experiment and Analysis

In this section, first we compare the prediction accuracy of sliding window algorithm with a popular time series prediction algorithm Auto Regressive Integrated Moving Average (ARIMA) when used for workload prediction. Then we perform evaluation of proactive resource provisioning in cloud federation.

4.1   Evaluation of Prediction Algorithms

We use the workload log obtained from The Los Alamos National Lab (LANL) which consists of incoming workload information that includes its resource requirements(CPU,memory) also. We predict the CPU and memory requirements for the next time interval using this history. Table 1 shows the MAPE(Mean Absolute Percentage Error) of the prediction algorithms. MAPE is given by the formula

$$\left(\frac{1}{n} \sum_{i=1}^{n} |a_i - p_i|/a_i \right) * 100 \tag{1}$$

Table 1. Comparison of MAPE of ARIMA and sliding window algorithm

	MAPE (%)	
	Memory prediction	CPU prediction
ARIMA	51.2	59.80
SW = 3	71.9	73.1
SW = 5	77.4	82.3
SW = 7	80.1	85.6

Table 2. Performance comparison of federation without prediction, with prediction using ARIMA and with prediction using sliding window

	Only Insourcing No Outsourcing		Insourcing and Outsourcing	
	Resource Util (%)	Profit ($)	Resource Util (%)	Profit ($)
Without Prediction	53.2	8541.46	55.6	13146
With Prediction(ARIMA)	54.5	8796.4	30.48	12840
With Prediction(Sliding window)	65.9	13736.8	67.7	15601.8

where a_i is the actual value, p_i is the predicted value and n is the number of observations. From Table 1, we learn that Sliding window algorithm is better in terms of accuracy when compared to ARIMA and also the accuracy of sliding window increases with increase in window size.

4.2   Evaluation of Proactive Cloud Federation Mechanism

We implemented a homogeneous cloud federation simulation environment. In reference to the utilization range defined by VMware in [7], we set the threshold values on utilization as $T_1 = 45\%$ and $T_2 = 81\%$ for our experimental purpose. Ideally, during outsourcing the best cloud has to be chosen based on various parameters like bandwidth, resource utilization and cost. But we assume that there is only one cloud called remote cloud to which a outsource requests are sent. We assume that price of a CPU per hour in home cloud is $0.7 and that in remote cloud during federation is $0.5, price of a memory unit per hour in home cloud is $0.5 and that in remote cloud is $0.4, operation cost of a VM in both the clouds is $0.1 per hour and outsourcing cost per VM is $0.2 per hour. From our experiment using the above mentioned data set, we identified that without federation the resource utilization of the home cloud was 24.6% and the profit gained was $4644. Table 2 shows that the resource utilization and profit of the home cloud during federation is better than that without federation. But the resource utilization and profit during federation with prediction using ARIMA is very closer to that without prediction when only insourcing is done.In the case when both insourcing and outsourcing are done, performance of federation using ARIMA dropped whereas federation with prediction using sliding window generated better performance in terms of utilization and profit in all cases.

5   Conclusion

In this paper, we have presented a proactive resource provisioning model for cloud federation that uses sliding window for workload prediction and we compared its accuracy with ARIMA. We have developed a simulation environment for federation for our experimental purpose and evaluated the results of proposed mechanism. Though its not experimentally shown, the proactive resource provisioning during federation decreases the SLA violations and better satisfies the QoS. We plan to prove this experimentally in our future work.

Acknowledgement. The research for this paper was financially supported by DST PURSE Phase II.

References

1. Goiri, I., Guitart, J., Torres, J.: Characterizing cloud federation for enhancing providers' profit. In: 2010 IEEE 3rd International Conference on Cloud Computing (CLOUD), pp. 123–130. IEEE (2010)
2. Toosi, A.N., Calheiros, R.N., Thulasiram, R.K., Buyya, R.: Resource provisioning policies to increase iaas provider's profit in a federated cloud environment. In: 2011 IEEE 13th International Conference on High Performance Computing and Communications (HPCC), pp. 279–287. IEEE (2011)
3. Samaan, N.: A novel economic sharing model in a federation of selfish cloud providers. IEEE Trans. Parallel Distrib. Syst. **25**(1), 12–21 (2014)
4. Mashayekhy, L., Nejad, M.M., Grosu, D.: Cloud federations in the sky: formation game and mechanism. IEEE Trans. Cloud Comput. **3**(1), 14–27 (2015)
5. Patel, K.S., Sarje, A.: VM provisioning method to improve the profit and SLA violation of cloud service providers. In: 2012 IEEE International Conference on Cloud Computing in Emerging Markets (CCEM), pp. 1–5. IEEE (2012)
6. Salehi, M.A., Toosi, A.N., Buyya, R.: Contention management in federated virtualized distributed systems: implementation and evaluation. Softw. Pract. Experience **44**(3), 353–368 (2014)
7. Gulati, A., Holler, A., Ji, M., Shanmuganathan, G., Waldspurger, C., Zhu, X.: Vmware distributed resource management: design, implementation, and lessons learned. VMware Tech. J. **1**(1), 45–64 (2012)

A Multiclass SVM Classification Approach for Intrusion Detection

Santosh Kumar Sahu$^{(\boxtimes)}$ and Sanjay Kumar Jena

National Institute of Technology, Rourkela, Odisha, India
santoshsahu@hotmail.co.in, skjena@nitrkl.ac.in

Abstract. As the number of threats to the computer network and network-based applications is increasing, there is a need for a robust intrusion detection system that can ensure security against threats. To detect and defend against a specific attack, the pattern of the attack should be known a priori. Classification of attacks is a useful way to identify the unique patterns of different type of attack. As a result, KDDCup99, NSLKDD and GureKDD datasets are used in this experiment to improve the learning process and study different attack patterns thoroughly. This paper proposed a multi-class Support Vector Machine classifier(MSVM), using one versus all method, to identify one attack uniquely, which in turn helps to defend against the known as well as unknown attacks. Experimentally, the proposed scheme provides better detection accuracy, fewer false positives, and lesser training and generalization error in comparison to the existing approach.

Keywords: MSVM · Threats · KDD corrected · NSL KDD · Gure KDD

1 Introduction

The highly integrated electronic world is an effect of technological development over decades. The number of malicious activities and attacks are also growing besides the advances in security against threats. To mitigate the situations, various attempts are made to control the attack activities. There is a need to improve and innovate different techniques for the detection of intrusion against the enormous amount of malicious attempts on networks [1]. To detect and countermeasures such attacks, multi-class problem should be adapted. Most of the learning methods are biased in multiclass problems. As a result proper combination approaches should be used to improve the detection rate, overcome the bias and over fitting situation. In this work, Support Vector Machine (SVM) learning approach is used as a base learner to solve the multi-class problem.

1.1 Support Vector Machine

The classification is used to achieve high accuracy for classifying the maximum number of instances with the small number of training samples. It gives better

© Springer International Publishing Switzerland 2016
N. Bjørner et al. (Eds.): ICDCIT 2016, LNCS 9581, pp. 175–181, 2016.
DOI: 10.1007/978-3-319-28034-9_23

result for two class classification problem [4]. It maps input vectors to a high dimensional feature space. Both linear and non-linear data is separated by a hyperplane in two classes. The hyperplane is found with the help of support vector (training tuples) and margin (defined by support vectors) [5]. SVMs are the successful and resilient classification algorithms [4]. The SVM supports only binary classification and deals with maximizing the margin which is the minimum distance from nearest example to the separating hyperplane. The concept of SVM can be extended to multiclass classification [6].

1.2 Multiclass Support Vector Machine

The multiclass problem needs to be decomposed into several binary class problems. Each of the binary classifiers is applied to new data point and the frequency of the number of times the point is assigned to the same label is counted and labeled with the highest count. The popular two methods for decomposition of multi-class problem discussed as follows: [7].

One-verses-all. One-verses-all is also called as winner takes all strategy. This is the simplest approach to reduce the problem of classification from k classes into k binary problems. Each problem is different from other k − 1 problems. This approach requires k binary classes in which we train kth classifier with positive example and belonging to class k and negative examples belonging to other k − 1 classes. An unknown example is tested and the classifier for which maximum output is produced is considered to be the winner class. That class label is assigned to that example. Although this approach is simple, its performance can be compared with more complicated approaches [8].

One-versus-one. For every pair of different classes, one binary classifier is constructed. In this way, the multi-class problem is broken into a series of a set of binary class problems; so that we can apply SVM model for each pair of classes. Total $k(k-1)/2$ classifiers are needed to classify the unknown data. The binary classifier is trained taking one class as positive and other class as negative. For a new data point x if that classifier classifies x in first class, then a vote is added to that class. If the classifier classifies x in second class the vote is added to the second class. This process is repeated for each of the $k(k-1)/2$ classifiers. Finally, label of the class with maximum number of votes is assigned to the new data point x. In this way the class to which the unknown data point belongs is predicted [8,9].

1.3 Intrusion Dataset

The intrusion dataset takes a vital role in model assessment and learning process. In this experiment the benchmarked intrusion datasets are used. The public datasets namely KDDCup99, NSLKDD, and GureKDD are used in learning and evaluation process. The details about the datasets are discussed in [10].

1.4 Motivation and Objective

As the number of attacks are growing day by day, it becomes utmost essential to classify the specific attack type with maximum accuracy that motivated to implement the MSVM IDS. The objective of this work is to detect the exact type of attacking effort to the network that helps to analyze, countermeasure and implement security policies.

The rest of the paper is organized as follows: The existing work on SVM and multiclass SVM discussed in Sect. 2. The result and discussion is presented in Sect. 3. The comparison of the proposed approach with existing approaches elaborated in Sect. 4, and finally, Sect. 5 conclude the work.

2 Related Work

Mathur et al. [3] has extended the SVM approach to multiclass SVM. He has undertaken a multiclass classification based on a single optimization. Chen et al. [12] uses hierarchical SVM for clustering the classes into binary tree. The clusters are formed by arranging the classes into undirected graph. Each node of the tree is a binary SVM classifier . Hsu et al. [14] has proposed two methods one by considering all data at once and second is a decomposition implementation.

According to latest research, there are a lot of attempts to improve IDS using the data mining and machine learning techniques. In this paper, a multi-class SVM approach is proposed to detect the specific attack types with low false alarm rate. The accuracy is calculated for each of the five classes i.e., Normal, DOS, U2R, R2L, and Probe attack.

3 Result and Discussion

In this paper, one against all approach of MSVM is implemented on Matlab R2015a. To improve the detection accuracy, cross validation and re-sampling

Table 1. The details of datasets

Dataset	No. of instances for training	No. of instances for testing	Number of instances correctly classified	No. of Class	Accuracy
KDD Corrected	77291	311029	284421	38	91.445 %
NSL-KDD	47736	125973	118447	23	94.025 %
Gure-KDD	160904	178810	177283	28	99.146 %

Table 2. The confusion matrix on KDD corrected dataset

790	2	0	0	0	0	0	0	0	0	0	2	0	0	0	0	0	0	0	0	0
16	98	0	0	0	0	0	0	0	0	0	984	0	0	0	0	0	0	0	0	0
0	0	12	0	0	0	0	0	0	0	0	6	0	0	0	0	0	0	0	4	0
0	0	0	0	0	0	0	0	0	0	0	2	0	0	0	0	0	0	0	1	0
2	0	0	3959	1	0	0	1	0	0	0	401	0	0	3	0	0	0	0	0	0
0	0	1	0	150	0	0	0	0	0	0	7	0	0	0	0	0	0	0	0	0
0	0	0	0	1	0	0	0	0	0	0	0	0	0	0	0	0	0	0	0	0
0	0	0	0	0	296	0	0	0	0	0	5	0	0	0	2	0	3	0	0	0
0	0	0	0	0	0	9	0	0	0	0	0	0	0	0	0	0	0	0	0	0
0	0	1	0	0	0	0	0	0	0	0	1	0	0	0	0	0	0	0	0	0
0	0	0	4421	0	0	0	579	0	0	0	0	0	0	0	0	0	0	0	0	0
0	0	0	1	6	0	0	0	1039	0	0	4	0	0	3	0	0	0	0	0	0
0	0	0	1	0	0	0	0	0	0	0	17	0	0	0	0	0	0	0	0	0
0	0	0	0	0	0	0	0	0	0	0	17	0	0	0	0	0	0	0	0	0
0	0	0	0	0	0	0	0	7	57989	0	5	0	0	0	0	0	0	0	0	0
0	0	0	0	0	0	0	0	0	0	84	0	0	0	0	0	0	0	0	0	0
1	9	1	46	2	1	0	15	4	5	0	48539	9	65	2	0	82	2	11707	103	0
0	0	1	0	0	0	0	0	0	0	0	1	0	0	0	0	0	0	0	0	0
0	0	0	0	0	0	0	0	0	0	0	2	0	0	0	0	0	0	0	0	0
0	0	0	0	0	0	0	0	0	0	0	13	73	0	0	0	0	1	0	0	0
0	0	0	0	23	0	0	0	0	0	0	1	0	330	0	0	0	0	0	0	0
0	0	0	0	0	0	0	0	3	0	0	0	0	0	756	0	0	0	0	0	0
0	0	0	0	0	0	0	0	0	0	0	14	0	0	0	0	0	0	0	2	0
0	0	0	0	0	0	0	0	0	0	0	12	0	0	0	0	0	0	0	0	1
0	0	0	0	0	0	0	0	1	0	0	17	0	0	0	104	614	0	0	0	0
0	0	0	0	0	0	0	0	0	0	0	9	0	0	0	0	1624	0	0	0	0
0	0	2	2	0	0	0	0	0	0	0	9	0	0	0	0	0	0	0	4	0
0	0	0	0	0	0	0	0	0	0	0	1	0	0	0	0	0	164090	0	0	0
0	0	0	0	0	0	0	0	0	0	0	106	0	0	0	0	0	0	7635	0	0
0	0	0	0	0	0	0	0	0	0	0	10	0	0	0	1	0	0	2395	0	0
0	0	2	0	0	0	0	0	0	0	0	0	0	0	0	0	0	0	0	0	0
0	0	0	0	0	0	0	0	0	0	0	12	0	0	0	0	0	0	0	0	0
0	0	0	0	0	0	0	0	0	0	0	2	0	0	0	0	0	0	0	0	0
0	0	0	0	0	0	0	0	0	0	0	97	0	0	0	0	0	0	0	1505	0
0	0	0	0	0	0	0	0	0	0	0	2	0	0	0	0	0	0	0	0	0
0	0	0	1	0	0	0	0	0	0	0	5	0	0	3	0	0	0	0	0	0
0	0	2	0	0	0	0	0	0	1	0	0	0	0	1	0	0	0	0	0	0
0	0	0	0	0	0	0	0	0	0	0	11	0	0	0	0	0	0	0	2	0

methods are applied on U2R and R2L distributions. The three intrusion datasets namely KDD corrected , NSL-KDD and Gure-KDD used for training and testing purpose. The details about the dataset and detection accuracy is given in the Table 1. The confusion matrices for KDD corrected, Gure-KDD and NSL-KDD dataset are given in Table 2, Fig. 1b and Table 3 respectively.

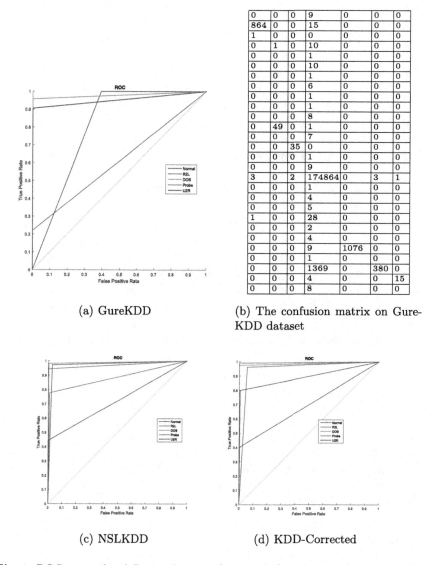

0	0	0	9	0	0	0
864	0	0	15	0	0	0
1	0	0	0	0	0	0
0	1	0	10	0	0	0
0	0	0	1	0	0	0
0	0	0	10	0	0	0
0	0	0	1	0	0	0
0	0	0	6	0	0	0
0	0	0	1	0	0	0
0	0	0	1	0	0	0
0	0	0	8	0	0	0
0	49	0	1	0	0	0
0	0	0	7	0	0	0
0	0	35	0	0	0	0
0	0	0	1	0	0	0
0	0	0	9	0	0	0
3	0	2	174864	0	3	1
0	0	0	1	0	0	0
0	0	0	4	0	0	0
0	0	0	5	0	0	0
1	0	0	28	0	0	0
0	0	0	2	0	0	0
0	0	0	4	0	0	0
0	0	0	9	1076	0	0
0	0	0	1	0	0	0
0	0	0	1369	0	380	0
0	0	0	4	0	0	15
0	0	0	8	0	0	0

(a) GureKDD

(b) The confusion matrix on Gure-KDD dataset

(c) NSLKDD

(d) KDD-Corrected

Fig. 1. ROC curve for different datasets (a, c and d) and confusion matrix (b) for GKDD dataset

Table 3. The confusion matrix on NSL-KDD dataset

65781	4	116	80	2	0	0	30	151	52	423	1	345	7	0	21	37	63	16	11	203
4	41200	0	0	0	0	0	0	0	0	0	0	0	0	0	0	0	1	9	0	0
380	0	492	0	0	0	0	0	0	0	18	0	0	0	0	0	0	0	0	0	0
111	0	0	3449	0	0	39	0	0	0	0	0	0	0	0	0	0	0	0	0	0
41	5	0	0	2852	0	0	0	0	0	0	0	0	0	0	0	27	2	4	0	0
7	0	0	0	0	884	0	0	0	1	0	0	0	0	0	0	0	0	0	0	0
271	0	0	13	0	0	1209	0	0	0	0	0	0	0	0	0	0	0	0	0	0
287	0	0	0	2	0	0	0	3325	0	0	1	0	0	0	13	0	5	0	0	0
66	0	0	0	0	0	0	2580	0	0	0	0	0	0	0	0	0	0	0	0	0
97	0	0	0	0	0	0	0	0	0	0	0	0	104	0	0	0	0	0	0	0
749	0	2	0	0	0	200	0	0	0	0	0	0	0	5	0	0	0	0	0	0
2	0	0	0	0	0	0	0	0	0	0	51	0	0	0	0	0	0	0	0	0
4	0	0	0	0	0	0	0	0	0	4	0	0	0	0	0	0	0	0	0	0
2	0	0	0	0	0	0	0	0	0	5	0	0	0	0	0	0	0	0	0	0
5	0	1	0	0	0	0	0	0	0	2	1	0	0	0	0	0	0	0	1	0
26	0	4	0	0	0	0	0	0	0	0	0	0	0	0	0	0	0	0	0	0
10	1	0	0	0	0	0	0	0	0	0	0	0	0	0	0	0	0	0	0	0
1	0	0	0	0	0	0	0	0	0	0	0	17	0	0	0	0	0	0	0	0
8	0	1	0	0	0	0	0	0	0	0	0	0	0	0	0	0	0	0	0	0
1	0	0	0	0	0	0	0	0	0	0	2	0	0	0	0	0	0	0	0	0
4	0	0	0	0	0	0	0	0	0	0	0	0	0	0	0	0	0	0	0	0
1	0	0	0	0	0	0	0	0	0	0	0	0	0	0	0	0	0	0	1	0
1	0	0	0	0	0	0	0	0	0	19	0	0	0	0	0	0	0	0	0	0

4   Comparison

The existing approach by [1] failed to detect the R2L and U2R attack patterns. As a result, the accuracy of that model is 91.67 % and only KDDCup99 dataset is used. In the proposed MSVM approach, three datasets are used and preprocessed properly before the model formation. The detection accuracy of the proposed scheme is 99.146 % on GureKDD, 94.025 % on NSLKDD and 91.445 % on KDDCorrected Dataset.

5   Conclusion

In this paper, an MSVM classifier is used to detect and identify the attacks by type. Evaluation has been done over the three benchmark intrusion datasets. Cross-validation and re-sampling methods are applied to improve the learning process to the datasets. The model can determine a particular known type of attack when the unknown instances need to be classified. This scheme provides a better detection accuracy and reduces the complexity of the model. Further, it can detect the least data distributions i.e. U2R and R2L attacks efficiently.

References

1. Ambwani, T.: Multi class support vector machine implementation to intrusion detection. In: Proceedings of the International Joint Conference on Neural Networks, vol. 3. IEEE (2003)
2. Mukkamala, S., Janoski, G., Sung, A.: Intrusion detection using neural networks and support vector machines. In: Proceedings of the 2002 International Joint Conference on Neural Networks, IJCNN 2002, vol. 2. IEEE (2002)
3. Mathur, A., Foody, G.M.: Multiclass and binary SVM classification: implications for training and classification users. IEEE Geosci. Remote Sens. Lett. 5(2), 241–245 (2008)
4. Cortes, C., Vapnik, V.: Support-vector networks. Mach. Learn. 20(3), 273–297 (1995)
5. Han, J., Kamber, M., Pei, J.: Data Mining, Southeast Asia Edition: Concepts and Techniques. Morgan kaufmann, Burlington (2006)
6. Lee, Y., Lin, Y., Wahba, G.: Multicategory support vector machines: theory and application to the classification of microarray data and satellite radiance data. J. Am. Stat. Assoc. 99(465), 67–81 (2004)
7. Allwein, E.L., Schapire, R.E., Singer, Y.: Reducing multiclass to binary: a unifying approach for margin classifiers. J. Mach. Learn. Res. 1, 113–141 (2001)
8. Aly, M.: Survey on multiclass classification methods. Neural Netw. 1–9 (2005)
9. Duan, K.-B., Keerthi, S.S.: Which is the best multiclass SVM method? An empirical study. In: Oza, N.C., Polikar, R., Kittler, J., Roli, F. (eds.) MCS 2005. LNCS, vol. 3541, pp. 278–285. Springer, Heidelberg (2005)
10. Sahu, S.K., Sarangi, S., Jena, S.K.: A detail analysis on intrusion detection datasets. In: 2014 IEEE International Advance Computing Conference (IACC). IEEE (2014)
11. Tavallaee, M., et al.: A detailed analysis of the KDD CUP 99 data set. In: Proceedings of the Second IEEE Symposium on Computational Intelligence for Security and Defence Applications (2009)
12. Chen, Y., Crawford, M.M., Ghosh, J.: Integrating support vector machines in a hierarchical output space decomposition framework. In: 2004 IEEE International Geoscience and Remote Sensing Symposium, IGARSS 2004, Proceedings, vol. 2. IEEE (2004)
13. Lee, H., Song, J., Park, D.: Intrusion detection system based on multi-class SVM. In: Ślęzak, D., Yao, J.T., Peters, J.F., Ziarko, W.P., Hu, X. (eds.) RSFDGrC 2005. LNCS (LNAI), vol. 3642, pp. 511–519. Springer, Heidelberg (2005)
14. Hsu, C.-W., Lin, C.-J.: A comparison of methods for multiclass support vector machines. IEEE Trans. Neural Netw. 13(2), 415–425 (2002)

Dynamic Data Replication Across Geo-Distributed Cloud Data Centres

D.S. Jayalakshmi[1], T.P. Rashmi Ranjana[1(✉)], and Srinivasan Ramaswamy[2]

[1] M. S. Ramaiah Institute of Technology, Bengaluru, India
jayalakshmids@msrit.edu, rashmiranjana23@gmail.com
[2] SRM University, Kattankulathur, Kancheepuram, India
rsv38@yahoo.co.in

Abstract. Cloud computing is being used for data-intensive computing for enterprise and scientific applications that process large data sets originating from globally distributed data centers. In this work, we propose a system model for multiple data centers cooperating to serve a client's request for data and to identify data centers which can provide the fastest response time to a client. Further, dynamic data replication strategy across geo-distributed data centers based on popularity is detailed. Simulation results are presented and the performance evaluation shows that our method consistently maintains the replica count to an optimal value.

Keywords: Data center selection · Dynamic data replication · Geo-distributed data centers · Data intensive applications

1 Introduction

Data-intensive mobile, enterprise and scientific applications are being run across geo-distributed data centers [1]. To perform analytics over the entire data, the geo-distributed data has to be transferred to a single data center which calls for costly data transfers across wide area networks or, the data sets have to be processed in the local data centers and the results aggregated [2]. In this paper, we consider data intensive applications running across geo-distributed data centers. Selecting the best data center based on the proximity to clients can significantly reduce the client response time and replicating data files in data centers that are close to the clients can benefit in reducing latency. Many variants of Hadoop for handling data across multiple data centers use static replication and do not consider replication across data centers. We propose a system model to reduce access latency by providing a method to determine the closest data center to the client [3] and to reduce data storage and transmission costs by dynamically creating or removing replicas of large data files based on their popularity [4]. The rest of the paper is organized as follows. In Sect. 2, we give the detailed information about the proposed system model and cloud data service architecture, while conclusions and final remarks are presented in Sect. 3.

D.S. Jayalakshmi—Research scholar, SRM University.

© Springer International Publishing Switzerland 2016
N. Bjørner et al. (Eds.): ICDCIT 2016, LNCS 9581, pp. 182–187, 2016.
DOI: 10.1007/978-3-319-28034-9_24

2 System Model

System Architecture. The cloud system architecture consists of a single Master Data-Centre (MDC) and two Ordinary DataCentres (ODCs) as shown in Fig. 1. Each data-centre comprises a Local Scheduling Broker (LSB), a Local Replica Manager (LRM), a Local Replica Catalog (LRC), and storage element. LSB is a scheduler which is responsible for selecting a datacenter on which the task must be executed. LRC is a catalog which has complete information about the blocks of files and the number of replicas of files which are stored in the datacenter. LRC is used by LRM for checking the requested file's availability in ODC. The MDC consists of Master Replica Manager (MRM) and Master Replica Catalog (MRC) which is held together as a single entity called Replica Broker (RB). Each ODC is assigned with unique IP address and unique datacenter id (ODCid). IP addresses are used for calculation of geographical distance between the client and datacenter.

During initialization of the system, files are stripped into blocks of equal size and stored with replica count as one. All files stored in this system are maintained as file set where each element file is defined as File Catalog Content/Local Replica Catalog. Each client is identified by a unique IP address assigned to it at the time of its creation. It creates tasks and submits them to the nearest datacenter in Poisson distribution using an External Scheduler.

Cloud Data Service. In the first phase of data service, a decision regarding task scheduling to a best suited datacenter is done by external scheduler and LSB; accordingly the task is routed to that datacenter for execution. The best datacenter is selected based on distance and file access cost between the client and datacenter.

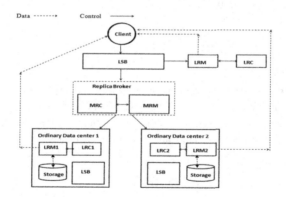

Fig. 1. Cloud system architecture

Datacenter Selection. The client submits tasks to the geographically closest datacenter which has all the resources to serve the request. File access cost from a datacentre DC j having the file to client 'i' is calculated. The formula of data transfer time $DT\ (C_i, DC_j)$ of a file 'f' is given by (1)

$$DT\left(C_i, DC_j\right) = Rt\left(DC_j\right) + \frac{Size\,(f)}{Bandwidth\left(link\left(C_i, DC_j\right)\right)} \tag{1}$$

where f - file requested, DC_j - data center which is considered for selection, $Rt(DC_j)$ - time span for requesting for 'f', C_i - client who has submitted the task, j can be $\{0,1,2\}$ - any one of the data center in cloud system. If a single data center does not have complete file required then the aggregated cost $DT(F)$, i.e. the total data transfer time, has to be calculated using (2).

$$DT\left(F\right) = DT\left(C_i, DC_j\right) + \sum_{k=1}^{k=n} DT\left(C_j, DC_k\right) \tag{2}$$

where DC_j is the data center at which task is submitted, DC_k is the data center having part of file 'f', k is the set of candidate data centers $(0 < k < n)$ having the blocks requested file, n is total number of data centers in the system. The total data file access cost in a data grid before replication is the total transmission time spent to get all needed data files for each site. The data file access cost $C_{ij}(F)$ between the client C_i and DC_j is obtained by (3) where $Cost_{bw}$ is cost associated with used network bandwidth.

$$C_{ij}\left(F\right) = Cost_{bw} * DT\left(F\right) \tag{3}$$

Dynamic Data Replication Strategy. Here a decision regarding creation of a replica for a file requested say $F(R_F)$ and deletion of replica to maintain optimal number of replicas in the system is made. The average amount of data accessed in some time interval is calculated. The MRM maintains a summarized access record for every file 'F' in the system for a certain time interval 't'. The formula for average amount of data accessed in time 't' is given by (4)

$$D_{avg}\left(t\right) = \frac{\sum_{i=1}^{T_f} n_t\left(F\right) * |F|}{T_f} \tag{4}$$

where $n_t(F)$ – the number of times file 'F' is accessed during 't', $N_t(F)$ - number of replicas of $F(R_F)$ in interval 't', T_f - total number of unique files in the system during 't'. A large file with more access time is suitable for replication when compared to a small file that is accessed many times. Thus amount of data accessed for a file 'F' in interval 't' is given by (5).

$$D_F\left(t\right) = n_t\left(F\right) * |F| \tag{5}$$

The decision on replica creation is made by the condition given in (6). If it satisfies, Stage 2 of this phase is entered; else exit.

$$\frac{D_{avg}\left(t\right)}{D_F\left(t\right)} > N_t\left(F\right) \tag{6}$$

Network topology that will be created from BRITE topology file is used to determine the hop count value. In this stage, the link H_i with minimum hop from a datacenter to another datacenter 'I' belonging to E_F, where E_F is the set of datacenters containing replica of file R_F is determined including maximum available bandwidth B_i, From the list of datacenters obtained, a datacenter 'k' is selected using (7).

$$min \left(\frac{H_i}{B_i} \right)^{|E_F|}_{i=1} \tag{7}$$

Least Recently Accessed (LRA) replacement strategy in combination with the popularity of that file is used as a criterion for deleting the replica which results in balanced number of replicas in the system.

3   Simulation and Results

The test environment is setup on CloudSim v3.0.3. A simulation is run with 3 datacentres MDC_0, ODC_1, and ODC_2. Each datacentre consists of 3 VMs and 3 Hosts with files that are stripped into blocks of equal size and loaded in to the datacenters randomly with initial replica count equal to 1. The storage capacity of each datacenter, IP address, Number of Requests, Poisson Mean, Replication Interval, Number of Files, and Size of each File can be changed for each simulation by the user and are given individually as shown in Table 1.

Table 1. Configuration parameters for simulation

Base Case / Cases Considered	Memory Storage of DC (in GB)			No. of Files	Size of File (in GB)				No. of Requests	Size of Blocks (in MB)
	ODC_1	ODC_2	MDC_0		F1	F2	F3	F4		
Cases Considered	1024	1024	512	2	400	750	-	-	25	204.8
Case 1: No. of Requests	1024	1024	512	2	400	750	-	-	75	204.8
Case 2: Memory Storage of DC (in GB)	1524	1524	1012	2	400	750	-	-	25	204.8
Case 3: No. of Files	1024	1024	512	4	400	200	750	400	25	204.8

3.1   Result Analysis

Simulation is performed extensively by varying parameters and there results are analyzed to give the inference and conclusions. The base case 1 simulation results are used for comparison with all the cases given in the following sections.

Number of Requests. It is inferred that as the number of requests increase the number of replicas also increase. It is observed that as the replicas increase the data transfer cost for that file decrease, decreasing the execution time as shown in the Fig. 2.

Memory Storage of Datacentres. It is inferred that as the number of replicas increases as there is empty storage space for the new replicas to be accommodated. Although there

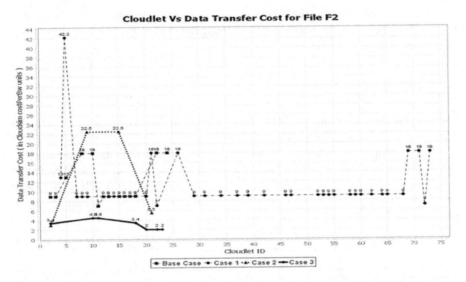

Fig. 2. Data transfer cost of a file F2 for all cases.

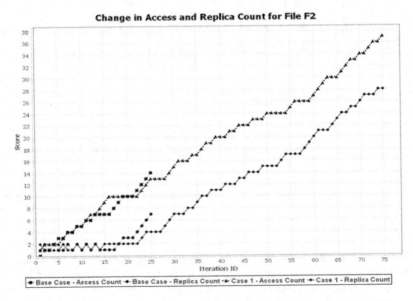

Fig. 3. Replica creation and deletion based on the access frequency for file F2.

is deletion for least recently accessed files, the number of replicas will be increased in line with access count as shown in Fig. 3. It is observed that as the replicas increase the data transfer cost or that file decrease which results in less execution time.

Number of Files in Datacentres. It is inferred that as the number of files increases; due to lack of storage space, the number of replicas will decrease.

4   Conclusions

The dynamic replication system proposed in this work aims at reducing the data transfer cost for a requested file as the closest datacenter will be selected for submitting the request. The performance evaluation shows that this reduces the execution time and data transfer cost in the course of time by increasing the number of replicas, the number of replicas will be increased only for the popular files and, the files with least access count and least recently accessed time will be deleted when a request is served. This dynamically controls the proliferation of replicas over a period of time and keeps the replica count constrained to an optimal value thereby bringing down storage costs.

References

1. Grozev, N., Buyya, R.: Inter-cloud architectures and application brokering: taxonomy andsurvey. J. Softw. Pract. Exp. **44**, 369–390 (2014). doi:10.1002/spe.2168. Wiley
2. Agrawal, D., El Abbadi, A., Mahmoud, H.A., Nawab, F., Salem, K.: Managing geo-replicated data in multi-datacenters. In: Madaan, A., Kikuchi, S., Bhalla, S. (eds.) DNIS 2013. LNCS, vol. 7813, pp. 23–43. Springer, Heidelberg (2013)
3. Kapgate, D.: Efficient service broker algorithm for datacentre selection in cloud computing. IJCSMC 3(1), 355–365 (2014). ISSN 2320–088X
4. Bsoul, M., Al-Khasawneh, A., Kilani, Y., Obeidat, I.: A threshold-based dynamic data replication strategy. J Supercomput **60**, 301–310 (2012). doi:10.1007/s11227-010-0466-3

Trust Based Target Coverage Protocol
for Wireless Sensor Networks
Using Fuzzy Logic

Pooja Chaturvedi[(✉)] and A.K. Daniel

M. M. M. University of Technology, Gorakhpur, India
chaturvedi.pooja03@gmail.com, danielak@rediffmail.com,
ajai.k.daniel@gmail.com

Abstract. Wireless sensor network constitute a class of real time embedded systems having limited resources. Target coverage problem is concerned with the continuous monitoring of a set of targets such that the network lifetime is maximized with the consideration of resource constraints. In this paper we propose a node scheduling protocol for target coverage problem on the basis of node contribution, coverage probability and trust values, where the set covers are computed dynamically using time stamping. The time stamping is a factor of threshold of the coverage level. We have evaluated the performance of the proposed protocol by varying the number of nodes and targets. The results show that the proposed scheme improves the network lifetime in terms of energy consumption and the reliability of the data communicated in comparison to the naïve approach in which all the nodes are activated at once. The results show that the network lifetime is proportional to the energy savings under a constant environment.

1 Introduction

Target coverage algorithms aim to have each critical region or area within the range of at least one sensor node. The scheduling of the nodes in a number of set covers can ensure the monitoring of the targets while conserving the energy. Consider the network as shown in Fig. 1. The set of sensor nodes as $S = \{s_1, s_2, s_3\}$ and set of targets as $T = \{t_1, t_2, t_3, t_4\}$ in which the nodes can monitor the targets as: $s_1 = \{t_1, t_2\}$, $s_2 = \{t_2, t_3\}, s_3 = \{t_3, t_4\}$.

Suppose each node can monitor the targets for 0.1 time unit, then if all the nodes are activated at once then the network lifetime will be 0.1. But if we schedule the nodes into various sets as: $C_1 = \{s_1, s_2, s_3\}, C_2 = \{s_1, s_3\}$ and suppose the monitoring time of each set covers is as: 0.3 and 0.2 then the network lifetime can be extended to 0.5 time units. Various approaches have been proposed for target coverage problem such as virtual force based approach, deployment based approach and geometrical constructs based approach. The most efficient way to improve the network lifetime while continuously monitoring a set of targets is to schedule the nodes in various set covers [1, 4]. The closest work related to our work is in [2], in which the authors have considered only the communication trust and one hop communication between the node and the base

© Springer International Publishing Switzerland 2016
N. Bjørner et al. (Eds.): ICDCIT 2016, LNCS 9581, pp. 188–192, 2016.
DOI: 10.1007/978-3-319-28034-9_25

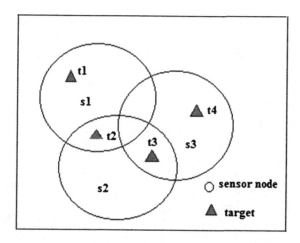

Fig. 1. Example of the sensor target relationship in a network

station. In the proposed approach we have considered the various trust metrics and also the multi hop communication between the nodes to ensure the desired coverage level and connectivity [5].

2 Proposed Node Scheduling Protocol

For a sensor network which consists of n sensor nodes $S = \{s_1, s_2 \ldots s_n\}$ and a set of m targets $T = \{t_1, t_2 \ldots t_m\}$, the coverage problem is formulated as an integer linear programming, in which the objective is to minimize the objective function $\sum_{j=1}^{n} x_j$

$$\text{subject to} \begin{cases} x_j \times \sum_{j=1}^{n} P_{ij}^{obs} > 0 & \forall T_i \in T \\ P_{cvr}(i) \geq RTL & \forall T_i \in T \\ x_j \in (0, 1) & \forall S_j \in S \end{cases}$$

where RTL is the required trust level of each target.

The objective of the function is to minimize the number of sensor nodes in active state. x_j is a Boolean variable which is set as 1 if the sensor node S_j is able to observe the target T_i and 0 otherwise. P_{ij}^{obs} represents the probability that the target is monitored by a sensor node and is obtained as:

$$P_{ij}^{obs} = Cov(i,j) \times STL \qquad (1)$$

STL represents the trust level of the node and it is calculated as the weighted average of the direct trust, recommendation trust and indirect trust [3]. $P_{cvr}(i)$ represents the probability that the target region is covered by any sensor node. The proposed protocol works in rounds, where every round consists of three phases: setup phase,

190 P. Chaturvedi and A.K. Daniel

Table 1. Rule base for the node status

Cov. prob.	Trust	Node status
Low	Low	Very poor
Low	Medium	Poor
Low	High	Poor
Medium	Low	Poor
Medium	Medium	Average
Medium	High	Good
High	Low	Poor
High	Medium	Good
High	High	Very good

Table 2. Values obtained in various experiments

S. no.	Node	Target	Energy saving	No. of active nodes	Set covers
1	10	5	60	4	9
2	15	5	67	5	15
3	20	5	80	4	10
4	25	10	76	6	20
5	40	10	78	9	25
6	50	10	82	9	30
7	70	10	85	10	35
8	45	15	76	11	40
9	70	15	81	13	50

sensing phase and transmission phase. In the setup phase the base station determines the status of the node to keep in active state on the basis of coverage probability and trust values using the fuzzy logic. We have considered the fuzzy process consisting of two input variables and single output variable and determined 9 rules for the observation probability of the nodes as shown in Table 1. The second phase is sensing phase in which the nodes senses the environmental phenomenon. In the transmission phase the nodes send their data to the base station in either single hop or multi hop communication [6, 7].

3 Experimental Results

We have considered a network of randomly and uniformly deployed nodes in the rectangular nodes of dimension 100×100. The experiments are carried out using the C language and MATLAB. Various experiments were carried out by varying the number of the sensor nodes from 10 to 70 and the number of target nodes from 5 to 15. The active set of nodes is computed by repeatedly observing the observing probability. We have considered the sensing radius $r_s = 20$ cm, detection error range $r_e = 10$ cm, coverage threshold value for every target = 0.5 and the various hardware parameters related to sensing and communication characteristics $\lambda = \alpha = \beta = 0.5$. The results obtained after varying the number of nodes and targets are shown in Fig. 2 and Table 2. Figure 2a represents the set of active nodes obtained by varying the number of nodes which is considerably less than the total number of nodes. In Fig. 2b the number of set covers obtained in each case is shown. It can be observed that the number of set covers increase linearly with the increase in the number of nodes and the targets. Figure 2c and d shows the energy saved in each case and the network lifetime in each case. The results shows that the network lifetime is increased by a factor of 4 for the considered iteration.

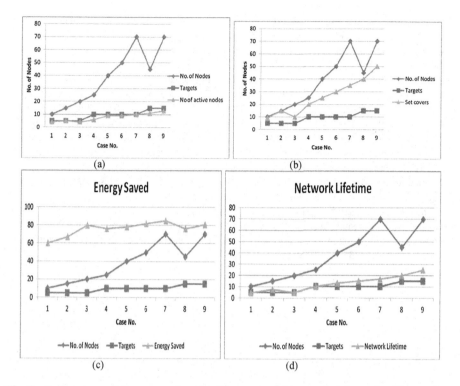

Fig. 2. Performance of the proposed protocol in terms of (a) no. of active nodes (b) no. of set covers (c) Energy savings (d) Network Lifetime

4 Conclusion

In this paper the proposed protocol is a node scheduling protocol for target coverage based on coverage probability, trust values and node contribution. The fuzzy inference is used for determining the node status to keep in active state. We have performed a number of experiments by varying the number of nodes and targets. The results show that the proposed protocol improves the network performance in terms of energy savings by a factor of 4 which implies that the lifetime is also improved by the same factor.

References

1. Akyildiz, I.F., Su, W., Sankarasubramaniam, Y., Cayirci, E.: A survey on sensor networks. IEEE Commun. Mag. **40**, 102–114 (2002)
2. Taghikhaki, Z., Meratnia, N., Havinga, P.J.M.: A trust-based probabilistic coverage algorithm for wireless sensor networks. In: 2013 International Workshop on Communications and Sensor Networks (ComSense 2013), Procedia, Computer Science, vol. 21, pp. 455–464 (2013)

3. Jiang, J., Han, G., Wang, F., Shu, L., Guizani, M.: An efficient distributed trust model for wireless sensor networks. IEEE Trans. Parallel Distrib. Syst. **26**, 1228–1237 (2014)
4. Cardei, M., Wu, J.: Energy-efficient coverage problems in wireless ad hoc sensor networks. Comput. Commun. J. **29**(4), 413–420 (2006)
5. Chaturvedi, P., Daniel, A.K.: An energy efficient node scheduling protocol for target coverage in wireless sensor networks. In: 5th International Conference on Communication System and Network Technologies (CSNT 2015), pp. 138–142, April 2015. doi:10.1109/CSNT.2015.10
6. Chaturvedi, P., Daniel, A.K.: Trust based node scheduling protocol for target coverage in wireless sensor networks. In: Shetty, N.R. et al. (eds.), 3rd International Conference on Emerging Research in Computing, Information, Communication & Applications (ERCICA 2015), Bangalore, Springer India (2015). doi:10.1007/978-81-322-2550-8_16
7. Chaturvedi, P., Daniel, A.K.: Trust based energy efficient coverage preserving protocol for wireless sensor networks. In: International Conference on Green Computing and Internet of Things (ICGCIOT 2015) (2015)
8. Chaturvedi, P., Daniel, A.K.: Lifetime optimization for target coverage in wireless sensor networks. In: 8th Annual ACM India Conference Compute 2015, pp. 47–53 (2015). http://dx.doi.org/10.1145/2835043.2835048

An Internet of Things Based Software Framework to Handle Medical Emergencies

K.G. Srinivasa, Kartik S. Gayatri, Maaz Syed Adeeb$^{(\boxtimes)}$, and Nikhil N. Jannu

M S Ramaiah Institute of Technology, Bangalore, India
maaz.adeeb@gmail.com

Abstract. A software framework is a reusable design that requires various software components to function, almost out of the box. To specify a framework, the creator must specify the different components that form the framework and how to instantiate them. Also, the communication interfaces between these various components must be defined. In this paper, we propose such a framework based on the Internet of Things (IoT) for developing applications for handling emergencies of some kind. We demonstrate the usage of our framework by explaining an application developed using it. The application is a system for tracking the status of autistic students in a school and also for alerting their parents/care takers in case of an emergency.

Keywords: Framework · Internet of Things · Autism · Emergency

1 Introduction

The Internet of Things (IoT) [1] based devices can be used to enable remote health monitoring and emergency notification systems. These health monitoring devices can range from blood pressure and heart rate monitors to advanced devices capable of monitoring specific patients, ensuring that proper treatment is being administered. This paper provides an IoT based framework to handle medical emergencies and takes up autistic student monitoring as a case study to analyse the application of this framework.

2 Architecture

The architecture (Refer Fig. 1) of the framework is divided into four modules:

- Data collection
- Representational State Transfer (REST) services
- Data storage and analysis
- Client applications

© Springer International Publishing Switzerland 2016
N. Bjørner et al. (Eds.): ICDCIT 2016, LNCS 9581, pp. 193–198, 2016.
DOI: 10.1007/978-3-319-28034-9_26

194   K.G. Srinivasa et al.

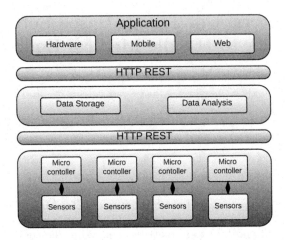

Fig. 1. Software architecture

2.1 Data Collection

Our framework requires an engineer to just plug the sensors required to his
microcontroller and write sensor specific code to access the data. We provide the
architecture for handling of various sensors and services to send over data to the
cloud.

The entire data collection module is run on the microcontroller. All the sensors need to be connected to the microcontroller. The main controller program
runs a forever loop and accesses data from each of the connected sensors or as
the engineer wishes to collect the data, serializes it and sends it over to the cloud,
at regular intervals of time.

2.2 REST Services

The entire communication between various components in our framework is built
on top of REST services. We provide a ready to use, simple REST API on the
cloud, where the engineer only needs to code how various end points are supposed
to behave.

2.3 Data Storage and Analysis

Our framework uses MongoDB [8] as the data storage. Data storage becomes
straight forward here as our data is being sent over as JSON, which reduces any
extra manipulation overhead on the cloud side. We do not provide any specific
features for data analysis in our framework, but it should be straight forward to
integrate third party libraries. The source code of our framework is available on
GitHub [6].

2.4 Client Applications

Client applications are basically the application layer. They can be web based, mobile or even hardware based. These applications consume the data from the cloud by using the REST services and give the engineer a freedom to create what ever he likes. We demonstrate one such application in the following sections.

3 Application

We demonstrate the application of our framework with an IoT based Autistic Student Health Tracking and Analysis system.

3.1 Autism

Autism is a neurodevelopmental disorder characterized by impaired social interaction, verbal and non-verbal communication and restricted and repetitive behavior. The signs typically develop gradually, but some children with autism will reach their developmental milestones at a normal pace and then regress [2].

3.2 Existing Solutions

Traditional measures relied on paper-and-pencil recordings of teachers and parents based on direct observations or video-based methods [4]. However, such methods are expensive, tedious and time consuming. The work done in [3] correlate environmental contexts with the occurrence of stereotypical behaviors to identify any environmental factors like sound, which may trigger such behaviors or emotional upsets.

3.3 Hardware

The sensors used are from Shimmer [7]. One of the key functions of the Shimmer board is its ability to communicate as a wireless platform. Shimmer uses a Bluetooth Radio module.

We have used Intel Edison as the microcontroller. It collects the data from the Shimmer sensors over bluetooth, processes it and sends it over for storage and analysis.

3.4 Analysis

Classification of actions performed by a person has been carried out using a two-step process.

In the first phase, training data is used to determine the reference index for each class and in the second phase, the real time data is analyzed to classify the action at any given interval of time.

Step 1: Learning from data

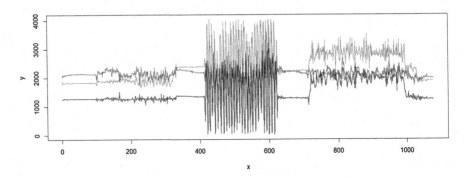

Fig. 2. Sample accelerometer readings

- Synthetic data was collected from 3 participants performing 3 different kinds of actions, namely Sitting, Walking and Vigorous hand movements.
- Statistical analysis was done on this data to derive a standard deviation (SD) of the recorded accelerometer readings for each of these participants.
- Mean of these deviations of all the participants was found and taken to be a reference index for further classification. This forms the reference model for further classification of real time data.

  Step 2: Classification of real time data.

- On receiving real time sensor data, the algorithm divides the data into windows of 500 continuous data points each, with a sliding range of 100 data points. Then it calculates the SD of the accelerometer readings of each window, in order to classify that window into some activity. It slides the window and repeats the process.
- If the algorithm figures out that there was a window in which the SD was in the range of vigorous hand motions activity, then an alert is triggered.

3.5   Client Application

- Web application has been written using Bootstrap and jQuery. The web application makes AJAX calls to the cloud to get the sensor data in real time and also the other details of the students.
- It also shows the results of the students data analysis in real time. Flot.js charting library is used for the creation of real time interactive charts.
- Push notifications are sent to registered android devices to raise an alert.

3.6   Overall View of Solution

Using body sensors, real time data of the student is collected. Using statistical analysis, we compare new readings with synthetic training data and classify the

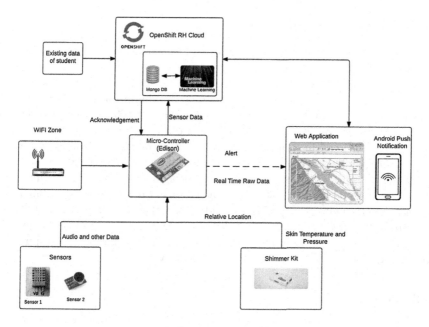

Fig. 3. Application architecture

readings as an alert or not. From the result of the analysis and the classification, we give an alert using an android application and a means to analyze the alert on a web application. Refer Fig. 3.

The implementation of the application is available on GitHub [5].

3.7 Results

The results of our analysis are tabulated in Table 1. Also, a sample graph of accelerometer readings of all 3 actions performed is shown in Fig. 2. The actions are siting, vigorous movement and walking respectively.

Clearly, there is considerable success in distinction between the vigorous movement action from the rest and can be used for triggering an alert.

Table 1. Standard deviations of accelerometer at various axes and our algorithm's accuracy to classify them

Action	X-axis	Y-axis	Z-axis	Accuracy
Sitting	45.43	24.56	36.76	91.34 %
Walking	153.29	167.41	154.65	34.67 %
Vigorous movement	702.34	723.9	847.34	93.91 %

3.8 Conclusion and Future Scope

Autism is a mental condition with a loss of social life and loss of ability to communicate with the public. This system provides a means of communication in times of emergencies and avoid the causes as a result of the mood swings in autistic students. The system comes with an android application for alerting the teachers and parents and a web application for analysis. The system provides the real time analysis on the various sensor data obtained by means of a wearable sensor and also helps in monitoring the condition of the student in real time. Abnormalities in the sensor readings are noted and alerts are sent.

The major work that can be taken is in designing a compact, non-intrusive wearable device. Better and stronger algorithms can be developed which can improve the efficiency of classification and reduce the latency. Sensors that take the surrounding noise for predicting the mood can be used. Also, mood swings can be calculated accurately by using PPG signals. Heart rate and respiratory rate can be used for calculations and analysis in various ways.

References

1. Atzori, L., Iera, A., Morabito, G.: The Internet of Things - A survey, May 2010
2. Myers, S.M., Johnson, C.P.: Management of children with autism spectrum disorders (2007)
3. Chuah, M., Diblasio, M.: Smartphone based autism social alert system. In: 2012 Eighth International Conference on Mobile Ad-hoc Sensor Networks (MSN), pp. 6–13, December 2012
4. Sturmey, P.: Video technology and persons with autism and other develop-mental disabilities: an emerging technology for positive behavior support. J. Positive Behav. Interv. **5**, 12–21 (2003)
5. Implementation of the health monitoring application. https://github.com/maaz93/iot-devs
6. Source code of the framework. https://github.com/maaz93/iot-framework
7. Shimmer sensor kit. http://www.shimmersensing.com/
8. MongoDB. https://www.mongodb.org/

Minimal Start Time Heuristics for Scheduling Workflows in Heterogeneous Computing Systems

D. Sirisha[1(✉)] and G. VijayaKumari[2]

[1] Department of CSE, Pragati Engineering College, Surampalem, India
sirishad998@gmail.com
[2] Department of CSE, JNTUH, Hyderabad, India
vijayakumari.gunta@gmail.com

Abstract. Heterogeneous computing systems require efficient task-to-processor mapping for attaining high performance. Scheduling workflows on heterogeneous environments is shown to be NP-Complete. Several heuristics were developed to attain minimum schedule lengths. However, these algorithms employ level-wise approach of scheduling tasks. This indirectly assigns higher priority to the tasks at lower levels than those at higher levels. Further, the start time of tasks at higher levels is constrained by the completion times of tasks at lower levels. The present work proposes a novel heuristic based global scheduling algorithm namely Minimal Start Time (MST) algorithm for workflows. The proposed approach focuses on minimizing the start times of tasks which are dependent on the tasks at lower levels to generate shorter span schedules. The primary merit of this scheme is due to the elimination of level constraints whenever there are no dependency constraints. The performance of MST algorithm is evaluated in terms of normalized makespan, speedup, efficiency and improvement of 5–20 % in 80 % of the cases is achieved in comparison to the earlier work.

Keywords: Task scheduling · Workflows · Heuristics · Schedule length · Heterogeneous computing systems

1 Introduction

Complex applications can be competently solved by decomposing into a set of tasks having dependencies, often modeled as workflow. Workflow applications can exploit Heterogeneous Computing Systems (HCS) to execute the parallel tasks for attaining high performance. High potentials of HCS which includes resources with a range of processing capabilities can be explored by efficiently scheduling the tasks in workflow. Scheduling defines the execution order of the tasks and maps the tasks to the appropriate processor. Obtaining an optimal schedule for a workflow is proven to be NP-Complete and cannot be solved unless P = NP [3]. Heuristics can be employed to generate near optimal solutions.

Heuristic approaches are static i.e., the tasks attributes such as processing time, inter-task dependencies and the structure of workflow are available a-prior [1, 2].

© Springer International Publishing Switzerland 2016
N. Bjørner et al. (Eds.): ICDCIT 2016, LNCS 9581, pp. 199–212, 2016.
DOI: 10.1007/978-3-319-28034-9_27

Heuristic algorithms are categorized into list based, task duplication based and cluster based scheduling. List based approach generates schedules in two phases. The first phase prioritizes the tasks and lists them in the decreasing order of priority. In the second phase, tasks are mapped to the fastest processor. In general, list based heuristics generate reasonable schedules with less complexity [5].

Heuristics used to assign priorities to tasks have considerable effect on the schedule and therefore have further scope for producing effective schedules. A major challenge in scheduling workflows is the inter-task dependencies besides resource heterogeneity and dynamism. A dependent task has to wait for its inflowing data from its prede-cessors while its executing processor runs idle. Motivated by this challenge, a global scheduling strategy namely MST algorithm is devised which examines the effect on the performance by queuing all tasks whose dependency constraints are satisfied and gives fair chance for the execution of such tasks. The proposed scheduling approach pro-duces shorter span schedules by efficiently minimizing the start time of dependant tasks and competently handles inter-task dependencies. The major scheduling aspects addressed by the proposed scheduling policy are: prevents a ready task in entering the wait state, guarantees fairness such that no ready task starves regardless of their size or processing times. That is, each ready task will eventually be executed.

The remaining of the paper is structured as follows. In Sect. 2, workflow scheduling problem with required terminology is presented. The related work is discussed in Sect. 3. The proposed MST algorithm is illustrated in Sect. 4. The performance eval-uation of MST algorithm with earlier work is presented in Sect. 5. Section 6 summarizes the findings of the work and outlines the future scope of research work on the same topic.

2   Workflow Scheduling Problem

The workflow scheduling problem essentially comprises of three components namely workflow application, a HCS and a scheduling strategy.

2.1   Workflow Model

A Workflow application consists of inter-dependent tasks modeled as Directed Acyclic Graph, $G = < V, E >$ where V represents a set of t tasks. And E is a set of directed edges with no cycles. Every directed edge $d_{i,j} \in E$ imposes dependency constraint between the tasks t_i and t_j where $i \neq j$, such that task t_j can be only be performed if its predecessor t_i is finished. Every edge $d_{i,j}$ is associated with a non-negative integer which indicates the data flow time between the tasks t_i and t_j. And $d_{i,j} = 0$, when both the tasks t_i and t_j are executed on the same processor. Satisfying the dependency constraints, the task becomes *free* and it is marked as *ready* after receiving the data from its predecessors.

2.2 The HCS Model

HCS consists of p processors with diverse processing capabilities. The processing time of t tasks on p processors is presented by Processing Time (*PT*) matrix of order $t \times p$ where each element $e_{i,j}$ denotes the estimation of processing time of task t_i on processor p_j. A $t \times t$ matrix indicates the Data Flow Time (*DFT*) among t tasks in a workflow where each element $d_{i,j}$ indicates data flow time between the tasks t_i and t_j. The processors are fully connected and tasks cannot be preempted while processing. A task having no predecessor is termed as *start task* and with no successor is defined as *sink task*. In general, a workflow is assumed to be consisting of a pair of start and sink tasks. If such tasks occur more than one in number then a pseudo task with zero processing time and zero flow times is connected to these tasks. An example application workflow and the processing time matrix are presented in Fig. 1 and Table 1 respectively.

The essential attributes for defining the workflow scheduling problem are Earliest Start Time (*EST*) and Earliest Finish Time (*EFT*) of a task [2]. *EST* is the earliest time a task t_i can start its processing on processor p_j and is denoted as $EST(t_i, p_j)$. It is determined either by the ready time of a task or by the available time of a processor, whichever is maximum. The ready time of task t_i is the time the dependency constraints of t_i are satisfied and t_i has obtained data from its predecessors, represented as *ready* (t_i) and computed using (1)

$$Ready(t_i) = max_{tm \in pred(ti)}\{AFT(t_m) + d_{m,i}\} \tag{1}$$

where $t_m \in pred\ (t_i)$ are a set of predecessors of t_i. $AFT(t_m)$ is the Actual Finish Time of the predecessor tasks. $d_{m,i}$ is the data flow time required to transmit the data between the tasks t_m and t_i. And $d_{m,i} = 0$, if the tasks t_m and t_i are executed on the same processor. For start task t_{start}, $ready(t_{start})$ is 0. The processor available time is the time the processor has finished executing the previous task and is prepared to perform the next task and denoted as *avail* (p_j). The $EST(t_i, p_j)$ is the maximum of these two parameters, defined using (2).

$$EST(t_i, p_j) = max\{ready(t_i), avail(p_j)\} \tag{2}$$

The *EFT* of task t_i on processor p_j is denoted by $EFT\ (t_i, p_j)$ and defined using (3)

$$EFT(t_i, p_j) = EST(t_i, p_j) + e_{i,j} \tag{3}$$

where $e_{i,j}$ is the processing time of task t_i on processor p_j. The schedule length known as makespan, is the *AFT* of sink task t_{sink}.

$$makespan = AFT(t_{sink}) \tag{4}$$

The objective of workflow scheduling problem is to define the scheduling order of the tasks and map them to processors so as to minimize the makespan of workflow by maximizing the parallelization of tasks.

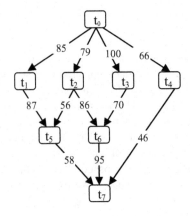

Fig. 1. An application workflow

Table 1. Processing time matrix

Task	p_1	p_2
t_0	70	84
t_1	68	49
t_2	78	96
t_3	89	26
t_4	30	88
t_5	66	86
t_6	25	21
t_7	96	26

3   Related Work

Effective scheduling of workflows in HCS has profound influence on the performance and hence motivated the researchers to study this area profusely. Heuristics for attaining minimum makespan abound in the literature [1, 4, 6, 8, 9]. The efficacy of list based heuristics is due to its near optimal solution generation with less complexity [1, 2, 4, 6, 9]. In this section, the most cited list scheduling algorithms namely Heterogeneous Earliest Finish Time (HEFT) [2], Performance Effective Task Scheduling (PETS) [4] and Critical Path On a Processor (CPOP) [2] are detailed.

HEFT scheduling strategy proceeds in two stages, task prioritization stage and processor selection stage. The tasks are prioritized using *upward rank* computed by summing the processing times and data flow times along the longest path from the task to the sink task. The tasks are then listed in the decreasing order of their *rank*. In the second stage, the selected task is paired with each processor and the processor which yields least *EFT* is selected for performing the task.

PETS algorithm works in three stages: In the first stage the tasks are grouped into levels to execute the entire level of parallel tasks. The second stage determines the execution order of tasks at each level based on the priority. Priority to a task is computed by summing up the attributes of task viz., average processing time, total data outflow time and highest rank of its immediate predecessor tasks. The third stage adopts HEFT's strategy to map a task-to-processor.

The CPOP algorithm assigns priority to tasks using *upward* and *downward ranks*. The *downward rank* of task t_i is the span of the longest path from start task to t_i, excluding t_i's processing time. In the second phase, CPOP algorithm identifies the critical path tasks and maps these tasks to the processor that yields minimum processing time. And the non-critical tasks are mapped to the processor with minimum *EFT*, as in HEFT.

4 The Proposed MST Algorithm

Mostly, list based scheduling heuristics [2, 4] from the literature execute the tasks level wise. The earlier algorithms imposed level-wise constraint in addition to the dependency constraint. The tasks are categorized level-wise to execute them in parallel. The tasks at lower level attain higher priority than the tasks in higher level. Within the same level, tasks are ordered for execution based upon their priority.

For workflow in Fig. 1, the execution of tasks employing level-wise strategy begins with start task t_0. The completion of task t_0 satisfies the dependency constraints for tasks t_1, t_2, t_3 and t_4 at level 1, hence these tasks get *free*. If however the tasks t_1, t_2 are executed ahead of t_3 and t_4 tasks, the task t_5 at level 2 which is dependent only on t_1 and t_2 tasks has to wait till t_3 and t_4 tasks are completed to become *free*. On close examination of these tasks it is evident that task t_5 can equally compete with tasks t_3 and t_4 when t_1 and t_2 are completed. The earlier algorithms imposed level-wise constraint on task t_5 though there was no dependency between the task t_5 at level 2 and the tasks t_3, t_4 at level 1. Moreover, t_6 becomes *free* after t_3 is executed. Though t_5 and t_6 tasks at level 2 are independent of t_4 at level 1, scheduling of these tasks is constrained by the completion time of t_4. The *EST* of the *free* tasks at higher levels must not be constrained by the finish times of tasks at lower levels. Therefore, it is proposed that the dependency constraints must be viewed globally and hence independent of levels.

For the same workflow, the *EST* of tasks t_5, t_6 and t_7 employing PETS, HEFT and CPOP algorithms is always greater than the *EST* of these tasks when MST algorithm is employed. For PETS and HEFT algorithms, *EST* of these tasks is same and it is 230, 300 and 420 time units while for CPOP algorithm it is 237, 206 and 379 time units. However, employing MST strategy the *EST* of these tasks is as low as 204, 237 and 357 time units. With the elimination of level constraints the *free* tasks are released and queued up, this led MST algorithm in reducing the *EST* of *free* tasks. This reduction in the *EST* of *free* tasks promotes MST approach in generating shorter makespans.

MST algorithm generates schedules in two stages namely task sequencing stage and task-to-processor mapping stage. The task sequencing stage sequences the order of execution of tasks. The second stage decides the suitable processor for performing the task and maps to the processor. The two stages are detailed below.

4.1 Task Sequencing Stage

This stage defines the sequence of processing tasks according to the priority of each task. Priority is assigned to tasks on the basis of *rank* computed using two parameters namely Average Processing Time (*APT*) and Total Data Flow Time (*TDFT*). The *APT* of task t_i is defined as the average processing time of t_i on p processors and computed using (5).

$$APT(t_i) = \sum_{j=1}^{p} e_{i,j}/p \tag{5}$$

where $1 \leq i \leq t$, t is the number of tasks and $1 \leq j \leq p$, p is the number of processors.

The *TDFT* (t_i) is defined as the sum of Data Inflow Time (*DIT*) and Data Outflow Time (*DOT*). *DIT* is defined as the time incurred for a task to receive the input data from its immediate predecessors, it is computed using (6).

$$DIT(t_j) = \sum_{i=1}^{m} d_{i,j} \tag{6}$$

where $1 \leq i \leq m$, m is the number of predecessors of task t_j. *DOT* is defined as the time required for a task to transfer the output data to its immediate successors.

$$DOT(t_j) = \sum_{k=1}^{n} d_{j,k} \tag{7}$$

where $1 \leq k \leq n$, n is the number of successors of task t_j. The *TDFT* of an intermediate task t_j is computed using (8).

$$TDFT(t_j) = DIT(t_j) + DOT(t_j) \tag{8}$$

where $1 \leq j \leq t$, t is the number of tasks. The *rank* of a task t_j is computed using *APT* and *TDFT* values and defined as

$$rank(t_j) = APT(t_j) + TDFT(t_j) \tag{9}$$

where $1 \leq j \leq t$, t is the number of tasks.

The tasks in workflow are assigned *ranks*. Initially, only the start task is *free* and is added to the ready queue. Tasks are inserted into the ready queue as they become *free* and are listed according to their *rank*. Maximum *rank* task attains utmost priority. Ties are solved using *APT* value i.e., task with higher *APT* value gains higher priority.

4.2   Task-to-Processor Mapping Stage

This stage selects the suitable processor for performing the task by computing the *EFT* of a task on p processors. The processor with least *EFT* is decided as the best processor for a task. To enhance the performance, this stage employs Insertion Based Policy (IBP) [7] which identifies the empty slots in the schedule and checks the likelihood of inserting a task if an empty slot is sufficient to execute the task. When such empty slot is unavailable, the task is performed after the selected processor is available. If the *EFT* of a task is same on more than one processor, then the processor which is sparingly utilized is preferred. Table 2 presents the stepwise trace of this stage.

For workflow in Fig. 1, the task sequence generated by MST algorithm is $\{t_0, t_2, t_1, t_5, t_3, t_6, t_4, t_7\}$. The makespan of MST, HEFT, PETS and CPOP algorithms is 383, 446, 446 and 405 time units respectively. MST algorithm generated shorter makespan compared to HEFT and PETS algorithm by 63 time units and 22 time units compared to CPOP algorithm.

Table 2. The stepwise trace of task-to-processor mapping phase of MST algorithm

Step	Ready queue	Task selected	p_1		p_2		Best processor
			EST	EFT	EST	EFT	
1	t_0	t_0	0	70	0	84	p_1
2	t_2, t_1, t_3, t_4	t_2	70	148	149	245	p_1
3	t_1, t_3, t_4	t_1	148	216	155	204	p_2
4	t_5, t_3, t_4	t_5	291	357	204	290	p_2
5	t_3, t_4	t_3	148	237	290	316	p_1
6	t_6, t_4	t_6	237	262	307	328	p_1
7	t_4	t_4	262	292	290	378	p_1
8	t_7	t_7	348	444	357	383	p_2

4.3   The MST Algorithm

In line 1 and 2, the algorithm computes *APT*, *TDFT* and *rank* values for all the tasks in workflow. In line 3, ready queue is constructed and the tasks which are *free* are queued up. Initially, the start task is ready and it is placed in the ready queue. In the while loop from lines 6–14, each iteration selects a task t_i with maximum *rank* from the ready queue. The *EFT* of t_i on p processors is computed using IBP in line 9. In line 11, task t_i is allocated to processor p_j with least *EFT* (t_i, p_j). In line 12, upon the completion of t_i, its successors which become *free* are identified and in line 13 they are inserted into the ready queue (Fig. 2).

Algorithm 1 MST (V, E, P, d, e)
Input :   A workflow, $G = (V, E)$ with $t \in V$ tasks, $e \in E$ edges
            $d[1: t,1: t]$: data flow time matrix for t tasks in a workflow
            $e[1: t,1: p]$: processing time matrix, where $e_{i,j}$ is the processing time of t_i on
                     processor p_j
Output : A Schedule

---

1. Calculate *APT* and *TDFT* values.
2. Calculate *rank* = *APT* + *TDFT*, for t tasks in workflow.
3. Construct ready queue Q and initialize with start task.
4. enqueue (t_i) // insert *free* tasks into Q.
5. Sort the tasks in Q in the non-increasing order of *rank* values.
6. while Q not empty do
7.   dequeue (t_i, Q) // delete the task with highest priority from Q.
8.   for each processor p_j do
9.   Compute *EFT(t_i, p_j)* using IBP
10.   end for
11.   map the task t_i to processor p_j with least *EFT*(t_i, p_j).
12.   if *succ* (t_i) is *free* // *succ* (t_i) is the successors of t_i
13.   enqueue *succ* (t_i) // insert successors of t_i to Q
14. end while.

Fig. 2. The MST algorithm

4.4 The Complexity Analysis of MST Algorithm

In general, the time complexity of scheduling algorithm is defined in terms of number of tasks t, number of edges e and the number of processors p. The analysis of time complexity of MST algorithm is as follows.

In step 1, *APT* and *TDFT* values for all tasks in workflow are computed with the time complexity of $O(t . p)$ and $O(e)$ respectively. In step 2, the *rank* is calculated for all tasks in time $O(t + e)$. The complexity for inserting each *free* task in the ready queue implemented using *binary heap* in step 4 is $O(log\ t)$ and for inserting t tasks it is $O(t\ log\ t)$. Sorting of tasks in the ready queue in step 5 is done in $O(t\ log\ t)$ steps. The highest priority task from the ready queue in step 7 is deleted with a complexity of $O(1)$. Therefore, the time complexity of task sequencing phase is $O(t\ log\ t + e)$. The *for* loop from the steps 8-10 determines the *EFT* of a task on p processors and the processor with minimum *EFT* is selected. The complexity of task-to-processor mapping phase is of order $O(t + e)\ p$. The overall time complexity of MST algorithm is $O(t\ log\ t + e)\ p$.

5 Performance Analysis

This section analyses and compares the performance of MST algorithm with the algorithms detailed in the related work. For experimental evaluations randomly generated and real world application workflows are considered. The scheduling strategies are evaluated by the following performance metrics as stated in [1, 2, 5].

Normalized Makespan (NM). Makespan is the primary metric used for analyzing the performance. This metric compares the workflows with diversified topologies and hence it is essential to normalize the makespan to its *lower bound lb*. *NM* is computed by relatively comparing the makespan with its *lb*. The value of *lb* is calculated by summing the minimum processing time of tasks on the critical path, computed using (10). Critical path of a workflow is the longest path from the start task to sink task. The algorithm which yields lowest *NM* is regarded as the better performing algorithm.

$$NM = \frac{\text{makespan of algorithm}}{lb} \tag{10}$$

Speedup. Speedup is the metric for relative performance. It determines the performance enhancement accomplished due to parallelization of tasks in a workflow in comparison to the sequential processing of tasks. The scheduling algorithm which maximizes the parallelization of tasks in a workflow is considered as superior. It is computed using (11)

$$Speedup = \frac{\text{sequential processing time}}{\text{parallel processing time}} \tag{11}$$

Efficiency. Efficiency measures the time for which the processors are employed. It is defined as the ratio of speedup to the number of processors employed in HCS, computed using (12). Usually, efficiency is in between 0 and 1. The scheduling algorithm with higher efficiency for a workflow nearing to 1 is considered as better.

$$Efficiency = \frac{Speedup}{number\ of\ processors} \tag{12}$$

Execution Time of Algorithm. Execution time of algorithm is the time required for algorithm to generate the schedule.

Frequency of Superior Schedules. This metric counts the frequency of superior, equivalent and inferior schedules generated by an algorithm in comparison with the related algorithms.

5.1 Randomly Generated Workflows

The input parameters essential for generating workflows with diverse topologies are presented below [2].

- *Workflow size (t).* The number of tasks t in a workflow.
- *Data flow time to Processing Ratio (DPR).* DPR is the ratio of average data flow time to the average processing time in a workflow. The workflow with very low DPR value is regarded as processing intensive.
- *Shape Factor (α).* The shape factor α determines the number of levels l in a workflow and the number of parallel tasks m at each level. The value of l and m varies from graph to graph. The maximum l value for a workflow is $\sqrt{t}/\alpha$ i.e., a sink task is at level $\sqrt{t}/\alpha$, where t is the workflow size. The t value is randomly selected with mean equal to $\sqrt{t} \times \alpha$. The smaller α values generate longer workflows with low parallelism while higher α values generate shorter workflows with high degree of parallelism.
- *Heterogeneity Factor (γ).* The deviation in the processing times of p processors in HCS is specified by γ. Higher γ values indicate wide range of processing times while lower γ values implies less variation. The processing time $e_{i,j}$ of task t_i on processor p_j is randomly selected from the range:

$$APT \times (1 - \gamma/2) \leq e_{i,j} \leq APT \times (1 + \gamma/2) \tag{13}$$

where *APT* is the average processing time. For the experimentations, workflows are generated considering the following values for the above stated parameters.

- $t = \{40,50,60,70,80,90,100,200,300,400,500\}$
- $APT = \{30,40,50,60,70,80,90,100\}$
- $DPR = \{0.1,0.5,0.75,1.0,2.0,5.0,7.5,10.0\}$
- $\alpha = \{0.5,1.0,1.5,2.0\}$
- $\gamma = \{0.1,0.25,0.5,0.75,1.0\}$

With the above combination 70,400 workflows are generated. The experimentations conducted through simulation with wide range of parametric values reduce the effect of dispersion in the schedule lengths.

5.2   Performance Analysis on Random Workflows

The performance of algorithms for average *NM* and average *speedup* with respect to various workflow sizes is shown in Fig. 3a and 3b. Each point plotted in the graphs (Fig. 3a and 3b) is the average of the data acquired from 6400 experimental results. The data trend in the graph depicted in Fig. 3a shows linear relationship between average *NM* and workflow size t. The percentage of improvement of MST algorithm over HEFT, PETS and CPOP algorithms for $t \leq 100$ is 5.07 %, 11.23 % and 17.11 % and for $t = 500$ it is 8.58 %, 13.77 % and 22.14 % respectively. For $t > 100$ the makespan drastically increased for all algorithms and the performance of MST algorithm gradually increased with t value over HEFT, PETS and CPOP algorithms.

The progress in the *speedup* of MST algorithm becomes more manifest with the increase in t value (shown in Fig. 3b) and it is 9.44 %, 10.97 % and 15.83 % compared to HEFT, PETS and CPOP algorithms. This performance gain achieved by MST algorithm is due to maximizing the parallelization of *free* tasks as these tasks are released instantaneously after satisfying their dependency constraints.

The effect of *DPR* on average *NM* is depicted in Fig. 3c. Every data point plotted in the graph is the average of 8800 experimentations. It can be observed from Fig. 3c that all the scheduling algorithms are affected when *DPR* values are high. The rise in *DPR* values causes data dependency overhead among the tasks to dominate the processing times in a workflow. The performance improvement (%) of MST algorithm over HEFT, PETS and CPOP algorithms for $DPR \leq 2$ is 8.96 %, 10.75 % and 22.98 % and increased to 11.28 %, 17.65 % and 29.28 % when $DPR \geq 5$. The significant growth in the performance of MST algorithm for higher DPR values can be is ascribed to its competency in handling heavily dependent tasks by determining an effective task sequence.

Figure 3d presents the average *NM* as a function of shape parameter (α). Each data point plotted in Fig. 3d is averaged from 17600 experimentations. The performance of the algorithms is found to deteriorate as the α value increases and much deviation in the makespan of the algorithms can be noticed for higher α values. However, MST algorithm surpasses HEFT, PETS and CPOP algorithms for varied α values and demonstrates the fact that the proposed strategy explores higher levels of task parallelism by eliminating level constraints. On average, the performance of MST algorithm is superior to HEFT, PETS and CPOP algorithms by 10.34 %, 20.54 % and 25.64 %.

The average efficiency of the algorithms is illustrated in Fig. 3e. The average efficiency of the algorithms dwindles with the increase in the number of processors. The efficiency (%) of MST algorithm is better by 11.53 %, 18.77 % and 25.04 % against HEFT, PETS and CPOP algorithms respectively. The average execution times of the algorithms for varied sized workflows are presented in Fig. 3f. When t value is small trivial difference in the execution times of algorithms can be observed, however this drastically increased with the workflow size. For various workflow sizes, MST algorithm is observed to be faster than HEFT, PETS and CPOP algorithms by 16.02 %, 41.07 % and 59.72 % respectively. The rationale behind the performance of MST algorithm is due to the advantage gained by preponing the start times of dependent tasks ensuing in the reduction of finish times of these tasks.

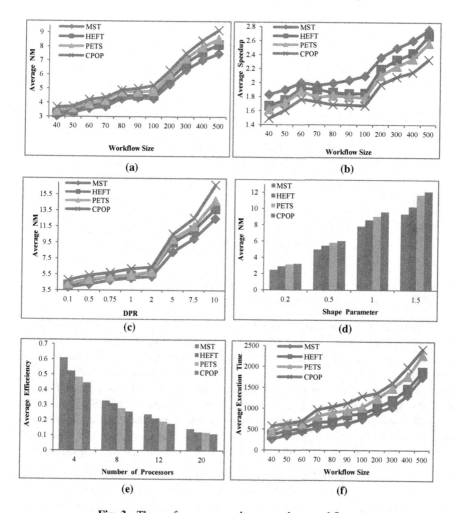

Fig. 3. The performance results on random workflows

Table 3 presents the relative comparison of the makespans generated by the scheduling algorithms for 70,400 randomly generated workflows. The data in each cell indicates the frequency of superior, equivalent or inferior makespans generated by algorithm on row head compared with the algorithm on column head. The overall column provides the number of cases (%) for which the algorithm on row head has generated superior, equivalent or inferior schedules against all other algorithms. It can be observed that MST algorithm produced superior schedules compared to HEFT, PETS and CPOP algorithms in 79 % of the cases.

5.3   Performance Analysis on Real World Application Workflows

The performance of scheduling strategies is also evaluated with respect to the real world application workflows. The structure of the application workflows is familiar,

Table 3. A global comparison of scheduling algorithms

		MST	HEFT	PETS	CPOP	Overall
MST	Superior	–	49984	55616	61248	79 %
	Equivalent		2816	2112	704	2.67 %
	Inferior		17600	12672	8448	18.33 %
HEFT	Superior	17600	–	44352	68288	56 %
	Equivalent	2816		4928	352	4 %
	Inferior	49984		21120	1527	40 %
PETS	Superior	12672	21120	–	54209	41.67 %
	Equivalent	2112	4928		6589	6.45 %
	Inferior	55616	44352		9602	51.88 %
CPOP	Superior	8448	1527	9602	–	9.27 %
	Equivalent	704	352	6589		3.62 %
	Inferior	61248	68288	54209		87 %

hence the parameters t and α are not required. The *DPR* and γ values are the only inputs essential for generating application workflows.

Fast Fourier Transformation (FFT). For generating FFT workflows [10], the parameter namely input points (*M*) is used to determine the workflow size t. The *M* value is varied from 2 to 32, incrementing by the power of 2. For *M* input points, the workflow size is $2 \times (M-1) + (M \log_2 M)$. Figure 4a depicts the graph plotted with average *NM* values as a function of various input points. The average *NM* of MST algorithm is lesser than HEFT, PETS and CPOP algorithms by 5.77 %, 13.825 % and 28.87 % respectively. Figure 4b presents the average efficiency of the algorithms for varied number of processors and MST algorithm has shown superior performance over HEFT, PETS and CPOP algorithms by 8.78 %, 13.5 % and 24.87 % respectively.

Gaussian Elimination (GE). The workflow size for GE algorithm [11] is characterized by the input points (*M*) which is varied from 4 to 32, incrementing by the power of 2. The workflow size for *M* input points is $(M^2 + M-2)/2$. The average *NM* obtained for various input points is shown in Fig. 5a and MST algorithm produced shorter span schedules in comparison to HEFT, PETS and CPOP algorithms by 6.83 %, 15.69 % and 19.65 %. Figure 5b depicts the average efficiency with respect to the varied processor set. MST algorithm has shown superior efficiency than HEFT, PETS and CPOP algorithms by 8.9 %, 14.44 % and 18.82 % respectively.

Molecular Dynamics Code (MDC). The irregular structure of MDC workflow [12] motivated to study the effect on the performance of the scheduling algorithms. Figure 6a plots the average *NM* values as a function of various *DPR* values and MST algorithm generated shorter span schedules compared to HEFT, PETS and CPOP by 3.76 %, 7.63 % and 12.57 %. The average efficiency of the scheduling algorithms is presented in Fig. 6b for varied processor sets used for experimentation. From Fig. 6b, it can be manifested that MST algorithm showed better efficiency than HEFT, PETS and CPOP by 6.64 %, 11.89 % and 18.83 % respectively.

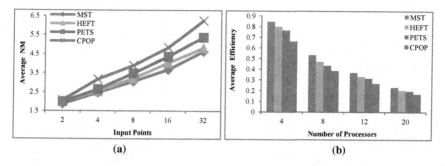

Fig. 4. (a) Average NM and (b) Average efficiency comparison for FFT workflows.

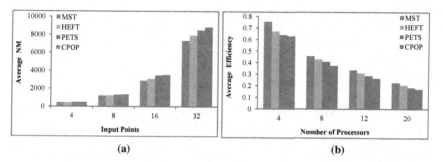

Fig. 5. (a) Average NM and (b) Average efficiency comparison for GE workflows.

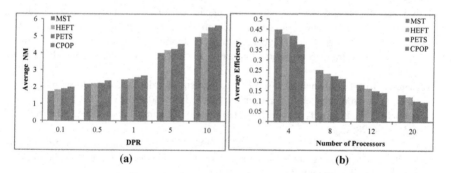

Fig. 6. (a) Average NM and (b) Average efficiency comparison for MDC workflow.

6 Conclusions

A new heuristic based global scheduling algorithm namely MST algorithm for work-flows in HCS is proposed in this paper. Earlier algorithms imposed level-wise con-straints due to which a *free* task at higher level has to wait for the entire level of parallel tasks to complete. MST algorithm eliminates the level constraints and releases the tasks as they become *free*, this reduces the *EST* of *free* tasks. Therefore, it is proposed that the dependency constraints must be viewed globally and hence independent of levels.

The proposed strategy effectively generates the task sequence by identifying the heavily processing and dependent tasks. This has potentially led the MST approach to generate shorter span schedules with less complexity of $O(t \log t + e) p$.

Experimentations are conducted on random and real world application workflows to evaluate the performance of the scheduling algorithms. The performance of MST algorithm is compared with most cited HEFT, PETS and CPOP algorithms. The experimental results reveal 5–20 % performance improvement of MST algorithm in 80 % of the cases against HEFT, PETS and CPOP algorithms. Much gain in the performance of MST algorithm is observed for higher shape parameter values. The reason behind this is due to maximizing the parallelization of tasks by releasing the *free* tasks. Moreover, significant performance improvement of MST algorithm can also be noticed for higher *DPR* values and this can be attributed to the fact that MST algorithm competently handles heavily dependent tasks. As future research work branch and bound technique can be implemented for accomplishing optimal schedules.

References

1. Arabnejad, H., Barbosa, J.M.: List scheduling algorithm for heterogeneous systems by an optimistic cost table. IEEE Trans. Parallel Distrib. Syst. **25**(3), 682–694 (2014)
2. Topcuoglu, H., Hariri, S., Wu, M.Y.: Performance effective and low complexity task scheduling for heterogeneous computing. IEEE Trans. Parallel Distrib. Syst. **13**(3), 260–274 (2002)
3. Gary, M.R., Johnson, D.S.: Computers and Intractability: a Guide to the Theory of NP-Completeness. W.H. Freeman and Co., San Francisco (1979)
4. Illavarasan, E., Thambidurai, P.: Low complexity performance effective task scheduling algorithm for heterogeneous computing environments. J. Comput. Sci. **3**(2), 94–103 (2007)
5. Daoud, M.I., Kharma, N.: A high performance algorithm for static task scheduling in heterogeneous distributed computing systems. J. Parallel Distrib. Comput. **68**, 399–409 (2008)
6. Falzon, G., Li, M.: Enhancing list scheduling heuristics for dependent job scheduling in grid computing environments. J. Super Comput. **59**(1), 104–130 (2012)
7. Kruatrachue, B., Lewis, T.: Grain size determination for parallel processing. IEEE Softw. **5**(1), 23–32 (1988)
8. Xu, Y., Li, K., He, L., Truong, T.K.: A DAG scheduling scheme on heterogeneous computing systems using double molecular structure-based chemical reaction optimization. J. Parallel Distrib. Comput. **73**, 1306–1322 (2013)
9. Khan, M.A.: Scheduling for heterogeneous systems using constrained critical paths. J. Parallel Comput. **38**, 175–193 (2012)
10. Chung, Y., Ranka, S.: Application and performance analysis of a compile time optimization approach for list scheduling algorithms on distributed memory multiprocessors. In: Super Computing, pp. 512–52 (1992)
11. Wu, M., Dajski, D.: Hypertool: a programming aid for message passing system. IEEE Trans. Parallel Distrib. Syst. **1**(3), 951–967 (1994)
12. Kim, S.J., Browne, J.C.: A general approach to mapping of parallel computation upon multiprocessor architectures. In: International Conference on Parallel Processing, pp. 1–8. Pennsylvania State University, University Park (1988)

FC-LID: File Classifier Based Linear Indexing for Deduplication in Cloud Backup Services

P. Neelaveni[(✉)] and M. Vijayalakshmi

Department of Information Science and Technology,
Anna University, Chennai, Tamilnadu, India
srirang.neels@gmail.com, vijim@annauniv.edu

Abstract. Data deduplication techniques are optimal solutions for reducing both bandwidth and storage space requirements for cloud backup services in data centers. During deduplication process, maintaining an index in RAM is a fundamental operation. Very large index needs more storage space. It is hard to put such a large index totally in RAM and accessing large disk also decreases throughput. To overcome this problem, index system is developed based on File classifier based Linear Indexing Deduplication called FC-LID which utilizes Linear Hashing with Representative Group (LHRG). The proposed Linear Index structure reduces deduplication computational overhead and increases deduplication efficiency.

Keywords: Deduplication · Cloud backup service · Linear hashing with representative group · File classifier

1 Introduction

Cloud computing consists of both applications and hardware delivered to users as services via the Internet. Cloud storage refers to a storage device accessed over the Internet via Web service application program interfaces (API) [1]. Cloud backup [2] stores data located at the client side into the cloud storage service provider through network so as to recover data in time [3]. Deduplication is an effective technique to optimally utilize the storage space in cloud backup services. Data deduplication method is an optimized technique for reducing both bandwidth and storage space requirements for cloud backup services in data centres.

Data deduplication technology identifies duplicate data, eliminate redundancy and reduce the need to transfer or store the data in the overall capacity [4]. Data deduplication can greatly reduce the amount of data, thereby reducing energy consumption and reduce network bandwidth in cloud data centres.

In the deduplication process, duplicate data is determined and only one copy of the data is stored, along with references to the unique copy of data thus redundant data is removed [5]. The most common deduplication technique partitions data into chunks of non-overlapping data blocks [6]. It calculates a fingerprint for each chunk using a cryptographic hash function (e.g. SHA-1) and stores the fingerprint of each chunk in a hash table (chunk index). Each chunk stored on the storage system has a unique fingerprint in the chunk index. To determine whether a chunk is already stored on the

N. Bjørner et al. (Eds.): ICDCIT 2016, LNCS 9581, pp. 213–222, 2016.
DOI: 10.1007/978-3-319-28034-9_28

system or not, the fingerprint of the incoming data item is first looked up in the chunk index and if there is a match, the system only stores a reference to the existing data. Otherwise the incoming chunk is considered unique and is stored on the system and its fingerprint inserted in the chunk index.

Data deduplication strategies [7] are basically classified into three types: (1) based on data unit (2) location where deduplication can be performed and (3) based on disk placement. The core of deduplication is the index store and index lookup mechanism and therefore, optimizing throughput at this critical path is vital for the performance of the whole cloud backup service. The main challenges to be considered in cloud back up services when deduplication is applied are high throughput, computational overhead, deduplication efficiency [2].

To find a duplicate chunk quickly, it is necessary to maintain an index of chunk IDs in RAM. A chunk ID is a signature of a chunk, which is usually computed by a cryptographic hash such as SHA-1 or MD5. When two chunk IDs are identical, the two corresponding chunks are duplicate. When the data size is not very large, it is easy to put the flat chunk index in RAM. Generally, the ratio of the size of the flat chunk index to the deduplicated data [8] consisting of unique chunks is about 1:100. It is hard to put such a huge index totally in RAM. Part of the index must be put in disk and is loaded to RAM when needed. Then, for searching every chunk in the index, part of the index should be loaded from disk to RAM, resulting in extremely low throughput.

We propose a novel File classifier based Linear Indexing Deduplication (FC-LID) method which eliminates the maintenance of index in RAM and thus reduces almost all RAM usage requirement to place an index. We only maintain 3 type of containers in disk, which mainly consists of number of chunk IDs for every type of a file called MFC (Most Frequently Changeable) files, LFC (Least Frequently Changeable) files and NC (Not Changeable) files and its corresponding containers. We designed variation of Linear Hashing called Linear Hashing with Representative Group (LHRG) to organize container and to compute the container address for a file. The proposed model is tested using university students datasets. Experimental results shows that our method eliminates the need of an index in RAM and the deduplication rate of our method is better than EB for the considered datasets.

The proposed deduplication system, which exploits file type attribute and File classifier based Linear indexing deduplication structure called FC-LID is used to reduces the RAM usage which in turn reduces deduplication computational overhead. The Index Structure used in the proposed deduplication method has effective impact in deduplication efficiency. The rest of the paper is organized as follows. Section 2 presents related work. The system design is in Sect. 3. Implementation details are given in Sect. 4. Section 5 evaluated FC-LID through experiments driven by real-world datasets and performance study is given. Section 6 concludes the paper.

2 Related Work

Several methods are proposed to solve issues involved in maintaining large index while cloud backup handles huge volume of data. To solve this problem, Bloom Filter [8] utilizes a summary vector to avoid the unnecessary index searches for new chunks, and utilizes Locality Preserved Caching (LPC) [12] to ensure the descriptors of a duplicate chunk are highly likely already in the cache. Sparse Indexing [8] utilizes a sparse index by sampling some chunk IDs to be placed in RAM at an exact rate per data segment. Both methods are very effective when there is high locality in the data stream. Extreme Binning (EB) [9] works very well even when there is low locality in the data stream. EB chooses the minimum chunk ID of all chunk IDs of a file as the representative chunk ID and places it in the index in RAM and puts all chunk IDs of the files with the same minimum chunk ID in the same bin in the disk.

All these methods can reduce the RAM usage, but the RAM usage is still too large [11]. If the average chunk size is 4 KB, for 100 TB of storage space utilization, Bloom Filter needs about 36 GB RAM while Sparse Indexing needs 17 GB RAM for an equivalent level of deduplication [3] compared with 1500 GB RAM required by the flat chunk index of Jumbo Store [10]. For 10 PB of storage space utilization, EB requires about 1500 GB RAM to hold the index [13, 14]. For a store with dozens of PB of storage space utilization, all these three methods require more than several TB of RAM to hold their indexes [15].

3   System Design

The architecture of proposed deduplication system given in Fig. 1 consists of the following components: File classifier, deduplication layer and storage layer.

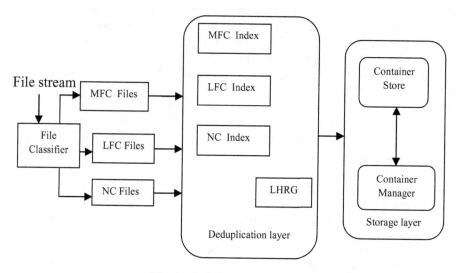

Fig. 1.   Architecture of FC-LID

3.1   File Classifier

The file type attribute is considered for deduplication process. Some specific files, such as compressed archives, multimedia files, that are semantically identical may share little redundant data in their binary presentations.

3.1.1 Classification of Files

MFC (Most Frequently Changeable) files: Files of types .txt, odt, .odp and .pdf are categorized as mutable file. They involve more modification and are most frequently accessed by the user. As the content of these files may get modified, content based chunking is used to divide the file to identify the duplicates effectively. LFC (Least Frequently Changeable) files: Files of types .exe and .rar are less mutable files as they contain only less modification. Duplicates among these types of files are efficiently identified by performing fixed size chunking method. NC (Not Changeable) files: Files of types .avi, .mp3 and .mp4 are categorized as immutable files. As the content of these types of files is not modified, such file can be compared in its entirety to identify the duplicates.

3.2 Deduplication Layer

Deduplication layer consist of index for MFC, LFC, NC files. The variation of linear hashing called LHRG based on file classifier described in the following section have the potential to reduce the Deduplication computational overhead.

Index for MFC files: There is a huge probability of multiple versions of the files with minor variations existing across the files of different users or within the files of the same user. These versions of files are similar files. According to Broder's theorem, files f1 and f2 are similar files, if their minimum chunkIDs are the same. Hence, it will be beneficial to maintain a hierarchical index. The primary index holds the representative chunkID and the secondary index accommodates the chunk IDs of similar files. Once the usage of hierarchical index is decided, it is necessary to choose suitable data structures for the primary and secondary index. B+ tree is a balanced tree from root to leaf level. A node in B+ tree constitutes a key and a pointer. Order of B + tree determines the number of representatives. **Index for LFC files:** The content of this kind of file is prone to minor modification only. ChunkIDs of these types of files are organized in a B+ tree to identify the duplicates and improve the retrieval time of the file. **Index for NC files:** Contents of these types of files will be the same across the users. Hence, it is enough to keep only the hashes of the files. Hash table is maintained to store the chunkIDs of files.

3.2.1 Linear Hashing with Representative Group (LHRG)

Deduplication Process: The key feature of our idea is that we can circumvent a main index in RAM by utilizing Linear Hashing with Representative Group (LHRG) to compute the address of container where classified files reside. Index is maintained to find the container where similar files are placed. When file stream comes into the deduplication system, the files are classified and processed one by one. A classified file is first chunked. Then the LHRG address of the classified file is computed. The deduplication system uses this LHRG address to load the container from the container store. New chunk IDs are found and inserted into this loaded container. After this, the old container is deleted and this new container is stored in the container store using the same LHs address as the old container. Then, new chunks are stored in disk. Finally, the file manifest of this file including all chunk IDs and other information are stored in the file manifest store.

When a file is being deduplicated, the address of the container, which this file is deduplicated against, should be computed. Then, the container with this address is loaded into memory to be searched for the duplicate chunk IDs. We design a variation of LH is used for container addressing, namely Linear Hashing with Representative Group (LHRG). LHRG consists of a group of container or bucket. Each container of LHRG contains a number of Representative Group which uses a group of keys for addressing and splitting of bucket. This difference results in a different addressing strategy of LHRG and a different splitting strategy of LHRG. All chunk IDs of a file constitutes a representative group of a LHRG container. The representative chunk ID of a file is the representative key of a group of LHRG. Firstly, we find the minimum chunk ID of a file as the representative chunk ID. And then, this minimum chunk ID is used as a LH key to compute a LH address, which is also the LHRG address. The LHRG address is the LH address of the representative of a group.

LHRG Addressing Algorithm. The LHRG is denoted by L. The initial number of container is denoted by C (C >= 1), the maximum size of container is specified by S, the Representative is denoted as R, the split pointer by p, the file level by $j + 1$ ($j = 0$, 1, 2 ...), the threshold of load factor by f, the addressing hash function by h. The addressing algorithm of LHRG, used to compute the container address of a Representative Group, is shown in Fig. 2.

```
Input: L, j, p:    Output: a
for all chunks
do   m = min(L);
     n = hi(m);
     if n < p then  n = hi+ f (m);
     end if
```

Fig. 2. LHRG addressing algorithm

3.3   Storage Layer

The proposed deduplication method FC-LID decreases the need of an index in RAM. We only maintain containers in disk, which mainly gives a number of chunk IDs. For every type of a file MFC, LFC, NC a separate container store is maintained called MFC container, LFC Container and LC Container. The container which holds the similar files is loaded from disk to RAM, and the file is deduplicated against this Container. We designed LHRG to organize container and to compute the container address for a file. For every type of file such as MFC, LFC and NC, the address of the container comprising the similar files is computed by the bin addressing algorithm of LHRG. The LHRG addressing algorithm only needs all chunk IDs of a file as input and output as the container address for this file. The file is deduplicated using this container after loading the container and new chunk IDs are inserted into this container. Then new chunks are stored in disk, and then the file metadata containing all information to reconstruct this file is also stored in disk. Container manager is responsible for storing, allocating, deallocating, reading, writing containers.

4   Implementation

A private cloud is set using Eucalyptus [16] open source software. The storage space in private cloud needs to be optimally utilized during cloud back up services Hence, deduplication technique has been incorporated in this to make this storage as an optimized one. Eucalyptus [16] consists of five functional components namely Cloud Controller (CLC), Cluster controller (CC), Storage controller (SC), Walrus and Node controller (NC). The Storage controller provides block storage services similar to Amazon's Elastic Block Service (EBS) [17]. The client can interact with cloud storage through Walrus via S3 interface or REST based tools similar to Amazon's Simple Storage Service (S3) [18]. The Walrus store the data in the installed machine [16]. The Node controller monitors and reins the hypervisor on each compute node an allows users to execute fundamental operations on the data. Gluster File System (GFS) is used to establish set up a storage with many storage servers that use GlusterFS [19]. It gives permission for a cloud client to accumulate the consolidated storage at a single mount point [20] and also gives the privilege to the clients user to control the storage and retrieval of the files [21]. Four machines are configured as CC, SC, CLC and Walrus. Rest of the machines are configured as Node controllers.

5   Performance Study

5.1   RAM Usage

In the proposed design, memory requirement for index in RAM is not necessary to decide whether a chunk exists in the deduplication systems. Also index is not required to determine the similar segment as it is done in Sparse Indexing or the similar file groups as Extreme Binning does. Instead minimum chunk IDs of 3 categories of file (MFC, LFC, NC) is used to compute the LHRG address and then the corresponding containers are loaded with this address. This methodology eliminates the maintenance of an index in RAM.

5.2   Analysis of FC-LID

Fixed sized chunking method is applied for files as they are prone to only less modification. Hence, it is assumed that chunks created for these types of files will be less compared to that of NC files. Due to the advantages of on-disk B + tree, it is chosen to hold the chunkIDs of these types of files.

Table 1. Performance analysis of FC-LID

Chunk entry	Sequential search (in sec)	FC-LID (in sec)
100	0.001	0.0
1000	0.172	0.0
10000	0.296	0.0
100000	0.431	0.0
2000000	0.740	0.001
2500000	0.973	0.001

Types of files like .avi, .mp3 and .mp4 involve no modification. Hence, hash for these types of files are enough to be maintained in index. Linear index and hash table are implemented to hold the chunkIDs of NC files. In worst case, sequential index is performed in O(n) time to retrieve a file. Whereas, linear index performs efficiently by retrieving the file in O(1) time. It is inferred from Table 1.

5.3   Deduplication Computational Overhead

De-duplication overhead, in terms of reduced throughput, is a critically important factor impacting cloud backup systems performance. The Performance analysis shows that the retrieval time for MFC, LFC, NC files. We use the retrieval time in deduplication process for each backup session as a metric to evaluate the deduplication overhead. The proposed deduplication process at the client site takes less time by singling out deduplicated files and small files with zero RAM access. Thus our system incurs much less deduplication overhead.

5.3.1   Analysis of Retrieval Time of MFC Files

When a request arrives to retrieve a file, the corresponding file recipe is obtained. It is forwarded to the storage node where the index for MFC files is maintained. The hierarchical index with on-disk B+ tree with linear hash table is implemented to hold reasonably large number of chunkID entries. The minimum and maximum size of the stored file is 10 KB and 1 MB respectively. Table 2 shows the time taken to retrieve a file of type MFC with various sizes.

Table 2. Retrieval time of MFC files

File size	No of chunks	Retrieval time (in sec)
10 KB	5	0.124
50 KB	10	0.313
100 KB	26	0.501
500 KB	112	1.1
1 MB	257	4.2

5.3.2   Analysis of Retrieval Time of LFC Files

Types of files .exe, and .rar are divided into fixed size of 8 KB and the chunkIDs are computed for those chunks. The minimum and maximum size of file that will be stored in OPCS are assumed to be 10 KB and 1 MB respectively. Table 3 shows the time taken to retrieve a file of type .rar with various file sizes.

Table 3. Retrieval time LFC files

File size	No of chunks	Retrieval time (in sec)
16 KB	2	0.24
50 KB	7	0.32
100 KB	13	0.50
500 KB	125	1.4
1 MB	248	4.7

5.3.3   Analysis of Retrieval Time of NC Files

Whole file chunking is performed for this file type and the chunkIDs of these types of files are maintained in hash table on-disk and sequential structure. The minimum size of these types of files are assumed to be 10 MB and the maximum size to be 1 GB. The time taken to retrieve these types of files with various sizes is tabulated in Table 4.

Table 4. Retrievaltime of NC Files

File size	Retrieval time (In sec)
10 MB	57
100 MB	792
250 MB	1447
500 MB	1935
1 GB	3245

5.4   Deduplication Efficiency

Deduplication efficiency is defined as the ratio between the amount of the redundant data actually removed and the total amount of the redundant data in each deduplication method. Our experimental results present both the cumulative deduplication efficiency in terms deduplication rate of each backup session for individual users. The results show that proposed method removes almost all the redundant data at the chunk level. The deduplication rate of FC-LID is compared with that of Extreme Binning (EB). For university student dataset, LHRG shows better deduplication efficiency than EB as shown in Fig. 3. When MFC, LFC, NC container size is varying from 1.2 MB to 2.0 MB, the deduplication rate of FC-LID is 24 % on the average better than EB. Usually, much more bigger container size brings much more larger chance to find duplicate chunks. Therefore, the deduplication FC-LID is better.

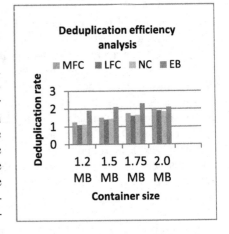

Fig. 3. Deduplication efficiency

When the container size is large, FC-LID performs better and the ratio of the deduplication rate is 92.87 % for MFC, 90.78 % for LFC, and 82.46 % for NC. The reason is that, in chosen dataset, files size is small, typically from several kilobytes to dozens of kilobytes. Thus, more similar files with different minimum chunk IDs exist in. At the same time, FC-LID selected the minimum chunk ID as the representative chunk ID, which means that, there are more similar files with different minimum chunk Ids are placed in different categories of containers. Therefore, deduplication efficiency is increased.

6 Conclusion

We have designed the FC-LID, File classifier based Linear Indexing for Deduplication in cloud backup services which eliminates the maintaining an index in RAM and LHRG is utilized to compute the address of a containers based on MFC, LFC, NC files. The corresponding containers holds the chunk IDs of similar files to a file. Then, maintain an index in RAM is not required to perform this operation. Our method computes the LHRG address for MFC, LFC, NC file, loads the container with this address, and deduplicates the file against the categorized container. Experimental results show that the deduplication efficiency is increased and reduces deduplication computational overhead. As a future work, we plan to design file classifier based probabilistic model using locality sensitive hashing for deduplication in cloud backup services.

References

1. Sun, Z., Shen, J., Yong, J.: DeDu: building a deduplication storage system over cloud computing. In: 15th IEEE International Conference on Computer Supported Cooperative Work in Design (2011)
2. Yinjin, F., et al.: AA-Dedupe: an application-aware source deduplication approach for cloud backup services in the personal computing environment. In: IEEE International Conference on Cluster Computing, pp. 112–120 (2011)
3. Zhonglin, H., Yuhua, H.: A study on cloud backup technology and its development. In: International Conference, ICCIC 2011, pp 1–7. Wuhan, China, 17–18 September 2011
4. Zhu, B., Li, K., Patterson, H.: Avoiding the disk bottleneck in the data domain deduplication file system. In: Proceedings of the 6th Conference on USENIX Conference on File and Storage Technologies, San Jose, CA, USA, pp. 269–282. USENIX Association, Berkeley, CA, USA, 26–29, 2008
5. Neelaveni, P., Vijayalakshmi, M.: A survey on deduplication in cloud storage. Asian J. Inf. Technol. **13**, 320–330 (2014)
6. Meyer, D.T., Bolosky, W.J.: A study of practical deduplication. In: FAST 2011: Proceedings of the 9th Conference on File and Storage Technologies (2011)
7. Harnik, D., Pinkas, B., Shulman-Peleg, A.: Side channels in cloud services: deduplication in cloud storage. IEEE Secur. Priv. **8**(6), 40–47 (2010)
8. Lillibridge, M., Eshghi, K., Bhagwat, D., Deolalikar, V., Trezise, G., Camble, P.: Sparse indexing: large scale, inline deduplication using sampling and locality. In: Proceedings of the 7th Conference on USENIX Conference on File and Storage Technologies, San Francisco, CA, USA, pp. 111–123. USENIX Association, Berkeley, CA, USA, 24–27, 2009
9. Bhagwat, D., Eshghi, K., Long, D., Lillibridge, M.: Extreme binning: scalable, parallel deduplication for chunk-based file backup. In: Proceedings of the 17th Annual Meeting of the IEEEIACM International Symposium on Modelling, Analysis and Simulation of Computer and Telecommunication Systems, London, UK, pp. 1–9. IEEE Computer Society, Washington, DC, USA, 21–23, 2014

10. Eshghi, K., Lillibridge, M., Wilcock, L., Belrose, G., Hawkes, R.: Jumbo store: providing efficient incremental upload and versioning for a utility rendering service. In: Proceedings of the 5th Conference on USENIX Conference on File and Storage Technologies, San Jose, CA, USA, pp. 123–138. USENIX Association, Berkeley, CA, USA, 13–16, 2007

11. Dong, W., Douglis, F., Li, K., Patterson, H., Reddy, S., Shilane, P.: Tradeoffs in scalable data routing for deduplication clusters. In: Proceedings of the 9th Conference on USENIX Conference on File and Storage Technologies, San Jose, CA, USA, pp. 15–29. USENIX Association, Berkeley, CA USA, 15–17, 2011

12. Mell, P., Grance, T.: The NIST Definition of Cloud Computing, Draft by The National Institute of Standards and Technology (NIST). United States Department of Commerce Version 15 (2009)

13. Tan, Y., Jiang, H., Sha, E.H.-M., Yan, Z., Feng, D.: SAFE: a source deduplication framework for efficient cloud backup services. J. Sign Process Syst. **72**, 209–228 (2013). Springer Science, Business Media, New York

14. Zhu, B., Li, K., Patterson, H.: Avoiding the disk bottleneck in the data domain deduplication file system. In: Proceedings of the 6th USENIX Conference on File and Storage Technologies, FAST 2008, pp. 18:1–18:14. USENIX Association, Berkeley, CA, USA

15. Wei, J., Jiang, H., Zhou, K., Feng, D.: Mad2: a scalable high-throughput exact deduplication approach for network backup services. In: IEEE NASA Goddard Conference on Mass Storage Systems and Technologies, pp. 1–14 (2010)

16. http://open.eucalyptus.com/wiki/EucalyptusInstall_v2.0

17. Amazon's Elastic Block Storage. Elastic Block Storage. http://aws.amazon.com/ebs/

18. Amazon's Simple Storage Service. Simple Storage Service. http://aws.amazon.com/s3/

19. Gluster file system. http://www.gluster.org

20. http://gluster.com/community/documentation/index.php/MainPag

21. http://open.eucalyptus.com/wiki/EucalyptusWalrusInteracting_v.0

Author Index

Printed in the United States
By Bookmasters